D1590913

OXFORD THEOLOGICAL MONOGRAPHS

Editorial Committee

Oxford Theological Monographs

THE ONTOLOGY OF
PAUL TILLICH

BY

ADRIAN THATCHER

1478

1978

OXFORD UNIVERSITY PRESS

Oxford University Press, Walton Street, Oxford OX2 6DP

OXFORD LONDON GLASGOW
NEW YORK TORONTO MELBOURNE WELLINGTON
IBADAN NAIROBI DAR ES SALAAM LUSAKA CAPE TOWN
KUALA LUMPUR SINGAPORE JAKARTA HONG KONG TOKYO
DELHI BOMBAY CALCUTTA MADRAS KARACHI

© *Adrian Thatcher, 1978*

British Library Cataloguing in Publication Data

Thatcher, Adrian
The ontology of Paul Tillich—(Oxford theological
monographs).
1. Tillich, Paul—Ontology
I. Title   II. Series
111'092'4   BX4827.T53   77-30288

ISBN 0-19-826715-0

Printed in Great Britain by
Butler & Tanner Ltd
Frome and London

PREFACE

Y ET another book on Tillich has to begin by justifying itself. The flood of books and articles examining his thought has now fortunately abated, but it has left behind a general consensus that his writings have already been over-researched and the effort expended in coming to grips with them has yielded only meagre results. Anyone glancing at a bibliography of work on Tillich might fairly conclude that all that could profitably be said about him has been said, and much of it has been said many times.

The justification of the present volume, late in the day and at the end of the field, lies in its historical method of approach to Tillich's work. A thorough-going historical approach to Tillich's thought is undertaken for several reasons. Much of the criticism directed against Tillich fails because it takes no account of the theological and philosophical traditions on which Tillich freely drew. A recent work, Alistair Macleod's *Tillich: An Essay on the Role of Ontology in his Philosophical Theology*, is perhaps an example of the rootlessness of much of the recent criticism of Tillich, for in the entire book there is scarcely a single historical reference. Before Tillich's achievement can be finally evaluated there is a need to examine his thought from the point of view of those philosophical and theological traditions which are incorporated into it. This is a task which, despite the weight of literature on Tillich, has still not been adequately done, and the present volume is intended to be a contribution to it. The historical approach to Tillich's thought is undertaken with the conviction that the meaning of many of the terms appearing in his philosophical theology can only be made evident by a patient and sympathetic unravelling of their history. There is no other way.

Where possible, the material chosen for inclusion in this book has had only a minimum of discussion elsewhere. While some repetition of some of the themes of earlier commentators is inevitable, the approach of this present volume is at least an attempt to present Tillich's basic ontology in a fresh light. The standpoint of the book is broadly sympathetic towards Tillich's theological aims and methods. This is acknowledged at the outset since commentators (including this one) are only too likely to elucidate their own positions as they elucidate Tillich's. Sympathy with Tillich's style of philosophical theology does not prevent one from being critical, sometimes severely, of lack of clarity or of inconsistency in his thought. I have approached Tillich's work from his own standpoint of liberal protestantism and in the belief both that the language of being is an asset to Christian theism, and that theism cannot finally avoid ontology.

I owe very much to my two teachers in philosophical theology at Oxford, the Revd. Dr. Gordon Pearce, formerly Dean and Senior Tutor at Regent's Park College, and the Revd. Professor John Macquarrie, Lady Margaret Professor of Divinity at Christ Church. Dr. Pearce led me through my studies as an undergraduate in modern doctrine and philosophy of religion, and constantly encouraged me to develop my interest in Tillich. I freely drew on his astonishing breadth and depth of scholarship, and he made available to me his Ph.D. thesis 'The Philosophical Theology of St. Augustine' (Aberdeen, 1960) and his unpublished translation of Tillich's 'Mystik und Schuldbewusstsein in Schellings Philosophischer Entwicklung'. His untimely death in 1974 was a sad loss, not only to his family, but to Regent's Park College, to the Baptist denomination, and to Oxford. Professor Macquarrie supervised the D.Phil. thesis which this work was originally, generously giving me his time and wisdom. He read the whole of the preliminary draft of the thesis, and provided me with a host of valuable suggestions and ideas. Finally, my thanks go to the deacons and members of the Baptist Church at Abingdon, who gave me full encouragement to engage in research while I was their Minister.

ADRIAN THATCHER

Cheltenham,
April 1976

CONTENTS

ABBREVIATIONS

(For full details see the Bibliography.)

BR	*Biblical Religion and the Search for Ultimate Reality*
CTB	*The Courage To Be*
GW	*Gesammelte Werke*
LPJ	*Love, Power and Justice*
PE	*The Protestant Era*
PTCT	*Paul Tillich in Catholic Thought*
ST	*Systematic Theology*
TC	*Theology of Culture*
TTP	'The Two Types of Philosophy of Religion', in *TC*
TPT	*The Theology of Paul Tillich*

I

ONTOLOGY AND THE
ONTOLOGICAL QUESTION

THE term 'ontology' was coined in the late seventeenth century. It seems to have occurred in a posthumous edition of *Elementa Philosophiae sive Ontosophia*, written and first published by the Cartesian Joannes Claubergius (1622–65) in 1647. Clauberg used the term 'ontosophy' almost as a synonym for the much older term 'metaphysics'. He wrote: 'Just as *theosophy* or *theology* is said to be a science about God, it seems we might be able, quite appropriately, to call that science which does not deal with this or that being . . . but with being in general, ontosophy or ontology'.[1] The term '*onto*logy' then, was suggested by the parallel term '*theo*logy'. Just as theology is said to be a science about God (*theos*), so Clauberg suggested, ontology should be the name for the science about being (*on*).

The term is also located in the seventeenth-century writings of Jean-Baptiste Duhamel (1624–1706) in his *Philosophia Universalis*.[2] In an undated fragment of Leibniz (1646–1716) ontology is called a 'general science' (*Scientia Generalis*) or a 'science about something and nothing, being and non-being, entities and their modes of existing, substance, and accident'.[3] The term was commonly used by the eighteenth-century rationalist Christian Wolff (1679–1754), who in 1730 produced a work entitled *Philosophia Prima sive Ontologia*, at the start of which he defined ontology as 'the science of being in general, or being as being'. Kant (1724–1804) called ontology 'the science of the general attributes of all things' or the science of 'the possibility of our knowledge of things *a priori*, i.e. independent

---

[1] My translation. Gilson refers to the passage in *L'Être et l'Essence*, 168n., but he is wrong to assume that the word *ontologia* occurs in the first edition of Clauberg's work in 1647.

[2] F. C. Copleston, *History of Philosophy*, vi. 108.

[3] 'Introductio ad Encyclopaediam Arcanam', *Phil.* 8.1: in Couturat, *Opuscules et fragments inédits de Leibniz* (1903), 512.

of experience'. Ontology, he wrote, 'can teach us nothing about things as they are in themselves, but only the *a priori* conditions under which we can know things in our general experience, i.e. principles of the possibility of experience'.[4] Ontology constitutes the contents of Hegel's (1770–1831) *Science of Logic*, and it is the title of the first section of the *Logic*, 'The Doctrine of Being'.[5] The term occurs in the systems of Herbart (1776–1841) and Lotze (1817–81)[6] and features prominently in the much neglected writings of Rosmini (1797–1855).[7]

Philosophers who produced ontology in the three centuries before our own can fairly be called either rationalists or idealists, and both kinds of ontology are present in the ontology of Paul Tillich. Tillich's particular indebtedness to the dialectical ontology of Hegel will be acknowledged and documented later. Rationalist and idealist ontology in their different ways classify and order what is by means of subdivisions, categories, properties, species, contrasts, and so on. It is the work of speculative reason projecting itself upon the external world and arriving at formal, general principles which the realm of existence is said to presuppose. But while it is important to acknowledge the earlier types of ontology, it is the existential or 'fundamental' ontology of the twentieth century which influences Tillich most. In this younger version of ontology, particularly in Martin Heidegger's (1889–1976) *Being and Time*, the approach to Being (*Sein*) is made through an existential description of the being of man (*Dasein*), so that if the meaning of Being is to be disclosed, an examination of the being of *Dasein* must first be undertaken. Heidegger writes '*Fundamental ontology*, from which alone all other ontologies can take their rise, must be sought in the *existential analytic of Dasein*'.[8]

The method and content of this kind of ontology is of course strikingly different from the earlier versions of the same subject. Tillich often speaks of the influence Heidegger had upon the

---

[4] See 'Nachrichten von der Einrichtung seiner Vorlesung im Winterhalbjahr 1765–6'; and 'Nachlass', 5936, cit. Eisler, *Kant Lexikon*, 400.

[5] *The Science of Logic* (tr. A. V. Miller), Foreword, § 33.

[6] 'Ontology' is the title of the first of three books comprising Lotze's *Metaphysic* (1878).

[7] The first three volumes of Rosmini's *Theosophy* (1859) were devoted to ontology.

[8] *Being and Time* (tr. Macquarrie and Robinson), 13. (As the book contains the paginations of the German *and* English versions, we have used the German version.)

development of his thinking,[9] and for a short period in 1924–5 both he and Heidegger were colleagues on the teaching staff of the University of Marburg. For Heidegger as for Tillich, philosophy is first of all ontology, and the task of ontology is to clarify the meaning of Being. In *Being and Time* Heidegger says

Basically, all ontology, no matter how rich and firmly compacted a system of categories it has at its disposal, remains blind and perverted from its ownmost aim, if it has not first adequately clarified the meaning of Being, and conceived this clarification as its fundamental task.[10]

Ontology then is an inquiry (*Frage*)[11] into the meaning of Being, and inquiry itself is a way of being which needs to be explicated because it is peculiar to man (*Dasein*). Inquiry, according to Heidegger, is 'the behaviour of a questioner, and therefore of an entity, and as such has its own character of being'. The interpretation of Being then, must be the task of an existential, not a traditional ontology: as such it will need to be grounded in an existential analysis of human being, and only through such an analysis does the meaning of Being-Itself (*Sein-Selbst*) begin to be disclosed.

Tillich, particularly in his later German period, follows Heidegger closely in his understanding of the nature of philosophy. He claims: 'philosophy is the attitude of explicit inquiry . . . *Philosophy is the attitude in which the specifically human power of inquiry becomes explicit*'.[12] Philosophy is called the 'inquiry into the nature of inquiry itself'.[13] And if philosophy is inquiry it is first of all inquiry into the being of an inquiring being, viz. *Dasein*. This is what gives philosophy an explicit ontological foundation and grounds philosophy in a specific and basic questioning, the 'ontological question' (the different formulations of the ontological question are the subject of the next section, below).

[9] e.g. *On the Boundary*, 48, 56: 'Autobiographical Reflections', in *The Theology of Paul Tillich* (eds. Kegley and Bretall): 'Sin and Grace', in *Reinhold Niebuhr: a Prophetic Voice in our Time*, 45n.

[10] *Being and Time*, 11.

[11] Ibid. 5. Heidegger's influence on Tillich's formulation of the ontological question is dealt with below, pp. 5, 14, 18, 22–4.

[12] 'Philosophie: Begriff und Wesen', in *Die Religion in Geschichte und Gegenwart* (2nd edn., 1927–32), iv. 1200. A translation appears as 'The Concept and Nature of Philosophy', in *Twentieth Century Theology in the Making* (ed. J. Pelikan), ii. 248.

[13] Ibid., 1204 (German), 256 (English).

In the thought of Tillich then, different types of ontology are blended together and each type must be recognized and separated out if his ontological thought is to be correctly placed and understood. It is one of the objectives of this study to do this.

Is there any difference between ontology and metaphysics? 'Metaphysics' is of course the traditional name given to ontology before Clauberg, and the original coining of the word by an early editor of the works of Aristotle is well known. What we know as metaphysics Aristotle (388–322 B.C) regarded as 'first philosophy', as that kind of philosophy which deals with 'reality as a whole' in contrast to, say, mathematics or physics which deal only with parts or segments of the former. Tillich's love of the classical tradition of philosophy makes him explicitly identify philosophy with metaphysics; in his thought they are always the same. Most commentators are unable to conceal their exasperation with Tillich's method at this point, for even a minimal acquaintance with the development of philosophy in the English-speaking world during the twentieth century shows how few philosophers understand the role of philosophy in quite this way.

Why then are the separate terms, ontology and metaphysics, each with their different etymological and historical backgrounds, retained throughout Tillich's writings? In fact their meanings were continually shifting and at the end of his life he came to abandon the distinction between them. In 1923 before Heidegger's existentialism was to influence him, Tillich published *The System of the Sciences*. Metaphysics is here assigned its due place in the System as 'first philosophy', but its object of inquiry is not, as might be expected, Being (*Sein*), but the closely related term Meaning (*Sinn*). The 'first and basic task' of metaphysics is said to be 'a theory of the elements of meaning'. 'Genuine metaphysics is meaning-metaphysics' (*Sinnmetaphysik*).[14] Ontology here plays a subsidiary role within metaphysics— its task is 'to represent the structure of all entities and their unity, as the expression of pure meaning'. Metaphysics then, deals with *Sinn*, ontology with *Sein*. How was each term understood in 1923? The 'metaphysics of being' is a description of 'that which is' (*das Seiende*), whereas the 'metaphysics of

---

[14] *Das System der Wissenschaften*, in *Gesammelte Werke*, i. 255.

meaning' is a description of the relation between the Unconditioned (Tillich's early characterization of God) and 'that which is'. The subsidiary role assigned to ontology as the metaphysics of being did not last long. After the influence of Heidegger, Being replaces Meaning as the ultimate philosophical absolute,[15] and ontology replaces metaphysics as Tillich's 'first philosophy'. However the question of the different roles assigned to each was still not finally settled. In the Firth lectures, *Love, Power and Justice* which Tillich gave at Nottingham in 1952 and were published two years later, there is still a place for the distinction between ontology and metaphysics. He asks: 'How is ontology distinguished from what has been called metaphysics? The answer is that ontology is the foundation of metaphysics, but not metaphysics itself' (*LPJ*, 28). Later in an article 'The Relation of Metaphysics and Theology' (1956) metaphysics appears as 'the rational inquiry into the structure of being, its polarities and categories as they appear in man's encounter with reality'.[16] Ontology, he agrees, has the same brief, though there is still a difference between them. While ontology deals with the 'universal structures of being', there are

structures of less universality like nature, man, history, which also precede in logical dignity anything concrete in their respective sphere but which are not structures of being as such, and which, consequently, are not objects of ontology in the strict sense of the word. Therefore, if the word 'metaphysics' can be saved from its supranaturalistic connotations, it should be used. If, however, this is impossible, the term ontology must be enlarged so that it embraces all structures which constitute reality. Both ways are open. (Ibid.; *ST* 1.24)

The passage contains a number of difficulties. Tillich means that while ontology deals strictly with the primary or universal structures of being, the secondary or less universal structures of being (nature, man, history, etc.) should be reserved for metaphysics provided the latter can be preserved from distortion. This distinction between ontology and metaphysics echoes

---

[15] For an elaboration of this view, see R. P. Scharlemann, 'The Scope of Systematics: an Analysis of Tillich's Two Systems', in *Journal of Religion*, xlviii (1968), 144 n. 17; and *Reflection and Doubt in the Thought of Paul Tillich*, 51–2.
[16] *Review of Metaphysics*, x (1956–7), 57.

Wolff's distinction two centuries earlier between *metaphysica generalis* and *metaphysica specialis*.[17] But why is metaphysics rather than ontology more able to deal with these 'structures of less universality'? In any case it must be doubtful whether the division between universal and less universal structures of being can be consistently maintained. Can metaphysics give an account, for example, of nature and its 'structures', which on the one hand is metaphysical (and not ontological), and on the other, does not trespass on the terrain of the empirical sciences? If it can, how does its account differ from the consideration of nature already included within an ontological account of the structure of being? In any case 'man' ought not to be included in the secondary list of structures of being, for without him there could be no approach to ontology at all, since man alone of all beings can ask the 'ontological question'. It is equally difficult to understand the precise objection that Tillich maintains against the 'supranaturalistic connotations' of metaphysics. 'Supranaturalism' is obviously used in a pejorative sense, Pejoratively it can refer to a rigorous, literally minded orthodoxy, but this does not seem to meet the force of Tillich's objection. More probably, Tillich means by 'supranaturalism' the old rationalistic types of metaphysics uninfluenced by existentialism and modern thought. In any case Tillich was soon to reject the term altogether. In 1962 he says he avoids the term because it 'means looking at the clouds; (*meta—above* the physical world)',[18] and because the suggestion of supranaturalism cannot be avoided. Perhaps a less obvious reason for dropping the term is that the subject-matter of both metaphysics and ontology is the same, and that Tillich was unnecessarily perplexed by assuming, wrongly, that because two different words were available to describe the same sort of enterprise, they must in some way be related. If not identical, the two words are at least interchangeable, despite their different histories and etymologies, and subtle attempts to contrast them failed.

What is the relationship between ontology and *theology* in Tillich's writings? This subject, culminating in Tillich's 'method of correlation' between philosophy and theology is already over-researched and commentators have in the main

---

[17] See G. Martin, *An Introduction to General Metaphysics*, 15.
[18] 'Sin and Grace', 45.

reached fairly critical conclusions about it. Our interest in the subject is confined mainly to Tillich's earlier and lesser-known German statements on the subject because they have received much less attention and because an understanding of them is essential to a grasp of the role of ontology in *ST* (1951–63), and in the one work devoted to the subject, *BR* (1955).

In a neglected article entitled 'Eschatology and History' published in 1927, Tillich devoted a section to what he called 'theological ontology'. The English version of the article appears in an early collection of translations by N. A. Rasetzki and E. L. Tabney published in 1936 under the title *The Interpretation of History*. Unfortunately the original article is badly paraphrased in the English and important sections of it are omitted altogether. Consequently its significance has been lost on succeeding generations of English readers. One piece omitted from the English is important enough to reproduce in full. Tillich writes

There can be no theological statement without theological ontology, or, if we are allowed to coin a new word, 'protology', the interpretation of the Unconditioned-Transcendent as that which is before all things, as that which gives being to all that is. We seek first of all to make clear theoretically the activity of the religious consciousness as far as it stands in the ontological intuition of things.

In the intuition of all that is in so far as it is, two things press themselves upon consciousness, the seriousness and the uncertainty of the being of things. Thus, if anything is, if it participates in being, it displays this dual character. This duality does not consist of characteristics which things possess through a particular structure: they come to things because they are. 'Seriousness' should be the term for the 'inescapableness', the 'uninventableness' of being, for the 'impenetrableness' of the 'core' of the being of each thing. The 'uncertainty' of being should be the term for that which in its being has a 'floating character', a 'weightlessness', an indication of possible non-being, a lack of unconditional consequence. Both seriousness and insecurity disclose themselves to an intuition of the being of things, supported by religious testimony. No entity has complete fullness of being, but each one participates in unconditional being. Its participation in being signifies its seriousness, the inescapableness of the 'is'. Its lack of fulness of being signifies its uncertainty, the 'passing away' of the 'is'. No entity is the *Proton* with regard to being, but each entity points positively and negatively to a *Proton* in which it participates. And the location of entities in this transcendental *locus* is the object of all statements of religious ontology or protology. . . .[19]

Beneath the obscurity and metaphorical character of much of the passage, Tillich's understanding of what ontology and theology are comes through strongly. He invents a neologism 'protology' which deals with 'that which is before all' (*Erstes*) or the *Proton*. Ontology is the same as protology, and without protology, theology cannot get off the ground. The term *Proton* perhaps suggested itself to Tillich because of its use in the *Enneads* of Plotinus (184/5–253/4) where it is a technical term for the 'One' (*to Prōton*), for the absolute first principle which is beyond all being and characterization while at the same time the source of all things. Consequently the term 'Unconditioned–Transcendent' which comes to Tillich via his knowledge of Kant and Hegel harmonizes well with Plotinus' thought because of its emphasis on the ineffable character of the absolute.

By 'ontological intuition' (*Anschauung*) Tillich means a direct and prior knowledge of what it means for anything at all to exist, a knowledge which is presupposed in any further attempt to characterize it. This knowledge is general in character and available to everyone, and while it is independent of religion, religious experience provides valuable testimony (*Evidenz*) in support of it. The content of the intuition is the dual character of the being of entities which manifests itself to the inquiring human mind. Each aspect of the being of things is described by a separate grouping of partly literal, partly metaphorical terms. If these groups of words are seen as important qualifiers of the key terms Tillich came to use later, 'being' and 'non-being', they are illuminating.

The group 'seriousness–inescapableness–uninventableness–impenetrableness' points to the factuality and concreteness of each thing, and to the permanence or dependability of the whole order of finite being which continues independently of our lack of complete knowledge of it. The group 'uncertainty–floatingness–weightlessness–insecurity–passing-away' describes the transient and precarious character of finite things, their

[19] My translation. The German text is found in *GW*, vi. 72–82 (§2, 'Theologische Ontologie', 74–5).

lack of necessity and permanence, the fleeting, uncertain being of each thing and the certainty of its ceasing to be. These two fundamental aspects of things, known by direct intuition, come to receive a variety of different systematic expressions. They provide us with the raw material for a polar approach to ontology and various polar schemes, e.g. ground–abyss, dynamics–form, courage–anxiety, divine–demonic (all to be examined in later chapters) are introduced to deal with them.

The passage translated above is, however, quite strikingly classical in its philosophical formulation, and very close to the understanding of the idea of being brought so fruitfully into Christian theism by St. Augustine (354–430). Here as in Augustine there are three orders of being: (i) the *Proton* who as such is prior to everything, and while not himself a being, his is the being in which all things stand: (ii) finite being or *das Seiende*, which in the German can be used in either a singular sense (an entity or a being) or a collective sense (all that is, what is): and (iii) nothing or nothingness, from which all beings metaphorically come and to which they return. As we shall see the philosophical theology of Augustine provides the key to this sort of categorization. His ontology has three similar levels, fullness of being or being-itself (*esse ipsum*), finite being (a mixture of being and non-being), and non-being or nothing.[20] Theological ontology describes what is, but from a specific point of view and commitment, viz. from the prior supposition that the being in which all things stand is the being of God, or more succinctly, that God is being-itself.[21] Theological ontology has other names. In *The System of the Sciences* he called it 'theonomous metaphysics' and 'theonomous systematics', but its task in all cases is the same, viz. 'to contemplate and describe reality in such a way that its supporting ground becomes transparent in it and through it'.[22] The language of classical theism provides a major contribution to Tillich's ontology and is an influence that firmly grounds it in the Christian faith.

So far we have briefly traced the history of ontology and suggested that an adequate appreciation of the ontology of Tillich must proceed by identifying the different influences and

[20] See below, pp. 26–31, 51.   [21] See below, p. 29.
[22] 'The Formative Power of Protestantism', *PE*, 217: German text in *GW*, vii. 66.

philosophical traditions which are represented in his thought. This is perhaps a daunting task but it is one of the justifications for the present monograph none the less. We have looked at the relation between ontology and metaphysics and suggested that attempts to distinguish them are failures. We have suggested that the early and wholly neglected account of 'theological ontology' yields illuminating insights into what Tillich thinks ontology is for. All this is preparatory to examining and evaluating the content of the ontology and assessing its significance for the interpretation of the Christian faith. The simplest and most direct way into Tillich's ontology is to ground it in the so-called 'ontological question' and to examine both its different formulations and the variety of answers it receives.

The Ontological Question

We have seen how Tillich follows Heidegger closely in his understanding of the role of philosophy as the elucidation of the elusive ontological question. Philosophy, says Tillich, asks 'the question of what being, simply being, means'.[23] The problem here of course is that most philosophers simply do not think that 'being' means anything at all: such a statement is usually regarded as a pseudo-problem, or a consequence of the simple logical fallacy of assuming that the word 'being' corresponds or refers to something describable: or, it is often objected, it turns 'being' or 'existence' into a special kind of predicate which mistakenly purports to give some further information about entities or attribute to them a special quality. The problem of philosophical hostility to the ontological question in principle is exacerbated by the variety of formulations the question receives in Tillich's own writings, so that it is easy to claim, with some justification, that Tillich does not have one basic ontological question but several. The confusion can be explained partly by the profusion of different sources from which his ontology is derived. What, for example, Aristotle, Schelling, Santayana, and Heidegger mean by the expression 'being' is not to be lightly dismissed merely because their accounts are importantly different and Tillich insufficiently distinguishes between them. Here as elsewhere, he has conflated several possible ways of ontological thinking. When they are

[23] 'Philosophy and Theology', *PE*, 85.

unravelled and identified, a clearer picture emerges, and the case of the logical critics loses some of its force.

Let us then look at some of the different formulations of the ontological question. In *ST* 1 (p. 181) the ontological question is 'What is being-itself?' or 'the question of being as being'. In *BR* (p. 6) the question of being is 'not the question of any special being, its existence and nature, but it is the question of what it means to *be*. It is the simplest, most profound, and absolutely inexhaustible question—the question of what it means to say that something is'. Alternatively it is 'the question of ultimate reality' or 'the question of being-itself' (*BR*, 19, 20). In *LPJ* (p. 19) the question has the form

What does it mean that something *is*? What are the characteristics of everything that participates in being? And this is the question of ontology . . . . Ontology asks the simple and infinitely difficult question: What does it mean to *be*? What are the structures, common to everything that is, to everything that participates in being?

Sometimes the ontological question is not about being generally, but about *human* being particularly. Tillich says: 'I will give a simple definition. The ontological question is the question: what makes man man in distinction from all other beings? Or in a more sophisticated form: what is the kind of being that characterizes man within the whole of being?'[24] At other times the question has a characteristically existential form and presupposes an ontological shock.[25] In such cases the question has the form 'Why is there being and not not-being'.[26]

Obviously there is some difficulty in these extracts over what the ontological question itself is, and how it is thought to arise. The suggestion is made here that the question arises in at least four distinct ways, and a different formulation of the question is appropriate to each. This suggestion arises naturally from a close study of the relevant passages and is hopefully more than a misguided attempt to expatiate Tillich's thought by imposing an over-simplified construction upon it. The questions can be said to arise in the first place as a purely rational inquiry into the structure of being; secondly, as a

[24] 'What is Basic in Human Nature', *Pastoral Psychology*, xiv (1963), 14.
[25] See below, p. 16 f.   [26] 'Philosophy and Theology', 85.

search for wisdom, or for something ultimate; thirdly, the question arises because it is the nature of man to ask questions; fourthly, and most commonly, the question is motivated by a profound negative human experience, usually referred to as the ontological shock, or the shock of non-being.

In the first sense the question of being is a theoretical or rationalistic inquiry into being, and is in good company with classical metaphysics. The ontological question understood as a rational inquiry into what is, corresponds well with Tillich's definition of philosophy as 'that cognitive endeavour in which the question of being is asked' (*BR*, 5). The 'question of being' in this sense is not in fact a question at all. Rather ontology is assigned a special task or subject, conceived along classical Aristotelian lines. 'The rational transformation of the manifestations of Being-itself is the task of ontology'.[27] Ontology in this first sense of the ontological question aims at a rational or theoretical description of the 'structure' or 'manifestation' of being-itself.

In our second sense of the term, the ontological question is more a '*quest for being*' than the 'question of being'. Tillich thinks that the second half of the title of *BR*, 'The Search for Ultimate Reality', 'gives an excellent interpretation of what is meant by the ontological question' (p. 12). The German title of the work is *Biblical Religion and the Question of Being*.[28] The question of being here is the search for the deepest level of being beneath the transitoriness of surface levels or appearances (*BR*, 12). Ontology is 'the basic work of those who aspire to wisdom' (*BR*, 8). It is 'the search for being-itself, for the power of being in everything that is. It is the ontological question, the root question of every philosophy' (*BR*, 12–13).

Plainly the ontological search is not the same as the rational inquiry into being. In the ontological search the seeker after wisdom already assumes the distinction between ultimate reality and mere appearance. He is, we might say, 'ultimately concerned'. He believes that there is some sort of ultimate reality to be searched for, or that such a search is at least a worthwhile undertaking. The rationalistic account of ontology proceeds by way of philosophical detachment: the search for the ontological ultimate proceeds by way of the existential in-

---

[27] 'Being and Love', in R. N. Anshen (ed.), *Moral Principles of Action*, 662.
[28] *Biblische Religion und die Frage nach dem Sein* (*GW*, v. 138–85).

volvement of the inquirer. The rational ontologist *describes* what he apprehends as the structure of being: the seeker after wisdom is not interested in what he apprehends because it only seems to be real. He is interested in discovering some hidden depths of being which rational description cannot open up to him.

Thirdly the question of being arises because it is the nature of man to ask questions, and particularly questions about his own being. 'One can rightly say that man is the being who is able to ask questions' (*BR*, 11). His preoccupation with the meaning of his existence singles him out as a unique entity among all other entities: 'Philosophy in this sense is not a matter of liking or disliking. It is a matter of man as man, for man is that being who asks the question of being' (*BR*, 8). The definition of man as the being who asks the question of being is made more explicit if we refer again to the corresponding German terms underlying Tillich's statement. The German makes explicit what is not clear in English, viz. the difference between the being of an entity (*Seiendes*) and being-itself (*Sein-Selbst*) which is exemplified by all entities and which instantiates them. God is being-itself, and not a being (*ein Seiendes*).[29] Man occupies a special place among entities (*Seienden*), for he alone is the entity who asks the question of being: 'Man occupies a pre-eminent position in ontology, not as an outstanding object among other objects, but as that being who asks the ontological question and in whose self-awareness the ontological answer can be found' (*ST* 1.187).

The understanding of man as the being who asks the question of being is expressly borrowed from Heidegger's doctrine of man as *Dasein*.[30] The need constantly arises when reading Tillich to differentiate between the being of man, the being of other entities, and being-itself which is the ground of the being of man and all other entities together. Failure to differentiate between these different uses of 'being' has thrown some of Tillich's critics into all kinds of errors. But Tillich's debt to

[29] 'Das Neue Sein als Zentralbegriff einer Christlichen Theologie', *Eranos-Jahrbuch*, xxiii (1955), 262.

[30] Macquarrie and Robinson leave the term untranslated. It is a compound word which combines the infinitive *sein* with the adverb *da*, 'there'. *Da* is the limiting factor on *sein*. M. Grene translates it 'human being' (*Heidegger*, 17): M. King prefers 'man', though she does not claim to use the term consistently (*Heidegger's Philosophy*, 66–9).

Heidegger does not end here. He follows Heidegger in affirming the need to explicate the kind of being which asks the question of being. *Dasein* is distinguished from other entities in that 'in its very Being, that Being is an *issue* for it'.[31] Some kind of 'understanding of Being' is already a peculiar characteristic of *Dasein*, for even as he asks the question of being, he has some kind of understanding of what he asks about.

What does this version of the ontological question, based on man's 'question-asking nature', amount to? Tillich seems to be advancing two quite separate arguments, each based on the universal, human characteristic of empirical, scientific inquiry into the diverse phenomena that constitute the world. Tillich seems to be saying both (i) Man asks specific questions about his world. These questions become ever more general until the wider general question of the nature of the world itself is asked. Ontology gives speculative answers about the nature of the world. And, (ii) Man asks specific questions about his world. Question-asking is a fundamental characteristic of human being-in-the-world such that it discloses something ontologically basic about it. What it discloses is that the *Seinsfrage* or question of being is an issue for *Dasein*, and by existential analysis it can be slowly and painfully uncovered.

The ontological question in (i) corresponds to our first sense of 'ontological question' above, where general metaphysical categories are regarded as providing a satisfactory rational framework within which all that is conveniently fits. In (ii) man's investigative nature, his incurable 'inquiringness' itself leads to another version of the ontological question, viz. a question about man's capacity for questioning. One of the formulations of the ontological question in an important, neglected article is 'How is it possible to ask about being at all? What is the structure of being that makes asking possible?'[32] But Heidegger's observation that the asking of a question presupposes some kind of understanding of what is asked about is developed by Tillich into a dubious deductive argument. He says

Let us think for a moment what it means to ask a question. It implies, first, that we do not have that for which we ask. If we had it,

---

[31] *Being and Time*, 12.

[32] 'Participation and Knowledge: Problems of an Ontology of Cognition', *Sociologica* i, Frankfurter Beiträge zur Soziologie (1955), 201.

we would not ask for it. But, in order to be able to ask for something, we must have it partially; otherwise it could not be the object of a question. He who asks has and has not at the same time. If man is that being who asks the question of being, he has and has not the being for which he asks. He is separated from it while belonging to it. (*BR*, 11)

Tillich is here propounding an argument which has four stages. He argues (a) if we ask a question we already have an understanding of what we ask about; (b) if we ask the question of being, we already have an understanding of being which enables us to ask the question; (c) man's understanding of being prior to his asking the question indicates that he 'belongs' to being, while his need to ask the question of being at all indicates his 'separation' from being; and (d) man's situation of belonging to being while at the same time remaining separate from it *compels* him to ask the question of being, for 'man can and must ask; he cannot avoid asking, because he belongs to the power of being from which he is separated, and he knows both that he belongs to it and that he is separated from it' (*BR*, 12: *ST* 1.208).

But Tillich overlooks at least two problems in this rather clumsily formulated version of the ontological question. He has over-emphasized the 'pre-understanding' of what is asked about before the question is put and an answer is received. For Heidegger, the understanding of being which is already present before the question of being is put is only a 'vague, average understanding'.[33] For Tillich, the same understanding is sufficiently developed to tell us that we 'belong' to being (whatever that means). In order to ask for something, says Tillich, we 'must have it partially'. But this partial possession of what we ask for when we ask a question becomes more than a partial possession when we ask the question of being. In the particular case of the ontological question, 'man has and has not the being for which he asks'. His *partial* knowledge of what he asks about when he asks the question of being becomes a *sufficient* knowledge of his 'belonging' to being ('he knows . . . that he belongs to it'). This is to read too much into what it means to ask an ordinary question. If a person knows of his belongingness to being and his separation from being *before* he asks the ontological question,

[33] *Being and Time*, 5.

he has asked *already* and received a preliminary ontological answer.

Tillich also assumes from his analysis of what it is to ask a question that the ontological question is both *universal* and necessary. Man 'must ask; he cannot avoid asking'. What compels man to ask the ontological question is the ambivalent situation of his belonging to being and his separation from being. This presumably constitutes man's existential situation. But Tillich should not assume that the existential situation will cause man to raise any question about it. Neither should he assume that, even if a person consciously asks the question of being, there need be any ontological pre-understanding at all on his part. He may simply be misled by the ambiguities of the word 'being'. Perhaps the very lack of preoccupation with the question of being is arguably a more urgent motive for asking the question than the complacent assumption that all men must, and in fact, do, ask it. Heidegger is conscious that the question of being as he raises it in *An Introduction to Metaphysics* is strange-sounding to most people. They cannot and they do not understand it.[34]

In its fourth and most common sense the ontological question is prompted by a negative human experience, variously described as the ontological, metaphysical, or philosophical 'shock', or just the 'shock of non-being'. In 1941, Tillich followed an analysis made by Santayana (1863–1962) of the breaking into human experience of determinative shocks which themselves raise metaphysical implications:

What is the meaning of being? Santayana, in a very fine analysis of experience, derives all experience from shocks which we receive and which disturb the smooth flux of our intuition. I think he is right . . . It is the philosophical shock, the tremendous impetus of the quest-ions: What is the meaning of being? Why is there being *and not not-being*? What is the structure in which every being participates?[35]

According to Tillich these questions, and the accompanying shocks with which they take hold of us, are 'essentially human'

[34] *An Introduction to Metaphysics* (tr. R. Manheim), 33.

[35] 'Philosophy and Theology', 85. The passage from Santayana is probably 'The Realm of Spirit' (*The Realms of Being*, iv), chs. 5 and 6, 'Intuition', and 'Distraction' (1940).

and the 'root of philosophy'. 'The question of being is produced by the "shock of non-being" ' (*ST* 1.207).

Ontology asks the question: 'What does it mean that something *is* and is not *not*?' . . . The ontological question presupposes the attitude of a man who has experienced the tremendous shock of the possibility that there is nothing, or—more practically speaking—who has looked into the threatening abyss of meaninglessness. Such a man is called a philospher.[36]

The 'tremendous impetus' or the 'tremendous shock' of the possibility of non-being, the shock which compels the philosopher to raise the ontological question, confronts the layman in the form of his 'having to die'. In one of his last lectures, *Absolutes in Human Knowledge*, Tillich speaks of a positive and a negative experience of being, and continues: 'The negative experience is the shock of non-being that can be experienced in theoretical imagination by those who are philosophers by nature. If one is not a philosopher, one can have it as a simple human being, in the practical experience of having to die.'[37]

The question of being is here raised for the 'non-philosopher' by the inevitability of not-being. Again the influence of Heidegger is apparent. Tillich has in mind Heidegger's description of man as a 'being-toward-death' (*Sein-zum-Tode*).[38] The inevitability of death, and the possibility of death at any moment, provide man with a negative experience against which the positive 'givenness' of his existence firmly stands out, enabling him to appreciate and assess it in a new light.

When the ontological question arises out of the shock of non-being, it gets grounded firmly in existential philosophy. This is perhaps the most characteristic form of the ontological question in Tillich's writings. The existential version of the ontological question sometimes appears in the causal form 'Why is there something rather than nothing?' (*ST* 1.181). In this form the question has an important philosophical history which goes back through Heidegger and Schelling (1775–1854) to Leibniz. In 1714 Leibniz asked 'Why does something exist rather than nothing?'[39] He used the question to illustrate the

[36] 'Being and Love', 661.   [37] *My Search for Absolutes*, 81–2.
[38] *Being and Time*, §53, 260 f.
[39] 'Pourquoi il y a plus tôt quelque chose que rien?', *Principes de la nature et de la grace fondés en raison*, 45.

truth of the principle of sufficient reason, viz. 'that nothing happens without its being possible . . . to give a reason which is sufficient to determine why things are so and not otherwise'. Nothing would be easier to explain than something, says Leibniz, so that something exists requires a causal explanation. According to the principle of sufficient reason there must be a 'reason why things exist'. Leibniz, innocent of modern difficulties with the cosmological argument, gave as his reason simply 'God'.

Schelling asked the same question nearly 130 years later, but his question was not 'rationalistic' in the sense that Leibniz's was. Schelling asks 'Why is there anything at all, why is there not nothing?'[40] This, says a recent American commentator on Schelling, is 'the existential question of him who has experienced the shock of non-being'.[41] But while Schelling's understanding of God is markedly different to that of Leibniz, his version of the ontological question also has God as its answer, designated as the primordial 'something that is', which generates existence from itself, the 'unquestionably existing'.[42] The existential version of the ontological question in Schelling and Heidegger is clearly an important strand in Tillich's ontology. Tillich uses Schelling's version of the ontological question in his early thesis on Schelling.[43] In Heidegger the question 'Why are there entities, why not nothing?' is the last sentence of *What is Metaphysics?* and the first sentence of *An Introduction to Metaphysics*.[44] The answer for Heidegger is not to posit God as in their different ways did Schelling and Leibniz, for Heidegger is not a traditional theist, not even in the sense that Schelling was. For Heidegger the question is the widest, most unfathomable question that can be asked, the basis of metaphysics, bringing into relief both the awful reality of nothingness and the being which sustains entities from falling back into the nothingness whence they came.

[40] '. . . warum ist überhaupt etwas, warum ist nicht nichts?"': *Der Philosophie der Offenbarung*, in *Schellings Werke*, vii.
[41] Gunter F. Sommer: 'The Significance of the Late Philosophy of Schelling for the Formation and Interpretation of the Thought of Paul Tillich', 209.
[42] 'Das unzweifelhaft Existirende', *Berlin Lectures* (1841–2): see below, pp. 80–3,
[43] 'Mystik und Schuldbewusstsein in Schellings philosophischer Entwicklung', *GW*, i. 27.
[44] *Was ist Metaphysik?* (1949 edn.), 38. And *Ein Einführung in die Metaphysik* (1953 edn.), 1.

The four versions of the ontological question separated out above locate four different ways of understanding ontology. These different ways are readily traceable to the various areas of Tillich's wide philosophical background. He brings together into an eclectic whole strands from classical, rationalist, and existentialist ontology, and in other areas of his thought (e.g the concepts of being and non-being) we shall see the net is yet more widely spread. The ontological question has first to be unravelled before it can be criticized. Unfortunately the unravelling has not yet gone quite far enough, for there are at least two areas in Tillich's thought where the way into ontology is not via an ontological question at all. In the book which deals specifically with the problem of the relation between being and non-being (*CTB*), the term 'anxiety' corresponds to the more formal term 'non-being'. But anxiety is nowhere expounded in the book as a 'shock': it is rather a 'state' or a general awareness. 'The first assertion about the nature of anxiety is this: anxiety is the state in which a being is aware of its possible non-being. The same statement, in a shorter form, would read: anxiety is the existential awareness of non-being' (*CTB*, 44). Perhaps it does not matter overmuch whether the term 'shock' or the term 'awareness' is used in the encounter with non-being. However it is incorrect to speak of awareness of 'possible non-being', for Tillich is clear that man already *is* a mixture of being and non-being (*ST* 1.108). Non-being is already an element of his being. If 'non-being is a part of one's own being', then we do not need to be ontologically shocked into realizing our predicament.[45] Non-being is already part of our created nature. 'Shock' implies a sudden, externally produced, instantaneous experience: 'awareness' is a more constant, internal phenomenon, which is itself the negative and disturbing side of the mystery of our being.

In another passage, the ontological question in its negative existential form is dispensed with altogether. In his elaboration of the doctrine of the 'ontological principle' (*TTP*, 22 f.), man is said to have an immediate awareness of God or Being-Itself through the principles of being, goodness, and truth. In the present context the important factor about the ontological

---

[45] The same point is made by J. Burnaby, 'Towards Understanding Paul Tillich', *Journal of Theological Studies*, v (pt. ii) (1954), 198.

principle is that it presupposes an ontological awareness already present in the human soul, without the need for an ontological shock to rouse it from its latency. The positive experience of being is itself sufficient for us to recognize the pressure of ultimate being within us, and around us. The ontological principle appears to render the ontological shock superfluous.

The ontological question is predictably singled out for special attack by critics writing from the standpoint of logical analysis. S. Hook dismisses the question 'Why is there something rather than nothing?' on the ground that 'why not nothing?' is logically meaningless. Following Bergson, Hook claims that one can only think the absence of a thing by thinking the presence of some other thing. Annihilation in thought is possible only by substitution. Blank nothing is unthinkable.[46] Consequently the ontological question is said to be 'devoid of sense except as a sign of emotional anxiety'. Tillich has assumed that because a sentence can be grammatically constructed in the form of a question, it must also have the logical form of a question.[47] G. Boas observes: 'to assume that any set of words preceded by "why" and ending with a question-mark is an answerable question is childish.'[48] Boas's objection to the ontological question is not just that, logically, it is not a question. He thinks that if it is to be allowed as a question it has to be asked on the basis of nothing or non-being. This not only hypostasizes the concept of nothing by giving it a referent; it presupposes the priority of non-being over being, and is said to validate the old myth of the cosmos arising out of the chaos.[49] E. Sprague also thinks the question assumes the priority of non-being over being and compares it with other pseudo-questions like 'Where is nowhere?', 'When is never?', 'How much is nothing?'[50] T. S. Knight thinks the question 'why?', the 'why-interrogative' as he calls it, is inadmissible within ontology.

---

[46] *The Quest for Being*, 147 (also *Journal of Philosophy*, 50 (1953), 711). The passage from Bergson is *Creative Evolution*, 283.

[47] *Jl. of Phil.* 50. 718.

[48] 'Being and Existence', *Journal of Philosophy*, liii (1956), 758.

[49] See also T. S. Knight, 'Why Not Nothing?', *Review of Metaphysics* (1956–7), 158.

[50] 'How To Avoid Being Professor Tillich', *Journal of Philosophy*, lvi (pt. ii) (1959), 969–70.

Whenever the 'why-interrogative' is used, he claims, it always demands an answer outside the field of inquiry to which it is addressed. One cannot ask, for example, the 'why' of gravity, without resorting to infinite regress or formulating a principle outside the domain of verifiable hypotheses. 'What is', it is claimed, is self-sufficient and necessary, and does not need the why interrogative to postulate an explanation outside itself. Such an answer would be 'extra-ontological'.[51]

These criticisms are directed against all attemps to formulate anything like an 'ontological question'. They have their value if they are understood as exposing the chronic unclarity of Tillich's presentation of his thought. The difficulty with them is that they are made without any attempt to understand the diverse philosophical background from which the ontology is derived. It is seriously to misunderstand Tillich to accuse him of committing the elementary philosophical howler of treating the concepts of being and non-being as if they were reifications or hypostatizations, as if their grammatical form by itself guaranteed their ontological intelligibility. But Tillich, in asking, say, 'Why is there something, and not nothing?' is not attempting to elicit an answer of the kind 'Because God made the world'; or 'Because there is an infinite Something'; or 'Because non-being is overcome by being'. His purpose in formulating this version of the ontological question is not in the first instance to elicit any kind of answer at all, but to articulate and bring into philosophy 'the shock of non-being'. It may of course be objected that the so-called shock of non-being is of no interest either to philosophy or to the great majority of people,[52] but this does not detract from what Tillich is doing. He is not asking a logical question. He is expressing the 'tremendous shock' which arises out of the encounter with non-being.

In the same issue of the *Journal of Philosophy* in which Boas attacks the ontological question, Tillich replies

These attacks would be justified if the logical form of the question were taken literally as a question about a cause or a reason in the realm of objects: for then it would lead to an infinite regression.

[51] T. S. Knight, *Rev. of Met.* x. 162.
[52] e.g. G. Tavard, 'Christianity and the Philosophies of Existence', *Theological Studies*, xviii (1957), 11–12: D. Emmet, 'Epistemology and the Idea of Revelation', *The Theology of Paul Tillich*, 211.

But the form of the question covers what one could call the basic philosophical shock about the brute fact of being.[53]

The question, then, is not logical: it is existential. Heidegger supplemented his question 'Why are there entities, why not nothing?' with a preliminary question 'How does it stand with being?',[54] a question which in its context evokes the uniquely difficult and extraordinary nature of the question of the being of entities. Neither Heidegger nor Tillich is articulating an ordinary question. Plainly, as an expression of 'ontological shock', the ontological question is existential in character. It generates a double response to the shock, viz. our horror in the face of non-being, and our wonderment that there is a world at all.[55] The use of the concept 'non-being' or 'nothing' need not mean the automatic exercise of a logical veto against its use. Two procedures need to be followed before any judgement about the use of the concept can be made: first, as a philosophical concept its use in a wide variety of philosophical contexts must be traced so that its diverse historical meanings can be uncovered: and second, that family of concepts it subsumes, e.g. anxiety, guilt, fate, having to die, etc., a family common to psychology and existential philosophy alike, must be understood as providing concrete empirical information about the character of the 'ontological shock'. The importance of this kind of thinking for philosophy should not be ruled out of order before it is even considered. A detailed attempt to evalute the significance of the concept non-being is attempted in chapter III below.

But in saying that the ontological question has an existential character, great care has to be taken in distinguishing between two different uses of 'existential'. Tillich means by 'existential' 'participating in a situation . . . with the whole of one's existence' (*CTB*, 124). For Heidegger, an existential question is a question about the meaning of the being of *Dasein*. But 'existential' means something quite different in Thomism and in modern logic. An 'existential' statement in Thomism is a state-

[53] 'The Nature and Significance of Existentialist Thought', *Journal of Philosophy*, liii, 744.

[54] 'Wie steht es um das Sein?' *Ein Einführung in die Metaphysik*, 25 (English, 27).

[55] On the close connection between the ontological shock and Otto's *mysterium tremendum et fascinans*, see below, pp. 57–8.

ment about whether such and such a thing is, or exists. It answers the question *an est*, whether a thing is. It affirms a judgement that such and such a thing exists or does not exist. But when Tillich asks 'Why is there something?' or 'What does it mean that something is?', it must be stressed that he is *not* inquiring into a kind of preliminary existential judgement through which it can be asserted that something exists. His intention is quite different. He is expressing in the legitimate form of a question a sense of wonderment that there is a world at all. This is a question which is *not* existential in the *logical* or Thomistic sense, but which *is* existential in the ontological sense.[56] Tillich in asking the ontological question is not seeking to establish the existence of anything, least of all the existence of God as the first cause of what exists, a doctrine which he greatly dislikes.[57] Instead he stands in the existentialist tradition of Schelling and Heidegger in articulating a question about the meaning of being, and in particular, human being, both in its facticity and its precariousness or nullity.[58] A much more careful use of the ontological question has recently been made by an analytical philosopher, M. Munitz. In *The Mystery of Existence* he argues that the ontological question in the form 'Why is there a world at all?' is a genuine question whose function is to state a genuine mystery. Munitz claims that there is a certain legitimate kind of 'unanswerability' which may attach itself to genuine logical questions, viz. 'the unavailability of a rational method for finding answers'.[59] The question 'Why is there a world at all?' is just such an unanswerable question. Munitz would not, of course, allow any kind of answer to the question, but he does allow the legitimacy of the question.

The logical critics, then, do not pay sufficient attention to the kind of job the ontological question is doing when it is put in an existential-ontological form and context. However the question receives a bewildering number of different formulations and arises in a number of different ways. Clarity and consistency are often lacking in Tillich. It is not a question

---

[56] As it is used by Heidegger, p. 18 above.   [57] See below, p. 71f.
[58] For the use of these terms in Christian theology, see J. Macquarrie, *Principles of Christian Theology*, 56, 77, etc.
[59] *The Mystery of Existence*, 46, 44.

that everyone necessarily asks. And according to at least one analysis of man, it seems there is no need to ask it. In one surprising passage Tillich himself even rejects the question in the form 'Why is there something; why not nothing?' as 'meaningless', on the ground that 'every possible answer would be subject to the same question in an infinite regression' (*ST* 1.181). He momentarily confuses the ontological question with a causal question about the origin of the world, and understood causally, he is right to reject it. But in another, almost contemporary passage, he remarks: 'He who seriously asks the question: "Why is there something, why not nothing?" has experienced the shock of non-being and has in thought transcended everything given in nature and mankind' (*BR*, 49). The second passage is the normative interpretation of the question as the basic articulation of the ontological shock. His ontology needs this version of the ontological question in order to ground it in existentialism. It guarantees that he is not merely engaged in the earlier type of rationalistic ontology, or in the creation of another system of idealism. It raises the issue of non-being in its acute existential. form. The existential basis which the ontological question guarantees is itself sufficient to turn ontology into what Tillich calls theology, for it easily satisfies Tillich's two well-known criteria of theology, viz. that a subject (i) 'concerns us ultimately' and (ii) 'determines our being or non-being' (*ST* 1.15, 17).

But the existentialist basis of part of the ontology should not blind us to the fact that not all Tillich's ontology is so based. We shall find many other elements which are not related in any way to existentialism or the ontological question. It is wrong to call Tillich's philosophy 'existential' as so many book-covers do. Existentialism is present as an important element in a highly eclectic ontology and it does not determine the whole. Heidegger believed the two types of ontology, the existentialist and the traditional were 'worlds apart' and 'should not bear the same name'.[60] But in Tillich they share the same status and validity and belong together in a single enterprise. Both alike are evident as we now turn to examine the all-important concept of being.

[60] *An Introduction to Metaphysics*, 34: see also *Being and Time*, 19 f.

II

BEING

CLARIFICATION of the fundamental pair of ontological concepts, being and non-being, is overdue. The procedure we shall follow consists largely of an historical inquiry into the philosophical and theological roots of both these concepts in the tradition of Western thought, and a comparison between the functions of each in Tillich's thought and in the earlier traditions to which he is the heir. Such an approach of course is bound to be selective. We consider first the concept of being in the present chapter, before examining the concept of non-being in chapter III. Then in chapter IV the implications for the doctrine of God which the prior analyses of being and non-being raise, will be considered. In the present chapter we shall note how Tillich identifies being with God, and we shall trace the influence on this part of the system of the kind of thought exemplified by Plato, Augustine, Plotinus, and Eckhart. We shall then inquire how this identity is to be understood. Finally we shall examine Tillich's development of the concept of being by the use of the two qualifying concepts power of being and love.

Tillich identifies God with Being, *Deus* with *Esse*. The identity is the keystone of his whole ontological-theological system, and the basis of the complex interplay between philosophy and theology. He asserts the identity of being and God in several widely differing passages:

Deus est esse, and the certainty of God is identical with the certainty of Being itself: God is the presupposition of the question of God. (*TTP*, 16)

In classical theology God is, first of all, Being as such. *Deus est esse*. Being in this sense is not the most abstract category, as a mistaken nominalism asserts; it is the power of Being in everything that is, in everything that participates in Being ... When Being as a symbol

O.P.T.—B

was lost, Being itself was lost. If it is denied that *Deus est esse, Deus* as well as *esse* is given up.[1]

The being of God is being-itself.(*ST* 1.261)

The statement that God is being-itself is a non-symbolic statement. It does not point beyond itself. It means what it says directly and properly; if we speak of the actuality of God we first assert that he is not God if he is not being-itself . . . Theologians must make explicit what is implicit in religious thought and expression; and, in order to do this they must begin with the most abstract and completely unsymbolic statement which is possible, namely, that God is being itself or the absolute. (*ST* 1.264–5)

Against Pascal I say: The God of Abraham, Isaac and Jacob and the God of the philosophers is the same God. (*BR*, 85)

The key statement 'God is being-itself', or *Deus est esse*, must first of all be seen as a genuinely attributive statement about God. The predicate 'being' or 'being-itself' might well seem to add nothing to the shorter statement 'God is'. It might be asked whether 'being' is tautologous and superfluous, merely adding to the statement 'God is' that God is 'existent'. The longer version 'God is being-itself' is however genuinely attributive because it attributes to God the peculiar property of 'fullness of being' which in Christian theism no other entity can by definition possess. The being which God has and nothing else has is 'being-itself'. God *is* being-itself because he is 'He Who Is',[2] i.e. he is the Supreme Being from whom all creatures derive their existence, and who, as being-itself, is infinitely greater than they.

The first statement on p. 25 above is taken from an important essay which deals with 'the problem of the two Absolutes' (*Deus* and *Esse*). The problem is the relationship between the religious and philosophical absolutes, God and being, or the problem of that to which both faith and thought are, in the last resort, directed. Is there an identity between God as apprehended by faith, and being, rationally understood? Tillich says there is. He outlines two solutions to the problem, or rather, a solution and a '*dis*solution'. The solution he outlines

---

[1] 'Religion and Secular Culture', *PE*, 63–4.
[2] *Qui est* (Exodus 3: 14, Vg.), see below, p. 28. It is not of course suggested that the traditional philosophical interpretation of this text can be sustained by modern etymological and critical scholarship.

is based on Augustine and is developed by the thirteenth-century Scholastics Alexander of Hales, Bonaventure, and Matthew of Aquasparta; it represents the *ontological* type of the philosophy of religion: the 'dissolution' begins with Aquinas, and gathers pace through Duns Scotus, William of Ockham, and the tradition of nominalism; this represents the *cosmological* type of philosophy of religion. According to Tillich, the cosmological type destroyed the ontological type and as a result 'religion itself was destroyed' (*TTP*, 22). The essay is a sustained attempt to reinstate the older, ontological approach to religion. In the 'Augustinian solution'

the question of the two Ultimates is solved in such a way that the religious Ultimate is presupposed in every philosophical question, including the question of God. *God is the presupposition of the question of God:* This is the ontological solution of the problem of the philosophy of religion. (*TTP*, 12–15)

The roots of this kind of thinking are discovered much earlier than the period of the medieval Scholastics. Tillich's concept of being is strikingly similar to two prominent features of Platonic thought, the Form of the Good, and the One.[3] We shall consider these in turn.

In the *Republic* of Plato (427–347 B.C.), the Form of the Good is an ineffable reality. It cannot be spoken of directly.[4] The Good is the source of knowledge and truth, yet it is not the same as either, and it is greater than both. Socrates is made to speak of the Good by using an analogy (the analogy of the sun). The Good (thus symbolized as the sun), brings entities

into existence and gives them growth and nourishment, yet he is not the same as existence. And so with the objects of knowledge: these derive from the Good not only their power of being known, but their very being and reality: and Goodness is not the same thing as being, but beyond even being, surpassing it in dignity and power.[5]

Being-itself in Tillich resembles Plato's 'Form of the Good' in several different ways. Just as the Good is sharply distinguished from existence or becoming (*genesis*) which it supports,

---

[3] Neither Tillich nor his critics draw attention to the remarkable affinities between the concept of being and the Hindu *Brahman*. See e.g. Radhakrishnan, *The Principal Upanisads*, 52–72.

[4] *Republic*, vi. 506 f.   [5] *Republic*, vi. 508 f.

so Tillich sharply distinguishes between being-itself and finite being: 'Being-itself is beyond finitude and infinity; otherwise it would be conditioned by something other than itself, and the real power of being would lie beyond both it and that which conditioned it. Being-itself infinitely transcends every finite being' (*ST* 1.263).

Again, just as existence depends on the Good for its 'very being and reality', so, continues Tillich, 'on the other hand, everything finite participates in being-itself and in its infinity'. Again, just as the Good is presupposed by any act of knowledge because it is that by which knower and known are held together, so Being-itself precedes 'the cleavage of subject and object'— it is the '*prius* of all that is'.[6] God as being-itself 'is knowable in Himself without media as the one which is common to all . . . He is the identity of subject and object' (*TTP*, 13). In each case, the Form of the Good or Being-itself is a kind of unifying principle between thinking and the objects of thought, or between the act of perception and what is perceived. It provides the essential conditions without which no knowledge or perception would be possible, conditions which are *a priori* and knowable directly by intuition.[7]

Augustine in several places gives the title *esse ipsum* to God.[8] God is also for Augustine 'He Who Is' (*qui est*) in accordance with the much renowned text of Exodus 3:14. For Augustine, the being of God differs from the being of the created world in that the former is supreme being, immutable and self-identical, whereas the created world is a mixture of being and non-being, and was created out of nothing. The difference between being-itself and the beings is made clear in the following well-known passage from the *Confessions*: 'I looked upon the things below Thee, and I saw that they neither wholly are nor wholly are not: they are indeed, since they exist from Thee; they are not, because that which Thou art, they are not. For that truly is which abides immutably.'[9] In so far as beings can be said to be, they have their being from being-itself or *esse ipsum*. But because beings come from and return to nothing,

[6] 'The Meaning and Justification of Religious Symbols', in S. Hook (ed.), *Religious Experience and Truth*, 7.

[7] See below, pp. 30. 115   [8] *Sermons* vi. 3–4; vii. 7: *De Trinitate* v. 2, 3.

[9] *Confessions*, vii. 11, 17.

i.e. because they change, they are compounds of being and non-being and can never be completely transparent to being-itself. Beings, or creatures, depend on God or being-itself for their being, but their dependence can never exhaust being-itself because the latter qualitatively transcends the former, or as we might say theologically, God transcends the world, and the Creator transcends the created.

In Augustine supreme being (*esse*) and finite being (a mixture of *esse* and *non-esse*) differ from one another in that, while the former is unchangeable, the latter changes, because it comes both from God *and* nothing.[10] God as *esse ipsum* also manifests himself as *verum ipsum* (truth itself) and *bonum ipsum* (goodness itself). Augustine, again betraying strong Platonic influence, states that anything true requires a prior notion of truth in the human soul, against which the judgement that something is true can be made. *Nihil verum sine veritate.*[11] The apprehension of truth is simultaneously the apprehension of God himself who as *esse ipsum* is also *verum ipsum* (or *veritas ipsa*) —*Ipsa veritas Deus est.*[12] The Good, or Goodness Itself, as in Plato, operates in the same way. Things have goodness only in so far as they participate in the *bonum ipsum*.[13] Goodness itself is prior to all relative 'goods' since 'we could not truly pronounce one of these good things to be better than another if the notion of what was good in itself had not been imprinted on our mind as the norm of our approach and preferment'. Thus, according to Augustine, we have a *notio impressa* of an unchangeable Good, which we know immediately, and without which our judgements about anything good would be inexplicable.

In *TTP* Tillich commits himself to the Augustinian doctrine of the knowledge of God whereby God is immediately known through the awareness of the 'principles' *esse ipsum, bonum ipsum*, and *verum ipsum*. On the basis of these principles Tillich forms a basic ontological principle of his own: 'The ontological principle in the philosophy of religion may be stated in the following way: *Man is immediately aware of something unconditional which is the prius of the separation and interaction of subject and object, theoretically and practically*' (*TTP*, 22). Plainly the 'ontological

[10] *Commentary on Psalms:* Psalm 121: 5. On the character of 'nothing' see below, p. 51f.

[11] *Soliloquies* ii. 15, 28: see also *TTP*, 12.

[12] *On Freedom of Choice*, ii. 15, 39.   [13] *De Trinitate* viii. 5.

principle' contrasts strikingly with the ontological question. Here there is no unpleasant ontological shock which jars us into asking for the meaning of our being. Neither do we need to make an ontological search, for *we already have an immediate ontological awareness of God* (*TTP*, 23). This prior awareness of God is built into the constitution of human existence. It cannot strictly speaking be an object of knowledge in a straightforward sense because it is rather the presupposition of all knowledge whatsoever. Knowledge itself, writes Tillich 'finally presupposes the separation of subject and object'. But God understood as *verum ipsum* is prior to any separation of subject and object. Consequently our awareness of the *verum ipsum* is said to give us certainty of God (*TTP*, 23). What man is actually aware of are the 'principles' of being, truth and goodness, the *principia per se nota*, which are not God's 'effects' as they are in Thomism (*TTP*, 17), but which are understood as God himself directly present to the human soul. Eleswhere Tillich calls this same awareness 'the presence of the element of "ultimacy" in the structure of our existence', or 'that in us which makes it impossible for us to escape God'.[14]

Failure to appreciate the extent of the Augustinian background of the concept of being is partly responsible for the unsympathetic treatment it has generally received. But Augustine's influence on Christian theism generally and on Tillich particularly cannot be so lightly overlooked. The question of the value or the appropriateness of Augustinian ontology for a contemporary theological outlook is of course another matter (to which we shall return). Whatever conclusions may be reached over *that* issue, our locating Augustine's *esse ipsum* as an important and classical model for understanding being-itself is not affected in the least. We must not assume, however, complete agreement between Augustine and Tillich over the *Deus est Esse* question. Tillich's ontology does not allow that being-itself is immutable in the manner Augustine assumes. Nor does Tillich consciously follow Augustine in making the ontological approach to God into an argument for God's existence by identifying the *verum ipsum* with the God of the Church (*ST* 1.230). None the less Tillich freely admits his dependence on Augustine to a degree no critic can afford to

---

[14] 'The Problem of Theological Method', *Journal of Religion*, xxvii (1947), 23.

overlook: 'If anyone wants to place a label on me, he can call
me an "Augustinian", and in this sense "anti-Aristotelian" and
"anti-Thomistic". I am in basic agreement with Augustine with
respect to the philosophy of religion.'[15]

If being-itself is understood as immediately present to the
human soul, supremely immanent in the constitution of the
created world, it is also for Augustine other than the world
as *idipsum* or 'fullness of being'. Tillich's being-itself suggests
both meanings; in fact the contrast between immanence and
transcendence is sometimes put so sharply[16] that as complementary terms they can scarcely be held together. The term
suggests both the manifestation of the Source of being in
beings (especially in the consciousness of human beings), and
the unknowability of that same Source in its unclouded reality
and otherness. The Platonic doctrine of the 'One' which
Plotinus found in Plato's dialogue *Parmenides* and developed
centuries later in his *Enneads* operates even more distinctly on
both these levels, and taken together with Augustine's *esse
ipsum* is a fertile source for understanding the modern concept
of being. The one in Plotinus is the remote, unknowable,
transcendent principle which is at the same time 'the author of
being to the universe'.[17] The One is, like the Good in Plato and
Augustine, above any kind of duality between subject and
object, knower and known, or intellect (*nous*) and 'object of
intellection' (*noēton*). The unity of the One is best illustrated by
a comparison with the second principle in Plotinus' divine
triad, Mind, or as McKenna translates it, 'Intellectual-Principle'.[18] In the Intellectual-Principle of Plotinus' 'Godhead'
'there is complete identity between Knower and Known . . .
by the fact that there, no distinction exists between Being and
Knowing'.[19] But not even the complete identity of the Intellectual-Principle can provide the key to the unity which alone
resides in the higher principle of the One, because even the
identity between knower and known in the divine 'Mind' can
be broken down into separate parts. Plotinus says: 'We cannot
stop at a principle containing separate parts; there must

[15] *A History of Christian Thought*, 112.
[16] See below, pp. 86–8.   [17] *Enneads* v. 3, 17.
[18] *Plotinus, The Enneads* (tr. McKenna). English quotations from *The Enneads* are
from this work.
[19] *Enneads* iii. 8, 8.

always be a yet higher, a principle above all such diversity.'[20] The One is 'absolutely simplex', a simple unity prior to any kind of quality. It transcends any name that can be predicated of it: and it is 'beyond being' while at the same time it gives being to each thing by its presence.[21] Plotinus asks

> What then is this in which every particular entity participates, the author of being to the universe and to each item of the total? Since it is the author of all that exists, and since the multiplicity in each thing is converted into a self-sufficing existence by this presence of the One, so that even the particular itself becomes self-sufficing, then clearly this principle, author at once of Being and self-sufficingness, is not itself a Being, but is above Being, and above even self-sufficing.[22]

Even in this short, isolated passage there are several remarkable parallels with Tillich's ontology. The passage mirrors the mutual participation of finite beings and being-itself. The designation of the One as the author of being suggests Tillich's fertile term 'ground of being', which engenders all finite being and sustains it. The 'self-sufficingness' of beings reflects Tillich's doctrine of the relative independence of beings from their divine ground. And, most striking of all, Plotinus' insistence that the author of being is not itself a being but above being is constantly reiterated throughout Tillich's writings. God is certainly, for Tillich, 'above being' if by 'being' is meant the being of entities, finite being or existence.

It is not suggested that Tillich was directly influenced by the *Enneads* in his ontology. It is truer to say that Plotinus was a major formative influence (through Origen, Augustine, and Pseudo-Dionysius the Areopagite) upon the Christian tradition in which Tillich stands. That is why Plotinus is important as a source, even though he writes from a standpoint quite outside the Christian Church. The similarity between Plotinus and Tillich extends beyond the restricted range of comparisons mentioned here.[23] One final comparison must be made—between the concepts of power. We shall see how Tillich qualifies his use of the concept of being by the phrase 'power of being', in an attempt to depart from the staticity of traditional

[20] *Enneads* v. 1, 5. [21] *Enneads* ii. 9, 1: iii. 8, 9: v. 3, 17.
[22] *Enneads* v. 3, 17.
[23] There are however important differences, e.g. the absence of a doctrine of evil in Plotinus (McKenna, xxix).

ontological concepts. In a remarkable passage in the Enneads, Plotinus writes: 'If the First is perfect, utterly perfect above all, and is the beginning of all power, it must be the most powerful of all that is, and all other powers must act in some partial imitation of it.'[24]

Important features of the Plotinian doctrine of the One, then, help us to understand the doctrine of being. The One, like being, is a philosophical concept which has had a marked influence on the Christian doctrine of God, notably through the theology of the *via negativa*. The identification of God with being-itself persists through the middle ages, and the writings of Meister Eckhart might be cited as our final example of the Platonic approach to being prior to Aquinas. Eckhart (1260–1327/8) stands firmly in the tradition of Augustinian theology and Tillich refers to him as a contributor to the 'Augustinian solution' (*TTP*, 14–15). That *Deus est Esse* is the cornerstone of Eckhart's theology: 'Being is the first name (for God). Everything that is defective is a falling away from being. All our life should be one being. As far as our life is being, it is in God.'[25] Gordon Leff interprets the meaning of 'God' in Eckhart as 'the source of all being (who) conferred being upon his creatures: in giving being to what had previously been non-being, he thereby enabled his creatures to participate in his own nature—which was being'.[26] For Eckhart, as well as for Augustine and Tillich, God alone is being. Creatures are partly being and partly not (i.e. partly not-being), standing on an ontological middle plane between God and nothing. In this tradition existence is a realm of ambiguity and a mixture of being and non-being, which constitutes finite being. These are themes which recur frequently in Tillich's ontology.

We have tried to anchor the basic statement 'God is being-itself' in a particular theological and historical tradition. We have already shown that the statement is genuinely attributive, and to that extent, literal. But just how literal is it? The scale of the confusion that has arisen over this particular issue can be seen by a glance at the statement about God and being-itself already quoted on p.25. In one statement ('When Being as a

[24] *Enneads* v. 4, 1.
[25] 'Sermons', 15, in J. M. Clark, *Meister Eckhart*, 195.
[26] *Heresy in the Later Middle Ages*, i. 269–70.

symbol was lost, Being itself was lost'), being is plainly a symbol. In another statement ('the most abstract and completely unsymbolic statement which is possible . . .') the meaning of being is entirely literal. In another context Tillich maintains that language about being is metaphorical. In *LPJ* he asks: 'What can we say fundamentally about the nature of being? . . . Nothing in terms of definition, but something in terms of metaphorical indication' (p. 37). Elsewhere being-itself cannot be entirely a *literal* term since it is said to *point to* something else, e.g. to the 'power of being inherent in everything' (*ST* 1.161) or to the 'original fact that there is something and not nothing' (*BR*, 16). And in yet other alternatives Tillich says that all concepts describing being-itself or ultimate reality are 'metaphorical or symbolic', or 'both literal and metaphorical' (*CTB*, 173; *LPJ*, 37).

The miscellany of pronouncements about the subject betray an uncertainty which was never satisfactorily resolved, and the confusion that has arisen over the relative merits of the literal or symbolic interpretations of being-itself is well known to Tillich's commentators. Is it worth pursuing any further? We think that the contrasting emphases are frankly irreconcilable and a legitimate source of impatience to Tillich's more sympathetic readers who try to keep an open mind about the philosophical plausibility of the concept of being. But by making a simple proposal, the cause of the confusion can be brought to light. When being-itself is affirmed literally of God, we are right to classify it as a concept: in classical language we may say it is *univocal*. When it is affirmed non-literally of God, then it is no longer merely a concept but a symbol: it is *equivocal*. When it is affirmed of God both literally and symbolically, it is both a concept and a symbol. Tillich oscillates between the first two positions, before adopting the third position in his later writings. When being-itself functions as a concept, literally ascribed to God, its use is ontological, and it is replaceable by the term 'structure of being'. When being-itself functions as a symbol, its use is theological, and is replaceable by the term 'depth of being'.[27] The ontological and theological uses of the term have been insufficiently distinguished with an inevitable consequence:

[27] I am indebted for this insight to R. P. Scharlemann's 'Tillich's Method of Correlation, Two Proposed Revisions', *Journal of Religion*, xlvi (1966), 95.

two different kinds of logical behaviour belonging to two separable uses of the same word 'being' have been hopelessly mixed up. Once their uses are distinguished a more precise account of the roles of being-itself in the ontology can be attempted. What must now be shown is how the ontological and theological uses can be separated out.

According to *ST* 1 the statement 'God is being-itself' is completely *un*symbolic (see statement 4 on p. 26). This position is qualified by Tillich a year later in his 'Reply to Interpretation and Criticism'. Here he acknowledges a criticism made as early as 1940 about the essay 'The Religious Symbol',[28] which, he says

forced me to acknowledge that in order to speak of symbolic knowledge *one must delimit the symbolic realm by an unsymbolic statement* . . . The unsymbolic statement which implies the necessity of religious symbolism is that God is being-itself, and as such *beyond the subject-object structure of everything that is.* [29]

It is uncertain whether the unsymbolic statement includes the last clause ('and as such . . .') or not. Tavard thinks it does.[30] More importantly the statement given here contradicts another in *ST* 1 where God is not beyond the subject-object structure but identical with it, i.e. 'Since God is the ground of being, he is the ground of the structure of being. He is not subject to this structure: the structure is grounded in him. He *is* this structure, and it is impossible to speak about him except in terms of this structure' (*ST* 1.264). Here then, God is literally being-itself, and he is identical with the structure of being.

A more serious variant of the single unsymbolic statement about God is found in *ST* 2 where the content of the statement is drastically revised:

. . . the question arises (and has arisen in public discussion) as to whether there is a point at which a non-symbolic assertion about God must be made. There is such a point, namely, the statement that everything we say about God is symbolic. Such a statement is an assertion about God which itself is not symbolic. (*ST* 2.10)

[28] 'Das religiöse Symbol' (1928). The article appeared in *Religiöse Verwirklichung* (1930). It was translated by J. Luther Adams and E. Fraenkel in *Journal of Liberal Religion* ii (1940), 13–33. This translation has appeared in *Daedalus* (Summer 1958), 301–21; in *Symbolism in Religion and Literature* (ed. R. May, 1961); and as an appendix to *Religious Experience and Truth*. The pagination is from *Sym. Rel. Lit.*
[29] *TPT*, 334–5 (my italics). [30] *Paul Tillich and the Christian Message*, 55–6.

Commentators have been quick to point out that the unsymbolic statement we can make about God is no longer that
God is being-itself, it is instead the statement that everything
we say about God is symbolic. Plainly this is not a statement
about God, but a statement about God-statements. It does not
directly refer to God at all. In another passage Tillich asks:
'Is there a nonsymbolic statement about the referent of religious
symbols? If this question could not be answered affirmatively
the necessity of symbolic language for religion could not be
proved and the whole argument would lead into a vicious
circle.'[31] But this time no attempt is made to indicate what the
statement is, and the matter becomes still more confused. He
continues: 'That to which our analysis leads is the referent in all
religious symbols. One can give it metaphoric names, like
"being-itself" or "power of being" or "ultimate concern" . . .
Such names are not names of a being but a quality of being.'[32]
The non-symbolic statement here seems to be the somewhat
vacuous pronouncement that religious symbols have a non-
symbolic referent. But the referent cannot be literally named,
and 'being-itself' can only be metaphorically predicated of it.
Here then, the necessity of saying something about God is
insisted upon, but what *can* be literally said is not specified.

At other times Tillich unmistakably discounts the need for
any kind of non-symbolic statements about God. He says

. . . every assertion about being-itself is either metaphorical or
symbolic . . . (*CTB*, 173)

To speak unsymbolically about being-itself is untrue. (*CTB*, 175)
. . . every statement about God is unavoidably symbolic.[33]

Everything we say about being-itself, the ground and abyss of
being, must be symbolic. (*LPJ*, 109)

. . . all . . . statements about God are symbols. In these, empirical
material is appropriated and transcended. (*ST* 3.118)

---

[31] 'The Meaning and Justification of Religious Symbols', *Religious Experience and Truth*, 6.
[32] Op. cit. 8. It is difficult to understand how being-itself can be a 'quality of being'. A quality presupposes a whole within which it has a qualitative part. In this case being-itself is both the whole and the quality. It would be more correct to say that *essence* is a quality of being.
[33] 'The Word of God', in *Language: an Enquiry into its Meaning and Function* (ed. R. Anshen), 131.

Here then the need to speak literally about God is simply given up.

In the discussion in *ST* 2 which replies to some of the criticisms of *ST* 1, Tillich says man's inability to speak directly or literally about God is due to his 'existential situation'. There is a 'boundary line at which both the symbolic and the non-symbolic coincide', so that 'If we say that God is the infinite, or the unconditional or being-itself, we speak rationally and ecstatically at the same time' (*ST* 2.11). The position outlined here, written in 1957, should be regarded as the least unsatisfactory of the three differing standpoints regarding the relation of being-itself to God. The position of *ST* 2 is partly anticipated by an article published in 1955. Here Tillich says,

We simply cannot say that God is a symbol. We must always say two things about him: we must say that there is a nonsymbolic element in our image of God—namely that he is ultimate reality, being itself, ground of being, power of being; and the other, that he is the highest being in which everything that we have does exist in the most perfect way ... That means we have a symbol for that which is not symbolic in the idea of God—namely, 'Being Itself'.[34]

Here language about God is partly symbolic, partly-non-symbolic, just as in *ST* 2.10 above, where symbolic and non-symbolic language about God reflects the ambiguity of the existential situation. Here, however, both elements occur because they are present in our 'image' or 'idea' of God. The non-symbolic element is that God is literally ultimate reality or being-itself: the symbolic element lies in our apprehension of him as a highest being. The two elements correspond to the philosophical and religious approaches to God respectively. In 1957 Tillich claimed that the 'ultimate of the philosophical question' and the 'ultimate of the religious concern' were to be expressed in concepts and symbols respectively: 'In both cases ultimate reality is sought and expressed—conceptually in philosophy, symbolically in religion. Philosophical truth consists in true concepts concerning the ultimate; the truth of faith consists in true symbols concerning the ultimate.'[35]

In the year of his death he partially clarified his position

---

[34] 'The Nature of Religious Language', *TC*, 61: see also 'The Religious Symbol', op. cit. 90.

[35] *Dynamics of Faith*, 91.

in a 'Rejoinder' to five articles criticizing different aspects of his thought, which together with 'Rejoinder' formed an *in memoriam* edition of the *Journal of Religion* in 1966. Here he says that he 'fully accepts' the statement of one of the contributors, R. P. Scharlemann, who assesses the difference between religious, ontological, and theological assertions as follows:

Religious assertions are symbolic (referring to the depth of being), ontological assertions are literal (referring to the structure of being), and theological assertions are literal descriptions of the correlation between the religious symbols and the ontological concepts.[36]

Tillich admits that the issue is unclear in his writings, and then goes on for the last time to try to outline the relation between God and Being-itself:

The more exact formulation, I think, should be that there is an element in the term God, namely, the fact that he is being-itself, which can become a concept if analytically separated, and that there is an element in the term 'being-itself' which can become a symbol if analytically separated. In the first case it is the answer to the question 'What does it mean that God "is"?' which drives to the concept of being-itself.

In the second case it is the element of mystery in the experience of being (in the sense of negation of non-being) that enables it to become a symbol.

Here an early difference between religious and theological or dogmatic statements is stressed. Only ontological statements remain completely literal. Theological statements are symbolic to the degree that they express a religious content. The term 'concept-symbol' is introduced to refer to terms which are both ontological and theological.

'Rejoinder' still leaves unresolved difficulties. It is difficult to classify statements into religious, ontological and theological types. The problematic 'God is being-itself' has elements of all three types (since 'God is both a religious and a theological word, and is for that reason a symbol[37]). At best it is possible to assess which element predominates. The problem of classifying

---

[36] 'Rejoinder', 184.
[37] That is why it is misleading to say that 'God is being-itself' is a literal *statement*. Only the predicate in the sentence can be literal. The word 'God', as Tillich repeatedly says, is a symbol.

assertions into one of three possible types arises more out of an analysis of the *terms* of the assertions rather than the *assertions* themselves. If there are ontological and theological elements in the single term 'God' which are always present and which do not depend on the context in which the term appears, then no sharp distinction between assertions about God is possible.

Despite the difficulties of the position outlined in 'Rejoinder', it is the best guide to Tillich's mature thought on the problem of how God and Being are to be understood. The term 'being-itself' can arise out of two different cognitive situations, the ontological and the religious. In the first we speak philosophically; in the second we speak theologically or religiously. What ontology calls 'being-itself' theology calls 'God'. In so far as being is a concept, it is predicated of God literally, and the predication is ontological rather than theological. In so far as being is a symbol its predication of God is obviously symbolic and therefore theological and only partially literal. It is a 'concept-symbol'. In the latter case it does not *define* God: as a symbol, being-itself 'opens up a stratum of reality, of meaning and being which otherwise we could not reach; and in doing so, it participates in that which it opens'.[38]

Tillich is right to say that some kind of literal predication of God is both possible and necessary. If God is being-itself and as such confers his being on his creatures, then there must be continuity of some kind between the being of God and the beings which together constitute the world. The continuity between God and the world is preserved by the use of the expression 'being' in each case—its use as a kind of semantic bridge between God and the world is actually an advantage to theology. To say 'God is being-itself' is to make a univocal statement. God is literally being-itself. If there is no continuity between being-itself and finite being, no understanding of being would be possible at all. There could be no guarantee that any analogous or symbolic statements corresponded in any way with their supposed referents.

On the other hand, the being that is literally predicated of God is more than being as we can experience it, and must remain, in Tillich's phrase, an 'infinite mystery'. God's being

[38] This is one of the functions of symbols. See 'Theology and Symbolism', in *Religious Symbolism* (ed. F. E. Johnson), 109.

is *esse ipsum*, being-itself, or fullness of being. God's nature cannot be exhausted by literal statements, particularly statements of the abstract philosophical type. There is therefore an element of symbolism or 'equivocity' in statements about God because they do not attempt to define the Indefinable, but point beyond themselves to the inscrutable depth which God is. Verbal symbols are not of course wholly non-literal. A verbal symbol according to Tillich is a word whose literal meaning is transcended when it is put to symbolic use. Some literal or non-symbolic knowledge of God is needed in order to know that when we talk about God *we know we have to use symbols*.[39] A symbolic interpretation of a statement implies that the literal interpretation of the statement does not go far enough. At least a rudimentary non-symbolic knowledge of God is needed in order to know that we have to go beyond a literal interpretation of the statements we use about him, in order to reach him.

When therefore we speak of God as being-itself we speak literally, and we affirm the univocal basis without which no equivocal or symbolic statement about God is possible. But to speak literally of God is not to speak exhaustively of him. There is always that within God which is inscrutable and inexhaustible, and therefore closed to literal characterization. The literal and symbolic uses of the term being-itself combine to suggest the traditional *via eminentiae*. God is being-itself in the eminent sense that when the literal predication 'being-itself' is made of him, the predication applies more eminently and fully than we can ever understand when we make it.

So far then, in our discussion of the concept of being in this chapter, we have located it in its traditional, historical context and noted important similarities between its use in classical theology and modern ontology. We have also examined the formula 'Deus est Esse' as the basis of an ontological approach to the philosophy of religion or theology, and inquired into the ways which Tillich meant the formula to be understood. We turn next to the two main qualifiers of the concept which are made to operate on it in an attempt to make it more concrete and identifiable. These two concepts, of course, are 'power of being', and 'love'.

[39] See R. C. Neville, *God the Creator*, 20.

In *LPJ* Tillich asked: 'What can we say fundamentally about the nature of being? . . . Nothing in terms of definition, but something in terms of metaphorical indication . . . We suggested the concept of power for this purpose: Being is the power of being!'(*LPJ*, 37). In this period (the early fifties) Tillich repeatedly qualified the concept of being with the help of 'power of being'. He writes:

God must be called the infinite power of being which resists the threat of non-being. In classical theology this is being-itself. (*ST* 1.72) Being can be described (not defined) as the power of resistance against non-Being, or simply as the power of being, whereby power means the chance of carrying through one's own self-realization.[40] Ever since the time of Plato it has been known—although it has often been disregarded, especially by the nominalists and their modern followers—that the concept of being as being, or being-itself, points to the power of being inherent in everything, the power of resisting non-being. Therefore, instead of saying that God is first of all being itself, it is possible to say that he is the power of being in everything and above everything, the infinite power of being.[41]

'Power of being' then, is almost as fundamental a concept as being or being itself. The 'first and fundamental statement about God' is that he is 'the power of being or the ground or the meaning of being'.[42] Power of being importantly narrows down the range of being-itself, and develops it in important directions. It requires, first, that the concept of being be understood *dynamically* as a fundamental, universal, active principle. It also requires (as we shall see in chapter III) an active principle of non-being against which the power of being gives beings power to be. Thirdly, it isolates a single quality of being, viz. power, and elevates it above all the other qualities being-itself might be said to have. Two German forms for 'power of being' are used, *Seinsmächtigkeit* and *die Macht des Seins*.[43] The former, literally 'powerfulness of being', particularly suggests that powerfulness is an attribute of being, and not being-itself. In another late German article Tillich even calls God

---

[40] 'Being and Love', 663–4.
[41] *ST* 1.161: see also *ST* 2.144 etc.: *CTB*, 153, 168, 173, 182: 'Being and Love', 664: 'Communicating the Christian Message: a Question to Ministers and Teachers', *TC*, 213: 'Religion and Secular Culture', *PE*, 63–4: *My Search for Absolutes*, 82 etc.
[42] 'Das neue Sein . . .', 262.   [43] 'Das neue Sein . . .', 255.

'the driving force of Being in all beings'.[44] Sometimes he admits
that when he speaks of power of being he is speaking not of
being but a *quality* of being.[45] But to speak of a quality of being
is perhaps not the same as to speak of being-itself, for there are
other qualities of being, apart from power, which equally can
be said to belong to it. If being is the power of being, the
introductory guidelines to the understanding of being-itself are
already laid down.

Once more we need to trace the philosophical history of
the concept in order to understand Tillich's use of it. Fortunately though, this time the derivation is simpler to detect.
Despite the reference to Plato, the philosophical background
of power of being is closer to hand. For once he is quite unusually
specific about his sources—power of being comes from Spinoza
(1632–77) and Nietzsche (1844–1900). Tillich confirms that
the concept of power which qualifies being-itself relies
specifically on Nietzsche's 'will to power' as it is interpreted
in Heidegger's *Holzwege* ('Forest Roads') (*LPJ*, 36). According
to Tillich, Nietzsche's 'will to power' is 'an ontological symbol
for man's natural self-affirmation in so far as man has the
power of being' (*ST* 2.63). It designates 'the dynamic self-
affirmation of life. It is, like all concepts describing ultimate
reality, both literal and metaphorical.' It is 'the drive of
everything living to realize itself with increasing intensity and
extensity'. It is 'the self-affirmation of life in its self-transcending
dynamics, overcoming internal and external resistance' (*LPJ*,
37).

Tillich's admiration for and dependence on Nietzsche's
will to power is expressed at greater length in *CTB*, the same
work in which he borrows for his own purposes, Spinoza's
concept of *conatus*.[46] The ontology of *CTB* is developed in
such a way that the terms 'courage' and 'anxiety' directly
represent the more formal and general terms 'being' and 'non-

---

[44] 'die treibende Kraft des Seins in allem Seienden', 'Die Wiederentdeckung der
prophetischen Tradition in der Reformation', *Neue Zeitschrift für systematische
Theologie*, iii (1961), 243. Tillich ascribes this view to Luther but clearly holds it
himself.

[45] Op. cit. n. 31 above, 6.

[46] *CTB*, 34–40. On Tillich and Spinoza, see Cornelius de Deugd, 'Old Wine in
New Bottles? Tillich and Spinoza', in *Talk of God* (ed. G. N. A. Vesey), 141: D.
Emmet, 'Review of *ST* 1', *Journal of Theological Studies*, iv (1953), 295.

being'. 'Courage can show us what being is, and being can show us what courage is' (*CTB*, 74). Courage is directly linked with Spinoza's *conatus* or 'striving'. Tillich cites the all-important seventh proposition of Spinoza's *Ethics*, Part Three: 'The *endeavour* (*conatus*), wherewith everything endeavours to persist in its own being, is nothing else but the actual essence of the thing in question.' Tillich rightly says that the *conatus* of a thing is, for Spinoza, its *essentia actualis*—

The *conatus* makes a thing what it is, so that if it disappears the thing itself disappears (*Eth.* 2, Def. 2). Striving towards self-preservation or self-affirmation makes a thing to be what it is. Spinoza calls this striving which is the essence of a thing also its power ... So we have the identification of actual essence, power of being, and self-affirmation. (*CTB*, 31)

'Self-affirmation' then, is not merely a human characteristic but an ontological element in all beings. And that power which is the self-affirmation of beings is divine, or the power of God, since, in Spinoza's view, 'The power whereby each particular thing, and consequently man, preserves his being is the power of God.'[47]

The unusualness of the background of power of being should not be allowed to escape comment, In the characterization of being-itself, material is borrowed both from a Jewish pantheist and a passionate anti-theist. Of course, Spinoza and Nietzsche were themselves heirs to the Judaeo-Christian tradition and were influenced by it, and Tillich's power of being is not *solely* derived from either of them.[48] Some commentators might want to protest against the inappropriateness of material from Spinoza and Nietzsche on the grounds that it is heretical and pagan respectively. Such criticism ignores both the freedom a Christian philosopher or theologian must be allowed to exercise with respect to his sources, and that the appropriateness of ideas in the service of Christian theology depends less on their intellectual origins and more on the uses to which

[47] *Ethics* 4, prop. 4: cit. *CTB*, 33.
[48] One notable commentator thinks the designation of God as power of being reinstates the biblical understanding of God against the 'Greek absolute'. G. Hammond thinks the use of 'power of being' is a 'partial victory' for the living God of the bible, and that 'it reflects the influence of the dynamism of the Judeo-Christian concept of God', *Man in Estrangement*, 96, 102.

they are put. The point we are making about the *conatus* and
will to power is not in fact a theological one at all. They
help us to understand what a diverse and eclectic concept
being becomes in Tillich's ontology. We have already traced
the influence of rationalism and existentialism on Tillich's
ontology in chapter I, and the influence of Platonism, Neoplatonism and Scholasticism in chapter II. We can now add to
the picture a dash of Jewish pantheism and anti-Christian
'philosophy of life'. The picture is still far from complete.

Power of being then is the basic model for understanding being-
itself, and occupies this role throughout the American period.
Love however is an alternative model with the same function, a
fact often overlooked by Tillich's commentators. In 1948
Tillich made a plea for a new Protestant interpretation of love.
He wanted this interpretation to show 'that love is basically not
an emotion but an ontological power, that it is the essence of life
itself, namely the dynamic reunion of that which is separated'.[49]
Love, like power of being, is dynamic and is 'an ontological
power'. It is in fact *the* ontological power for it soon gets identified with the concept being-itself:

... God is love. And, since God is being itself, one must say that
being-itself is love ... The process of the divine life has the character
of love. (*ST* 1.310)

If we speak of the ontology of love we indicate that Love belongs to
the structure of Being-itself, that every special being with its special
nature participates in the nature of Love since it participates in
Being-itself.[50]

Love and power of being then, are alternative character-
izations of being-itself. But is there any difference between them?
Once again the answer to the question is only possible after a
thorough look at the historical sources that inform Tillich's use
of each. The background to the concept of love is understand-
ably more difficult to unravel, but it is not difficult to show the
influence of two sources in particular, Plato and Hegel. What
the New Testament has to say on the subject seems not to
matter in the ontology, though in his sermons the biblical
influence is of course much more marked.

Frequent mention of 'separation' and 'reunion' within the

[49] 'Author's Introduction', *PE*, xxv.   [50] 'Being and Love', 661.

BEING 45

process of the divine love bespeaks the influence of Plato's
eros. The following passages are typical of Tillich's understanding of the ontological concept of love:

> The answer to the question: what does it mean that God is Love, is
> this: The Ground of being from which every being takes its power
> of being has the character of self-separating and self-returning life.
> Self-separating is the abbreviation for the return of life to itself in
> the power of reuniting love.[51]

> ... being is not actual without the love which drives everything
> that is towards everything else that is ... Love is the drive towards
> the unity of the separated ... Unity embraces itself and separation,
> just as being comprises itself and non-being. (*LPJ*, 25)

The ground of being then, separates from itself and returns
to itself. What can such an extraordinary statement mean? A
look at Plato's *Symposium* might make the matter clearer. In
the *Symposium* it is argued that if the nature of *eros* is 'desire'
or 'longing', then love must by definition be without that
which it loves, or it would not desire it.[52] Already then,
love is portrayed as the movement of the lover towards that
which is loved. Love exists between the divine and the mortal,
mediates between gods and men, and spans the chasm which
divides them. Through love, Socrates says, 'all the intercourse
and converse of gods with men, whether they be awake or
asleep, is carried on'.[53]

In the familiar tale of the birth of Love, Love is made to be
the child of Plenty (*Poros*) and Poverty (*Penia*). Love is thus a
union of opposites, and 'as his parentage is, so also are his
fortunes'. The union of opposites is then, the work of love
everywhere. Love is 'in a mean', not only between the divine
and the mortal, and the rich and poor, but even between ignorance and knowledge. Love is also the desire or thirst for
wisdom, since love can only motivate a desire for something
which is not already possessed, and knowledge is not possessed
in ignorance. Indeed, the desire of love is not only a desire for

[51] 'Being and Love', 671.
[52] *Symposium*, 199 c–202 d. Subsequent references to the *Symposium* can all be
found in 199–208.
[53] 203 a. *Erōs* is used interchangeably with *daimonion*, 'the spiritual', but Jowett
translates both as 'love'. See *The Dialogues of Plato*, i (4th edn.), 531 f. English
quotations are from this work.

knowledge but 'all desire of good and happiness is only the
great and subtle power of love'.

Eros here is plainly ontological, for it is the movement of
a basic life-process. Tillich's constantly recurring definition of
love as the drive toward the reunion of the separated harmonizes
well with it. Love in the *Symposium* is also ontological in the
sense that it is not confined to human beings only. It is manifested in the union of man and woman in conception and
generation, and the union of animals and birds 'which begins
with the desire of union and then passes to the care of offspring'
is also due simply to the power of love within them. Significantly
even the process of bodily physical change, and the corresponding changes within the soul, are cited as evidences of love, in
that the constant movement of life ahead of itself is a sign of
the desire for immortality, and is therefore one of love's
fruits.[54]

The Platonic *eros* is implicit in the accounts of love provided
by Hegel and Schelling which Tillich knew well. Hegel
in an early fragment entitled 'Love', spoke of love as 'union'.[55]
In an elusive illustration he speaks of the union of parents in the
conceiving of a child. As separate persons they come together,
separate again, but in their child they are reunited since he is a
product of the living elements of both.[56] Commenting on the
illustration, Hegel adds: 'Thus the process is: unity, separated
opposites, reunion. After their union the lovers separate again,
but in their child their union has become unseparated.' While
Tillich's account of love is not apparently influenced by this
specific passage, it provides an instance of what Hegel meant by
love, and already a dialectical pattern, with its all-inclusive
implications, can be distinguished. In Schelling God or
'Spirit' is the unity which pertains between two potencies
or opposites, just as love is the unity between lover and loved.
Love is the name given to the unity of ontological potencies,
and in the state of love the disruption of the potencies is impossible.[57] Love then, or Spirit, or God is the unity of opposites. In
Tillich's doctrine of love, the two potencies (he prefers the word

[54] 207 d–208 b.
[55] cit. J. Heywood Thomas, *Paul Tillich: An Appraisal*, 171.
[56] 'Love', in *Hegel: Early Theological Writings* (tr. Knox and Kroner), 307–8.
[57] See Sommer, 89.

'principles') are otherness and reunion. God, love, or being-itself constitutes their harmony.

Our concern here is with love only so far as it acts as a model for the basic ontological concept being-itself. Love is a much abused word, and if it is to function at all as a model for being-itself, its meaning in those philosophical traditions which influenced Tillich must be traced and made explicit. Tillich wrote extensively about the concept of love, but we are concerned only with its primary ontological meaning. He had to withstand a barrage of criticism that he had ontologized love, and allowed the philosophical account to dominate the biblical *agape*. These criticisms in the main are justified. But a more subtle criticism which ought to have been made is that in modelling the concept of being-itself by the Platonic *eros*, Tillich is giving the concept an ontological ultimacy which Plato himself would have firmly repudiated. Plato taught that *eros can never be applied to a god or gods*. If love desires the beautiful and the good, it cannot be itself beautiful and good, for it must lack those things which it desires. Love is 'in a mean' between the divine and the mortal, and between the other opposites in which desire is active. In the same way 'no god is a philosopher or seeker after wisdom, for he is wise already'. Love is not a god. Instead, 'He is a great spirit, and like all spirits he is intermediate between the divine and the mortal.'[58] Now when Tillich speaks of the divine love in terms of *eros*, or when he equates love with being-itself, he has not only Platon-ized the Christian account of the divine love, but *elevated the Platonic love to a position even higher than that which Plato intended in the Symposium*. Plato, like Augustine after him, speaks of *a* trio of that which loves (*to erōn*), that which is loved (*to erōmenon*) and love (*erōs*). But Plato uses the trio to expose the error of assuming that love is divine or beautiful. *Eros* cannot be beautiful because it is the principle of desire, not that which is desired: 'The beloved is the truly beautiful, and delicate, and perfect, and blessed; but the actual principle of love is of another nature.'[59]

Eros then, as Plato himself says, is an inadequate model for being or God because it pertains only to the intermediate relationship between God and the creature, and between

[58] 200 c–202 c.   [59] 204 c.

other opposites or contrasts. For Plato *eros* characterizes the relationship between the world and God, but is neither. For Tillich *eros* includes both the world and God, *and* the relationship between them. It is this very all-inclusive quality that makes *eros* a model for being-itself, and which unintentionally assigns to it an ontological range which Plato himself never intended. Plato's *eros* is allowed to qualify being-itself because Tillich wants to introduce into it an ontological dynamism, a basic life-principle. Power of being is the device which is normally used to do this, for power of being is in constant dialectical tension with non-being. When being-itself is alternatively understood as love, the account of love which is made to act as a model is the one which is the bringing together of all contrasts and opposites into an essential harmony within the unity of a single life-process. There is more of Plato and Hegel in all this than there is of conventionally religious sources. Dialectical and di-polar thinking have an enormous influence on the shaping of the doctrines of God and being-itself. The clue to the scope of the dialectic lies in an examination of the different types of non-being to be found in Tillich's system, the task of the next chapter.

III

NON-BEING

UP to now we have been unable to speak of being without constant references to its opposite, non-being, a notoriously difficult and diffuse concept. Non-being has already featured in the analysis of the ontological shock, the elucidation of the ontological question and in the description of power of being. We have seen how the encounter with non-being or nothing grounds Tillich's ontology in existentialism. As non-being plays such a key role within the doctrine of being, it must now be examined before the analysis of being can be completed. In this chapter we shall (i) trace out some of the different historical sources of the idea of non-being; (ii) enumerate some of the different uses to which the concept is put; and (iii) examine the dialectic between being and non-being as it works itself out in three other areas of the ontology— between the ground and abyss of being, between the divine and demonic, and between dynamics and form.

Non-being has a complicated history in Greek, Christian, mystical, idealist, and existentialist thought. Tillich often drew upon a distinction found in Plato's writings between the expressions *ouk on* and *me on*. The Greek language of course has two negative particles, *ou(k)* and *me*, and the use of each depends on varying syntactical and grammatical contexts. Both particles are translated 'not', so that *ouk on* and *me on* represent two different grammatical ways of talking about 'nothing'. They also provide a good starting point for a discussion of non-being in Tillich, for he builds on both of them, and as we shall see confuses them.

Plato's *ouk on* and *me on* are said, e.g. *ST* 2.22, to refer respectively to absolute and relative non-being. *Ouk on* is 'utterly unknown and unknowable'.[1] It is sheer nothingness or negation of fact, and is altogether void of ontological status.

---

[1] *Republic*, v. 477.

Me on is more difficult to elaborate. It can mean the principle of difference or otherness,[2] in the sense that a particular entity is what it is and *not* otherwise. The best discussion of non-being in Plato is in the *Sophist*[3] where *me on* is described as 'otherness' or 'difference'. He writes: 'When we speak of not-being, we speak not of something opposed to being, but only different.' It is important to realize that the full-blown dialectical concept of non-being which Tillich says resists the power of being, gets no support from the discussion of non-being in the *Sophist*. Not-being in this passage is a kind of negative pre-dicate of things because in its relative form it means something like 'difference' or 'limitedness'. 'Let us not say then', con-tinues the same passage, 'that while affirming the being of not-being, we still assert the opposition of not-being to being, for we have long ago *given up speaking of an opposition to being*.'

A careful study of Plato's remark about *me on* should pay dividends, for while we can affirm with Tillich that there is a difference between *ouk on* and *me on*, we should deny that the difference is at all what Tillich wants to make of it. *Me on* is not an active ontological principle but simple logical negation. Plato says in the passage that he affirms the being of not-being. This need not mean that not-being is a property or quality of things like colour or shape: it need mean nothing more than that it makes sense to make negations. We do not need, for example, to say that a cup participates in non-being in order for it *not* to be a saucer; it is simply other than anything that is not a cup. Hegel was to pick up Plato's idea of 'otherness' in his definition of finite determinations. A determinate being is something that is circumscribed or bounded by what it is not, and for Hegel this plunges it into the non-being of differentia-tion or limitedness.[4]

John Hick has recently drawn attention to the use of the Platonic *me on* in the Western tradition where it has been interpreted and developed as a kind of potentiality out of which evil arises.[5] He too thinks the use of the concept in this way is invalid, and calls it 'a fertile source of conceptual confusion', 'poetic diction', and 'a mistaken hypostatization

[2] Jowett, *The Dialogues of Plato*, iv. 386.   [3] *Sophist*, 237–59.
[4] *The Science of Logic*, 109 f., 115, 126.
[5] *Evil and the God of Love*, 47–8 (paperback edn.).

of language'.[6] He sees *me on* to have been misused by Plotinus and Augustine, and among modern writers by Berdyaev, Tillich, and Barth.[7] Hick is right to assume that Tillich's non-being is more than the mere nothingness of the *ouk on*, though it was not part of Hick's intentions to specify the philosophical influences which led Tillich to trespass as it were beyond the logical limits of the concept. The confusion between *ouk on* and *me on* becomes particularly apparent in Tillich's treatment of the doctrine of creation *ex nihilo*. On the one hand he says: 'The *nihil* out of which God creates is *ouk on*, the undialectical negation of being.' On the other hand he draws on Augustine and the 'many theologians and mystics who followed him' who 'interpreted non-being in terms of resistance against being and perversion of being' (*ST* 1.209). It soon becomes plain that the nothing out of which God made the world is in fact *me on* or 'dialectical non-being', for this nothing has a direct relation to finite beings and is the cause of their finitude and sinfulness. 'Being created out of nothing means having to return to nothing. The stigma of having originated out of nothing is impressed on every creature.' So the created world is limited and indeed 'infected' by the relative or dialectical non-being out of which it came. Everything 'created' bears evidence of its origin out of dialectical nothingness. It is circumscribed by limit (the non-being of *differentiation*); it might not have been (the non-being of *contingency*); and it will inevitably cease to be (the non-being of *impermanence*). *Me on* is responsible for all such characteristics of creatures or 'marks of finitude'.

Plainly the range of Tillich's concept of non-being quickly extends beyond what can be inferred from Plato's use of it. It also extends beyond Augustine's teaching that creatures are a mixture of being and non-being on an ontological middle-plane between God and absolute nothing. Other philosophical influences are operating here which we shall identify as Boehme, Schelling, and Hegel. Once again the problem for the interpreter of Tillich is not simply that of uncovering logical confusions in the use of a key term: it is instead the tracing out of its use in the different philosophical traditions from which it is derived, and unravelling the different strands of thought which are knitted together in an uneven pattern in the ontological system.

Me on becomes a full-blown dialectical principle within God or being-itself. Tillich asks, tentatively at first,

If God is called the living God, if he is the ground of the creative processes of life, if history has significance for him, if there is no negative principle in addition to him which could account for evil and sin, how can one avoid positing a dialectical negativity in God himself? (*ST* 1.210)

The status of non-being in this passage at any rate is now explicit. It is neither *ouk on* nor *me on* in the classical sense of those terms. It is a divine principle *within God himself*. It is an element in the divine life. It is dialectical in the full Hegelian sense, a polar element within God without which he would not be active or 'the living God'. Non-being on this account is therefore positive, essential both to the creative process of life and to God himself. The elevation of non-being to a creative principle within God is emphasized in a remarkable passage in *CTB*:

Being could not be the ground of life without non-being. The self-affirmation of being without non-being would not even be self-affirmation but an immovable self-identity. Nothing would be manifest, nothing expressed, nothing revealed. But non-being drives being out of its seclusion, it forces it to affirm itself dynamically . . . Non-being (that in God which makes his self-affirmation dynamic) opens up the divine self seclusion and reveals him as power and love. Non-being makes God a living God. Without the No he has to overcome in himself and in his creature, the divine Yes to himself would be lifeless. There would be no revelation of the ground of being, there would be no life. (*CTB*, 774)

Tillich makes it clear that any such description of non-being is 'highly symbolic', but its symbolic character must not be construed as a licence for ambiguity, a sort of blanket excuse for vagueness. In this 'highly symbolic' passage, non-being is without doubt the source of life even in God himself. No other interpretation can be plausibly found for the statement 'non-being drives being out of its seclusion, it forces it to affirm itself dynamically'. Despite the cautious deference to the role of non-being in the Christian account of creation *ex-nihilo*, non-being in this passage differs fundamentally from it in at least two important respects: (i) the *nihil* of the creation account is an absolute nothingness which has no ontological power or status whatever, especially in relation to God; and (ii) the dialectical concept of non-being is firmly within God himself, forming an internal dualism within him, so that his life or activity can be said to consist in the constant interrelatedness of the polar opposites being and non-being. God first of all has a 'No to overcome in himself', a kind of principle of divine self-activation which 'makes God a living God'. Without this principle there can be no divine revelation or life.

Hegel is, of course, associated more than any other philosopher with dialectic, and his dialectical account of the relation between being and non-being in the synthesis of becoming is well known.[8] His influence on Tillich's doctrine of the Trinity and on the development of the form of Tillich's three-volume *Systematic Theology* is sketched out below.[9] But Hegel is not the only writer in the modern period to influence Tillich's understanding of non-being: one must look to his erstwhile colleague Friedrich Schelling and before either of them the Protestant mystic and cobbler, Jacob Boehme. Tillich wrote an appreciation of Boehme in a rare English commentary on Boehme's thought by J. J. Stoudt, the first edition of which was entitled *From Sunrise to Eternity*. In this introduction he stated his preference for Boehme's language and thought against the static categories of Aristotelianism. He wrote elsewhere of his interest in Boehme and Schelling (which he shared with Martin Buber):[10] and he regarded Boehme as the author of an important though much neglected post-renaissance philosophical tradition which was revived in the nineteenth century by Schelling, Schopenhauer, and Nietzsche.[11] Tillich's first two works were of course theses on Schelling, who was himself an ardent admirer of Boehme.

A brief look at each writer shows that the familiar concepts non-being, ground, and abyss bring into Tillich's ontology meanings which belong in highly unusual and obscure mystical contexts, which must be uncovered if these terms are ever to be

[8] *The Science of Logic*, 82 f.   [9] See below, pp. 89f., 155f.

[10] 'Martin Buber and Christian Thought', *Commentary*, v–vi (1948), 515.

[11] 'Kairos and Logos', *The Interpretation of History*, 123–9: summarized by K. Osborne, *New Being*, 207–15.

properly elucidated. They represent a distinct style of thought almost unknown to English readers, and they influence Tillich's understanding of dialectical thinking. In Boehme, non-being or nothing is an element in God which brings him to self-realization, consciousness, and life: in Schelling, non-being is the positive principle of potentiality from which all change and movement is derived. As we shall see, these notions do not easily blend with the Platonic-Augustinian tradition of philosophy in which Tillich's ontology is steeped.

Boehme's God is 'an eternal Nothing',[12] totally incommunicable and uncharacterizable, but who, as a 'Nothing' (*Nichts*) must become a 'Something' (*Ichts*).[13] God is an eternal abyss,[14] but within the abyss there is a 'will' through which the abyss generates itself into a Ground, in a mysterious, inscrutable process of theogony. The *Nichts* generates the *Ichts*. Consequently the *Nichts*, despite its negative connotation, is also a positive, creative principle within God, which as Boehme says is like a seed which contains in itself all it can ever become.[15]

The theogonistic process whereby God himself, and not merely creatures, arises out of nothing, is a description of a self-generating, self-producing movement between two principles or 'ternaries' where God is neither merely one principle nor the other, but the movement between them. This movement, says Boehme, is more then just 'dynamic'—it is a violent, spontaneous fracas, 'the contrariety and combat in the being of all beings, how that one does oppose, poison and kill another'.[16] Boehme's imagery here (and of course almost everywhere else) is uncouth and unpolished, but there can be no doubt that he depicts the generation of being out of non-being in the manner of much Eastern mysticism. The self-generation of being is a violent though provisional conquest of non-being, which makes God actual and brings him out of his 'eternal silence'.[17] The word 'explosion' more befits Boehme's description than 'generation'.

---

[12] 'ein ewig Nichts', *Mysterium Magnum*, 1.2.

[13] *De Electione Gratiae*, 1. 6–8: *Behmen's Works* (1772), iii. 155.

[14] *Epistolae Theosophicae*, 47.37.

[15] A. Koyré, *La Philosophie de Jacob Boehme*, 323: based on *Quaestiones Theosophicae*, 2. 12.

[16] *Signatura Rerum*, 2.1–2. This is an early work which reflects the coarse extravagance of Boehme's language.

[17] *De Triplici Vita*, 275.

The similarity of this kind of thinking with the passage quoted from *CTB* is obvious. In each case there is both a negative principle in God, which provides the philosophical and theological guarantee that he is 'living'; and a positive static or changeless principle. God's life is the union of them both. In each case there is a strong analogy between the principles of being and non-being as they appear in life ('the actuality of being') and in the divine life. Without non-being neither concept of God would be viable.

There is also a remarkable affinity between the concepts of non-being in Tillich and Schelling. Schelling posits a type of non-being in God which is 'a potential good'.[18] It is the basic activating principle from which all goodness comes. As for Boehme it is the eternal principle of becoming in God which must be accorded equal status with the eternal principle of being, the good, creative element in the internal dualism within God. In the same way that God for Boehme arises out of his own nothingness, Schelling's God is activated by the first potency or principle in the Godhead which is given the title, among countless others, of 'pure potentiality'.[19] It is not generally recognized how close Tillich stands to Boehme and Schelling at this point, for the God of Tillich too, 'eternally "creates himself" ' (*ST* i. 280), and everlastingly overcomes the negative pole of being in the first place within himself in his ceaseless activity.

So far then, we have located strands of thought behind the diffuse concept non-being, noting that the *dialectical* version of non-being as a creative principle within God far exceeds what can be inferred from both the *nihil* of the doctrine of creation and the *non-esse* which Augustine (sometimes) dubiously interpreted as the stigma of everything created. But non-being, and its correlate being-itself or power of being, has an alternative, almost synonymous form in Tillich's writings, i.e. in the pair of concepts *ground* and *abyss* of being. When the historical roots of this latter pair of terms are uncovered, the influence of Boehme and Schelling is shown to be even more marked than in the case of non-being by itself. We consider them next.

Tillich uses the term ground of being and the corresponding

[18] *Sammelte Werke*, viii. 75–6: Sommer, 25.
[19] Sommer, 78: see also 18, 79, 127.

term abyss to express the relation between being and non-being *in a parallel systematic form*. Ground of being is, like power of being, an alternative to being-itself as a characterization of God,[20] and when it is predicated of God it shares the same ambiguities that afflict the use of being-itself.[21] Life is said to be rooted in the ground of being. Tillich expresses the hope that the use of the concept *ground* in speaking of God will obviate some of the difficulties in referring to God as cause or substance. The term, he writes,

oscillates between cause and substance and transcends both of them. It indicates that the ground of revelation is neither a cause which keeps itself at a distance from the revelatory effect nor a substance which effuses itself into the effect, but rather the mystery which appears in revelation and which remains a mystery in its appearance (*ST* 1.173; 227)

Allegedly then, there are considerable apologetic gains in speaking of God as 'ground of being'. The ground of being is also synonymous with the term 'dimension of depth' (*ST* 3.120). It points symbolically to that depth in God in which all distinctions and polarities disappear. It is manifest in both the structure of being ('the physical world') and meaning ('the good, true and beautiful') while yet remaining in its inexhaustible depth.[22] In an unusual display of wishful thinking Tillich believes that the suggestion of fecundity in the term ground of being (presumably the fertile character of earth which the material connotation of 'ground' connotes) might restore the female element in the Protestant religious consciousness of God! And not only does 'ground' suggest birth, it suggests death! '. . . it points to the mother-quality of giving birth, carrying, and embracing, and, at the same time, of calling back, resisting independence of the created, and swallowing it' (*ST* 3.313).

But, more important than any practical religious consideration *the ground of being is also the abyss of being*, a fact not widely recognized by Tillich's commentators. 'Ground of being' is in

[20] 'Reply', 335: *ST* 1. 173.
[21] *ST* 1.261; 'Reply', ibid.; *CTB*, 153; 'The Nature of Religious Language', *TC*, 61; *ST* 3.313; *Ultimate Concern*, 46 etc.
[22] 'Science and Theology: A Discussion with Einstein', *TC*, 130. The identification of the structure of being with the physical world is unfortunate.

fact a convenient abbreviation of 'ground and abyss of being', even though the linking of abyss with ground appears to destroy any suggestion of firmness, immovability, or fecundity that the term 'ground' by itself might provide.[23] Ground and abyss are dialectically related to one another, and in constant interplay between one another. This dialectical relation mirrors the parallel dialectical relation in God, i.e., between being and non-being.

The pair of terms ground and abyss is used to provide a safeguard for the inscrutable mystery of God. Tillich calls God an 'infinite mystery' who maintains his mysterious character after he has revealed himself (ST 1.278). The mystery of being appears when being-itself is encountered in both negative and positive experiences. These correspond to the experiences of non-being in the ontological shock and of the power of being which resists non-being. But these same ontological experiences both can equally well be interpreted in terms of the abyss and ground of being. Both the 'stigma' of finitude and the shock of non-being are said to 'reveal the negative side of the mystery, the *abysmal* element in the ground of being'. Conversely, 'The positive side of the mystery—which includes the negative side —becomes manifest in actual revelation. Here the mystery appears as ground and not only as abyss. It appears as the power of being, conquering non-being' (ST 1.122).

The passage assumes a dialectical relation between ground and abyss. The abyss is not just a figure of speech—it is a polar element within God as ground of being. The positive side of the mystery cannot appear except as the conquest of the negative side—that is why 'it includes the negative side' in its actual manifestation. Even negative experiences are experiences of God—they reveal his character as abyss. The ground of being is also 'the abyss in which every form disappears' (ST 1.172). The notion of the divine mystery manifest both negatively and positively, is derived in part from Otto's *The Idea of the Holy*. Tillich expressly acknowledges that he interprets Otto's *mysterium tremendum et fascinosum* in this way. The *tremendum* is the abyss, and the *fascinosum* the ground of man's being (ST 1.239). Elsewhere he calls the *tremendum* the

---

[23] See D. Emmet, 'The Ground of Being', *Journal of Theological Studies*, xv (1964), 292.

'annihilating power of the divine presence' and the *fascinosum*
the 'elevating power of the divine presence' (*ST* 1.126).

The abyss then, is the negative side of the mystery of being,
its "abysmal element". In positive revelation, experience of the
abyss is always overcome by the positive experience of the
ground. Alternatively abyss is used as a symbol for the divine
limitlessness or inexhaustibility.[24] The abyss engages in a
dialectical tension with everything it encounters, and everything that is is *limited* by it. In God the abyss is what makes his
being so mysterious no revelation can exhaust it (*ST* 1.173). It
is a symbol for God apart from and prior to his self-revelation,
in his 'uncovered divinity'.[25] The ground of being manifest in
existence is the ground of revelation (*ST* 1.172–3), but the
revelation is always qualified by the abyss which safeguards the
mysterious character of the divine. The abyss is paradoxical in
that it is both creative and destructive. In God it is always
creative, for as with non-being it is that which makes God
dynamic. Within existence, however, it acts negatively as the
non-being that limits every being. The change of character of
the abyss within existence is due to its manifestation after the
irrational transition from essence to existence has taken place.[26]
Elsewhere the abyss is called the 'dark ground' of life (a phrase
borrowed from Boehme) and identified with the 'unconscious'.[27]

Clearly Tillich is more influenced here by that 'post-
renaissance philosophical tradition' which was revived by
Schelling, than by Plato, Augustine or Hegel. In the article
'Realism and Faith' Tillich calls Schelling's concept of *das
Unvordenkliche* ('that before which thinking cannot penetrate'),
'the originally given, the ground and abyss of everything that
is'.[28] But one must go behind Schelling to Boehme to find the
origin and significance of the pair of terms ground and abyss.
Several of Tillich's commentators presume that Boehme stands
behind Tillich at this point, but no work has yet been done to
assess the similarity of these concepts in both authors. Boehme
coined his own word for abyss, *Ungrund*, literally 'not-ground',

---

[24] e.g. *The Interpretation of History*, 80.
[25] Luther's phrase. See A. A. Miller, 'The Theologies of Luther and Boehme in
the Light of their Genesis Commentaries', *Harvard Theological Review*, lxiii (1970),
281 f.
[26] See below, p. 63.
[27] 'The Idea and the Ideal of Personality', *PE*, 134.   [28] *PE*, 76.

an untranslatable combination of the negative *un-* and *Grund*. Eckhart four centuries before had used the word *Abgrund* for abyss, and he too had posited an abyss within God himself. The use of *Ungrund* by Boehme is, however, unprecedented.

Boehme's *Ungrund* is the self-generating aspect of the divine Ground—'The Unground introduces and generates itself into a Ground'.[29] The abyss is not the negation of being, but rather the *generation* of being, for prior to the realization of the Ground from the Unground, God himself had not yet come to full self-consciousness.[30] There is an element within the abyss called variously hunger, desire, craving, or will. This is the first stirring within God to become recognizable, in the first instance to himself: 'The nothing hungers after the something, and this hunger is the desire . . . For the desire has nothing that it is able to conceive. It conceives only itself, and draws itself to itself . . . and brings itself from Abyss to Byss (*vom Ungrunde in Grund*) . . . and yet remains a nothing.'[31] The most important 'moment' for the divine being in its 'eternal birth' is its self-realization or 'apprehension'.[32] Its 'place of apprehensibility', wrote Boehme, 'is a ground and beginning of all beings, and possesses in turn the unfathomable will which is God the Father'. Elsewhere the will[33] in the abyss is identified with God the Father, and that which is realized out of the Father is the Son: 'For the eternal will is Father. And that which is eternally grasped in wisdom, the grasp comprehending a basis or centre in itself, passing out of the ungroundedness into a ground, is Son or heart . . .'[34]

This short summary of Boehme's theogonistic account is scarcely able to do justice to the spirit of his thought or to the unique (and Protestant) mystical vision which inspired them. The strange neglect until very recently of Boehme's writings has made his language still less palatable than it was when John Wesley rejected it as the 'most sublime nonsense'.[35]

[28] *Clavis Specialis*, 1.58.   [30] *Aurora*, 23.17 b.

[31] *Mysterium Magnum* 3.5, cit. J. J. Stoudt, *Jacob Boehme: His Life and Thought*, 200.

[32] *De Electione Gratiae*, 1.8. See also 2.7.

[33] For an account of the rise of the 'will' in God, see Martensen and Hobhouse, *Studies in the Life and Teaching of Jacob Boehme* (1949), 40 f.

[34] *Six Theosophic Points* (tr. J. E. Earle, 1968), 8.

[35] Stoudt, 19: his source is G. C. Cell, *The Rediscovery of John Wesley*, 117.

Nevertheless Boehme is beyond doubt the source of Tillich's ground of being, and the phrase cannot be properly evaluated unless it is seen in its proper historical and theological context. Our modern impatience with the kind of language Boehme uses should be tempered first by two considerations. First he was uneducated, and in any case the modern psychological terminology through which he could have better expressed his insights was at the time unavailable to him. Second, he makes plain that his theogony is highly symbolic and he sometimes denies that he wishes to posit a time when God was not or once came to be.[36] Neither, we might add, are his writings in any way systematic. If his work were more widely known it would doubtless attract the criticism that it is simply inconsistent with mainstream Christian theism; or that the suggestion, made frequently in his writings that God himself has a beginning from nothing, is either confused, or heretical, or just plain blasphemous. Probably there would be some point to such criticisms. What Boehme has done is to allow his mystical enthusiasm to press the analogy between the processes of earthly life and God's life beyond the bounds of orthodoxy. At some point the analogy between earthly life and God's life must be seen to be only an analogy and to be equivocal in some important aspects. Boehme's bold placing of non-being before being in God is due to his technique of applying to God the detail from a general description of an earthly life process, that anything created has a beginning from nothing. It would not be entirely fair, however, to accuse Boehme of reducing the ontological status of God to that of finite living creatures, for there still remains a distinct difference between them. The difference is that the nothing from which God himself arises turns out after all to be an aspect of his eternal being, an unfathomable abyss which had yet to take shape as a ground; whereas the nothing from which creatures come into being functions simply as a pointer to the fact that once they did not exist as the creatures they now are.

But the point of our discussion about the influence of Boehme is not to bring against him or his later sympathizers a charge of heterodoxy. Such a charge would have to be grounded on

---

[36] *Epistolae Theosophicae*, 17.10. See Martensen and Hobhouse, 37; and N. Berdyaev, 'Unground and Freedom', in *Six Theosophic Points*, 2.

something more concrete than a strong dislike of his style, or its uncontrolled manner, or simple unfamiliarity with his thought and the innocent motives behind it. We want to suggest that Boehme's theogonistic musings are incompatible, not with Christian theism generally, but with the other philosophical and theological traditions which are brought into association with it in Tillich's ontology. This is the major criticism we wish to mount against Tillich, that the apparent unity of his ontological system is in fact quite markedly eclectic, and that some at least of the difficulty theologians have experienced in trying to understand him can be pinned down to his habit of drawing key terms from a bewildering variety of theological and philosophical backgrounds, while neglecting to specify either their original meanings or the newer subtler meanings they seem to acquire when he presses them into service. This criticism will be developed later. Non-being is a good example of such eclecticism. The term covers such a wide range of meanings that they cannot all be compatible with each other. We have already uncovered no fewer than five, viz.(1) negation of fact (*ouk on*); (2) negation of thought (*me on*); (3) the infecting agent which constitutes the 'marks of finitude'; (4) dialectical non-being, where non-being is a positive principle within God, the source of his own life and self-manifestation; and (5) dialectical non-being where non-being is a negative principle, encounterable as the abyss, or the ontological shock, or anxiety, or having to die. And there are still other important areas of the ontology where non-being plays a leading role, yet to be examined. We may also mention (6) mystical non-being, which tends to be rather gratuitously associated with the preceding five. There is of course a legitimate sense in which Christians have sometimes called God 'Nothing'. Examples of this proliferate in Christian mysticism. But this Nothing must be carefully distinguished from a kind of hypostatized nothing which is then posited either within God or outside him. The distinction is well described by Helmut Kuhn in a comparison between the Nothingness of existentialism and the Nothing of the Christian mystics. He writes,

But when the mystic speaks of God as Nought, as darkness, or as abyss, he means to say that God appears so to us. The God-Nothing is really our own nothingness which is unable to comprehend God. It is the inadequacy of our own human language which, in the vain attempt to express God, is finally reduced to stammering 'Nothing', thus confessing that our words are too narrow to hold God and that He can be expressed only negatively and indirectly by the admission of our failure to express Him.[37]

Tillich too, sometimes confuses the Nothing of mystical devotion, the characteristic of the Christian *via negativa*, with an actual nothingness that he locates within God. This is precisely what Boehme and Schelling did.

The dialectical concept of non-being is located both in God and creatures, though the relation between the pairs of opposites being and non-being is different in each case. In God the polar opposites are held in creative tension: in the world the tension between being-itself and non-being becomes a disruption. In the divine life non-being is always overcome even though it offers infinite resistance to being. In human life and finite being generally, the tension between being and non-being is disrupted so that non-being threatens and 'swallows up' being. 'Man participates not only in being but also in non-being' (*ST* 1.208). This is said to be a 'double participation' of man both in being and non-being, which constitutes the state of finitude and anxiety: 'Anxiety is the awareness of that element of non-being (of the negation of what one is) which is identical with finitude, the coming from nothing and the going toward nothing. This anxiety is as basic as finitude is basic.'[38]

The dialectical relation of opposites within God was expressed in Tillich's early period by a third pair of terms, divine –demonic. In *Religionsphilosophie* (1925) he wrote: 'In the sphere of the Holy itself there arises the polarity of the divine and the demonic. The demonic is the holy (or the sacred) with a minus sign before it, the sacred anti-divine (*das heilig Gegengöttliche*).'[39] A year later in the essay 'The Demonic' demonic power is placed firmly in God. Tillich speaks here of the tension between 'form-creation' and 'form-destruction', and of two corresponding and opposing principles, the

---

[37] *Encounter with Nothingness*, 91–2.
[38] 'What is Basic in Human Nature', 19.
[39] Tr. J. Luther Adams, and others, in *What is Religion?*, 85: German in *GW* i. 338.

'positive, creative, meaningful principle' and the 'negative, destructive principle'. The relation between them is the 'dialectics of the demonic'.[40] In this early essay depth (not ground) is paired with abyss, and the positive and negative principles correspond respectively with them. The depth of things, 'their basis of existence, is at the same time their abyss; or in other words ... the depth of things is inexhaustible'.

In the ontology of the essay 'The Demonic' the being of things lies in the depth and abyss of all being, which are the positive and negative principles in the Unconditioned or God. Things are said to derive their 'form' from the depth of being, their transitoriness from the abyss. In so far as the demonic is experienced in human life, it is the premature eruption of the abyss of things into form, a movement which in God is impossible because there depth and abyss are wholly creative. In existence though, on a lower ontological plane, the demonic is manifested as an irrational, uncontrollable 'form-destroying' power. 'Form of being and inexhaustibility of being belong together. Their unity in the depth of essential nature is the divine, their separation in existence, the relatively independent eruption of the "abyss" in things, is the demonic.' The power of the demonic is therefore divine power. There is no power at all outside or other than the power of God, but the manner of the manifestation of demonic power within existence is what makes it perverse and destructive:

The demonic is the perversion of the creative, and as such belongs to the phenomena that are contrary to essential nature, or sin. In the creative in itself the demonic is bottom and depth, but it does not break out as demonic; it supports, but it does not appear; it is bound to the form.[41]

The major difficulty in this early account of the demonic, bearing the influences of Boehme and Schelling, is that existence appears to impose upon divine power a compulsion to act destructively upon it, 'contrary to essential nature'. It does not explain why the divine abyss erupts perversely and destructively into form, only that within existence it does so. The character of the language Tillich has chosen is unlikely to appeal

---

[40] 'Das Dämonische': tr. in *The Interpretation of History*, 80–1. See also 83–4.
[41] Op. cit. 93. See R. A. Killen, *The Ontological Theology of Paul Tillich* (173 f.), for an accurate account of the demonic in Tillich.

to English readers, any more than the monistic view of God which it presupposes. In the divine–demonic polarity we encounter an earlier version of the being-itself (power of being) —non-being polarity, and its counterpart, ground and abyss of being. But the concept 'demonic' features prominently in later writings. In *CTB* he speaks of 'the courage to take the anxiety of the demonic upon oneself', of 'one's own demonic depth', and of the discovery of 'the demonic as the ambiguous ground of the creative' (pp. 122–3). And in his description of life-processes in the third volume of *ST*, where his systematic writing is at its most refined, he still posits 'an element of chaos' which, on the different levels of being-itself and finite being, echoes exactly the earlier sense of the demonic. In the divine life, says Tillich,

the element of chaos does not endanger its eternal fulfilment, whereas in the life of the creature, under the conditions of estrangement, it leads to the ambiguity of self-creativity and destructiveness. Destruction can then be described as the prevalence of the elements of chaos over against the pole of form in the dynamics of life (*ST* 3.54).

We have seen the dialectical relation between being-itself and non-being reflected in two further pairs of contrasts, ground and abyss, and divine-demonic. We need now to examine a final pair where the same dialectic again works through the system, viz. the polar elements of dynamics and form.

There is no room in the limited scope of this book to expound either the three pairs of ontological elements (individualization/ participation, dynamics/form, and freedom/destiny) or the counterparts of the first two pairs on the level of personal being (person/communion, vitality/intentionality or self-transcendence/self-conservation) (*ST* 1.183, 195 f.). This is a baffling area of ontology, and we shall simply confine our preliminary remarks about it to two, viz. (i) that the three pairs of elements constitute the formal structure of being prior to its actualization in existence (*ST* 1.182); and (ii) that the basic polar ontological structure presupposes a 'subject–object structure' of knowing, and a 'self-world structure' as the 'basic articulation of being' (*ST* 1.183). We have chosen to

NON-BEING 65

analyse the second polarity because of its bearing upon the basic being-itself/non-being dialectic.

The form side of the dynamics-form polarity determines what a being is. 'Being something', says Tillich, '*means* having a form.' The form of a being is a more basic element of it than its content: 'Whatever loses its form loses its being. Form should not be contrasted with content. The form which makes a thing what it is, is its content, its *essentia*, its definite power of being' (*ST* 1.197: also 3.53). The form of a thing, then, is much the same as its essence, content or 'power of being' which 'makes a thing what it is'. An important feature of the behaviour of the concept *form* is that it should not be contrasted with matter or content. Its proper contrast in the ontology is dynamics, which in turn is qualified as '*me on*, the potentiality of being' (*ST* 1.198). Of dynamics, one can neither say that it is nor that it is not: rather it is a concept which cannot be understood conceptually. It is a dialectical concept prefigured in the primeval chaos and in the concepts of '*Urgrund* (Boehme), will (Schopenhauer), will to power (Nietzsche), the unconscious (Hartmann, Freud), *élan vital* (Bergson), strife (Scheler, Jung)' (*ST* 1.198). Dynamics is 'non-being in contrast to things that have a form'. Equally it is becoming—it is 'the power of being in contrast to pure non-being'. It is the 'not yet' of being and the 'no more' of being (*ST* 1.210). The dynamics/form polarity shows how 'it is impossible to speak of being without also speaking of becoming. Becoming is just as genuine in the structure of being as is that which remains unchanged in the process of becoming' (*ST* 1.200). Form represents the being of an entity, dynamics represents its becoming, its coming from and returning to nothing. In entities both sides of the polarity are prominent, each side contributing to what they are. Plainly this polarity mirrors the dialectic between being and non-being, but at a lower ontological level, i.e. that of the formal structure of being prior to the transition to existence. The language of dynamics and form, or becoming and rest, is used to portray the basic dialectic as creatures actually participate in it.

This second polarity directly reflects the influence of Schelling. Perhaps the term 'dynamics' was suggested by his term 'potency' (*Potenz*). According to Schelling God equally contains within himself eternal becoming and eternal being.[42] There is in God a vitalistic, unformed principle, and a principle of form. Together these two principles receive an astonishing number of different formulations. Schelling's first potency is the irrational element in God which balances the rational or *logos* element.[43] It is the principle of contingency or freedom over against necessity.[44] It is the 'will of the ground' in God which is balanced by the 'will of love'.[45] the subjectivity of God ranged against his objectivity, the 'primordial matter' or 'nature principle' in God over against God as Spirit. Alternatively dynamics in Schelling is God's existence, defying all conceptualization and contrasted with his essence or ideality.[46] Sometimes the two principles in God are simply called 'A' and 'B' and not further qualified,[47] for the names given to the principles are less important than their interrelationship. Tillich's pair of terms dynamics and form adequately reflects their meaning. The first principle in God is the principle of darkness[48] (as in Boehme) or the 'barbaric principle'. It contains all potentiality there 'is' within God and outside him, a blind power principle which is tamed by the structure-imposing *logos* and which, together with the *logos*, comprise God in his 'true duality'.[49] The bewildering variety of language, drawn from poetry, mythology, theology, philosophy, and mysticism renders this nature-principle almost impossible to define. Perhaps its very defiance of definition is the best clue to an understanding of it, and the reason why Tillich says it is a concept which cannot be understood conceptually. But its plurality of verbal forms it receives renders it a most unreliable component in a system of ontology. And as we have seen in the analysis of non-being, Schelling's treatment of it (he also calls it *me on*) converts it into the source of *all* power and life, albeit chaotic, unformed and undirected. Beyond doubt the classical *me on* has now been transformed beyond recognition.

In conclusion we suggest that the second ontological polarity reconceptualizes what has already been said at a higher level of the system in the discussion of the being–non-

42 See Sommer, 78.   43 See Sommer, 209.
44 *The Ages of the World* (tr. F. de W. Bolman, 1942), 96.
45 *Schellings Werke*, vii. 395.   46 Sommer, 10–12.
47 As in *The Ages of the World*.   48 Sommer, 74.
49 *Schellings Werke*, vii. 395.

being dialectic. Considered on its own the polarity has to overcome many difficulties. The pairing of form with *dynamics* provides an unusual departure from its traditional Aristotelian relation to the matter. To anticipate for a moment our discussion of Tillich's treatment of Aquinas in chapter IV,[50] one major difficulty with this polarity is that it bears the marks of Tillich's unfortunate misinterpretation of Aquinas's living principle of *actus purus* as a dead static identity, which he then identifies with form, and then has to supplement by the addition of some new living ontological principle of his own. Tillich's misunderstanding of Aquinas's term can be expressed in a single sentence: he confuses 'pure act' with 'pure actuality'. Wrongly assuming that *actus* means *actuality* rather than *activity*, Tillich places it on the fixed, static form side of the polarity. We shall see that the Greek concept underlying the *actus purus* is *energeia*, and that as the English word 'energy' suggests, it is dynamic in character. *Energeia* or *actus purus* then, ought to be associated with the *dynamics* side, *not* the form side of the polarity. We contend that Tillich has made a major error in associating the *actus purus* with form.

The consequence of the error renders the entire polarity misleading and even contradictory. When the misinterpretation of Aquinas is added to the largely mythological theory of potencies the polarity becomes almost impossible to elaborate. It makes little sense to claim, as Tillich does, that dynamics is both 'non-being in contrast to things that have form, and the power of being in contrast to pure non-being' (*ST* 1.198). Dynamics is given the range of Schelling's first potency with the result that it takes upon itself contradictory connotations. Dynamics cannot be both the negative power of being (the Augustinian *me on*) *and* the positive power of being (the Schellingian *me on*) because non-being is what being-itself or the power of being actively resists and overcomes. Dynamics stands for the source of anything whatever which 'acts' or is alive, which is not, like Tillich's *actus purus*, fixed, static, and a dead identity with itself. Consequently on the dynamics side of the polarity we have, as in Schelling, a blind power principle, whether it acts creatively or destructively, whether it results in courage or despair, whether it represents the power of being

[50] See below, pp. 72–5.

conquering non-being, or the power of *non*-being conquering being. Anything which is not fixed or immovable is placed on this side of the polarity.

The form side of the polarity is equally unbalanced. Tillich is wrong to assume that form functions solely as identity or permanence, a kind of inert stability that constantly needs to be supplemented by dynamics or growth. Form is a flexible kind of concept. The form of the entity 'person' is not compromised or destroyed by the natural process of growth and decline. The form of a person, we might say, includes his process of development and does not need the notion of dynamics to complement it. Even if we were inclined to accept Tillich's account of dynamics and to agree with his use of form as a polar correlate, it would still be almost impossibly difficult to reconcile the static account of form with the earlier contention that form is to be best understood as the *essentia*, the 'definite power of being' of a thing.[51] For essence and power of being alike express a thing's movement from potentiality to actuality and its ability to maintain itself in its actuality. But both these characteristics of entities have nothing to do with their form as form is understood in polar contrast with dynamics. They belong on the dynamics side of the polarity and are in polar opposition to form.

Again it is misleading to associate this polarity as Tillich does with the old controversy between being and becoming.[52] If dynamics represents becoming, then obviously form represents being. And it is impossible to speak of one without the other. But the issue of the priority of being over becoming can never be settled on the basis of this polarity, for it is a *condition of polar contrasts* that neither element essentially can be dominant. The issue has already been decided, on a higher ontological level. Being-itself is the dominant concept, and any becoming must take place within the structure of being. It is only on the lower level of the ontological elements that being and becoming appear as equal in ontological status. And there the polar contrast is not really between becoming and being, but between becoming and *rest*.

One final criticism of the unfortunate second polarity throws doubt on the question of the consistency of the system itself.

[51] *ST* 1.197: see below, pp. 113-4.   [52] See Plato, *Sophist*, 251 f.

The presence of the ontological elements in the system contradicts the character of the concept of being as power of being. What is described is the structure of *das Seiende*, of beings, of the world as a whole as it becomes accessible to ontological description. Power of being, *Seinsmächtigkeit*, appears among the elements as dynamics, as one side of one of them, and *not* as the source or *being of them all*. The presence of the ontological elements introduces an incompatibility between being-itself qualified as the power of being, and being-itself qualified as a formal structure. The ontological structure risks the validity of characterizing the concept of being by power.

If the second polarity is to be retained in any ontological-theological system it will have to be recast. The dynamics side will need to be represented by a principle of power which need not be as chaotic as Boehme's *Ungrund* or Schelling's first potency. It is a wholly creative principle, which is well conceptualized by the traditional *actus purus* or pure *activity* of God. The form side is a principle of order or structure which interacts with power, and is perhaps better expressed by the traditional term *logos* than by either *actus purus* or form. But before such a suggestion could ever be adopted, general agreement would have to be obtained about the desirability of attempting a di-polar account of the divine life.

In our discussion of non-being in this chapter we have traced some of the complex historical sources of the concept, separated out some of the different meanings the term assumes in Tillich's ontology, and noted that the dialectic between being and non-being is reflected in three other contrasts, between ground and abyss, divine and demonic, and dynamics and form. These contrasts were themselves analysed and the influence of Boehme and Schelling on all of them was documented and held to be more dominant than that of the classical or existentialist ontology we examined in chapters I and II. Non-being has at least one further central role in part of the ontology yet to be considered, the transition from essence to existence (chapter VI). The historical data we have uncovered enable us to appreciate the variety of meanings which are subsumed beneath the concept non-being which, because of its careless homonymous use, are clouded over. In the attempt to understand Tillich we have preferred the historical approach to his work because it yields fruitful conclusions and because it is more constructive than the mere raking up of logical fallacies (of which his work abounds), a method which, necessary though it is, never gets beneath the grammatical surface of the text. The one major criticism we are now in a better position to bring against Tillich than before is that of ill-considered eclecticism. Plato and Boehme simply do not harmonize within the unity of a single ontological system. Schelling's mystical, mythical style of writing is inappropriate, even after revision, in the more formal ontological style of the *ST*. Absolute non-being and dialectical non-being are so far apart they should not share the same name. Neither can the anxiety-producing type of non-being have much in common with the non-being of pure potentiality. There are some of the incompatibilities. Others soon emerge as we consider next the doctrine of God.

IV

GOD

THE doctrine of God is primarily a theological, not an ontological matter. Ontology however raises implications and difficulties for the doctrine of God, over and above the cluster of problems attaching to the statement 'God is being-itself'. Sometimes key words borrowed from the ontology decisively colour the theological content (e.g. existence); sometimes the ontology brings suppositions into theology which subtly influence its character (as in the ontological argument); sometimes the theological content cannot be satisfactorily expressed in ontological terms at all (e.g. the God above God); and sometimes theology and ontology are just plain irreconcilable (e.g. the Trinitarian and dialectical understanding of God). Thus the four areas of the doctrine of God examined in this chapter are chosen because they highlight some of the ways in which theology and ontology are uneasily related to each other in the unity of the theological system. They are (a) the non-existence of God; (b) the ontological argument; (c) the God above God; and (d) the Holy Trinity. We shall look at each in turn and conclude the chapter with a short comment about Tillich's use of sources.

(a) The Non-Existence of God

It is a notorious fact that Tillich has from his earliest writings refused to allow the statement that God exists, usually on the ground that to apply the concept of existence to God makes him into a being alongside other beings, and less than being-itself or the ground of being. Thus to argue that God exists is to 'deny him' (*ST* 1.227) and to 'encourage atheism'.[1] The existence of God is said to be a 'half-blasphemous and mythological' concept.[2] Essence similarly cannot be predicated of God

---

[1] *On the Boundary*, 65.

[2] 'Religion as a Dimension in Man's Spiritual Life', *TC*, 5: *TTP*, 25. For a few of the many trenchant criticisms of the existence of God as a highest being, see

either because this would confine him to the realm of potential-ities (*ST* 1.262). The being of God is being-itself. And being-itself is beyond the contrast between essence and existence.[3] Therefore God as being-itself is neither essence nor existence. Neither term can be predicted of him.

In denying the appropriateness of talk about the existence of God Tillich is making a conscious protest against the doctrine of God's existence in Thomas Aquinas. He believes the theological motive behind Thomas's attempt to demonstrate the existence of God is itself a disturbing feature of the 'Thomistic dissolution' of religion (*TTP*, 18 f.). It belongs to the discredited cosmological type of philosophy of religion. Tillich thinks,

grave difficulties attend the attempt to speak of God as existing. In order to maintain the truth that God is beyond essence and exis-tence while simultaneously arguing for the existence of God, Thomas Aquinas is forced to distinguish between two kinds of divine exis-tence: that which is identical with essence and that which is not . . . What really has happened is that Thomas has had to unite two different traditions: the Augustinian, in which the divine existence is included in his essence, and the Aristotelian, which derives the existence of God from the existence of the world and then asserts, in a second step, that his existence is identical with his essence. (*ST* 1.262)

Tillich's insistence on rejecting belief in the existence of God is part of his full-scale rejection of that particular type of philosophy of religion associated with it, namely the 'cosmo-logical type' whose chief representative is Thomas Aquinas. Obviously there is a head-on clash between his thought and mainstream Catholic theology at this point, and Tillich certainly regarded his 'ontological' type of philosophy of religion as a radical philosophical alternative to it. In fact they stand considerably nearer to each other than is commonly supposed. Both authors agree in referring to God as *esse ipsum*. Both authors moreover, regard the created world as a mixture or composition of essence and existence. The first step towards a reappraisal of the gulf between Tillich and Thomas is to realize that each writer uses the family of concepts 'being–

'Science and Theology', *TC*, 130–1; *Dynamics of Faith*, 47; *ST* 1.82, 227, 231, 261, 271; *The Shaking of the Foundations*, 52 f.; *CTB*, 178; 'Being and Love', 662.

[3] *ST* 1.227, 262: *ST* 2.170: 'Afterword: Appreciation and Reply', *PTCT*, 307.

essence–existence' differently. Some of the supposed disagreement between the two writers simply disappears when their
differing uses of those concepts which share the same grammatical form in English are traced out.

Two leading Thomist scholars E. Gilson and E. L. Mascall
both agree that *esse* or *esse ipsum* in Thomas does not simply
mean being or being-itself but 'act of being'.[4] Gilson claims that
esse is used 'existentially'[5] so that when *ipsum* is conjoined with
esse, the *ipsum* emphasizes the meaning of *esse* as *act*ual existence.
Ipsum esse means the same as *actus essendi* (act of being). Beings,
on this view are themselves acts, and Pure Act or *esse ipsum* 'is
the ceaselessly overflowing source of its effects',[6] that is, being-
itself or pure act is related to beings or acts just as Tillich's
ground of being is related to beings. In a Thomist metaphysic,
being-itself is God as an active, engendering principle, the
pure act which instantiates entities and invests them with
their unique and individual acts of being. According to Gilson
the infinitive *esse* should not be translated as a noun (i. e. with
a static implication) but as a verb (i.e. with a dynamic implication). As a verb, he observes, 'it no longer signifies something
that is, nor even existence in general, but rather the very act
whereby any given reality actually is, or exists'.[7] (Unlike the
English word 'being', the French *l'exister* and the German *Sein*
are better suited to bring out Gilson's meaning.)

Tillich however seems quite unaware that *esse ipsum* in
Aquinas is capable of being interpreted in this manner.[8] What
is still more surprising is Tillich's definition of the *actus purus* as

[4] E. Gilson, *The Christian Philosophy of Thomas Aquinas*, 29. See L. Ford, 'Tillich
and Thomas: the Analogy of Being', *Journal of Religion* (memorial issue, op. cit.),
237: G. F. McLean, 'Paul Tillich's Existential Philosophy of Protestantism',
PTCT, 78.

[5] It is most confusing that Gilson's interpretation of Thomas should have been
called 'existentialist metaphysics', and that the Thomist *esse ipsum* should be
regarded as an 'existential' term. Gilson stresses that the concept of being refers to
actual existence, and that there is therefore more to 'being' than a formal, general
concept. But this use of the adjective 'existential' is not what the term suggests to
most modern readers. They rightly assume that the term refers to the existentialism
of the last and present centuries where the account of existence is very different from
that of St. Thomas.

[6] Gilson, *Being and Some Philosophers*, 185.

[7] *Being and Some Philosophers*, 2 f.

[8] R. Demos ('Review of *ST* 1', *Journal of Philosophy*, xlix (1952), 704), and L.
Ford (op. cit. 239) both come to the same conclusion.

'pure form'.[9] He thinks that Aquinas's doctrine of God as *actus purus* has done irreparable damage in the history of theology because it has made God into a static, i.e. non-living identity (*ST* 1.199). But this is certainly not the interpretation that recent Thomist thought has put upon the matter. A recent account of active and passive potency in Aquinas stresses that God is called 'pure act' or 'pure actuality' in contrast to created beings which are necessarily only potential, because they fall short of complete perfection or perfect actuality.[10] God is thus called a pure actuality *in contrast to creatures* which by definition can never be as perfectly actual as God himself. It does not seem to follow from such an account of pure act that it must be static. The doctrine of pure act is based on Aristotle's doctrine of being as *energeia* or actuality.[11] But *energeia* as the English word 'energy' suggests is a most appropriate word for expressing the dynamism of which Tillich so frequently speaks. We suggest the point that Tillich strenuously tries to make when he says that the *actus purus* entails a static conception of God is that the Aristotelian-Thomist metaphysic is not *dialectical*, not that it is not dynamic.[12] It is wrong to assume, as Tillich does, that the only available dynamic doctrine of God is that provided by the dialectical tradition of Boehme, Schelling, and German idealism.

The concepts of essence and existence and their relation are the subject of a later chapter, but already Tillich's doctrine of God has shed sufficient light on both concepts to see their marked difference between his use and that of Thomas Aquinas. In Thomas existence is both more positive and fundamental, akin to Tillich's being. As Mascall comments, 'To exist is not just to lie about the place exemplifying characteristics; it is to *do something*, to be exercising an activity . . .'[13] Mascall uses the verbal form 'existing' as an alternative to the abstract 'existence', because existence as a noun is said to imply a concept, and existing cannot be conceptualized—it is always something actual. That a thing exists is not a statement deducible from a

[9] See above, p. 67.
[10] H. P. Kainz, *Active and Passive Potency in Thomistic Angelology*, 30.
[11] *Metaphysics*, Λ 1071b 19–20.
[12] So Demos, ibid.
[13] *Existence and Analogy*, 74.

concept; it is the expression of a judgement,[14] so that when one says a thing 'is' or 'exists' one 'conveys assent to the "truth" of the mind's simple apprehension or reflection'. On this basis existence is logically prior to essence. The judgement *that* a thing is (its existence) precedes the assertion *what* a thing is (its essence). In Thomas, essence belongs to the defining, ordering, and classifying approach of the mind toward existence.[15] It is 'quiddity' (*quidditas*), i.e. it answers the question about something, *quid sit*? Thus reference to the essence of a thing can never establish its existence. Thomas writes:

Now every essence or quiddity can be understood without anything being known of its existing. I can know what a man or a phoenix is and still be ignorant whether it exists in reality. From this it is clear that the act of existing is other than essence or quiddity, unless, perhaps, there is a being whose quiddity is its very act of existing. And there can be only one such being, the first being.[16]

In Thomas then, the essence of a thing is *the mode of its existing*. Existence and essence are distinct in creatures but identical in God. The essences of simple things on this view are determined mainly by linguistic conventions which assign to them their names. In God however essence is not at all like learning the definition or nature of anything. God's essence *is* his existing. Existing is what God does: to exist is the most fundamental thing we can say about God's nature; and his unique act of existing is logically and ontologically prior to the existence of anything else.

It should now be plain that the deep gulf between Tillich and Thomism is partly terminological. For Aquinas, God, angels and creatures all alike exist. They are. But Tillich's concept of existence is drawn, not from Thomas or the Scholastics, but from the modern existentialists. That is the reason why, in his ontology, it cannot be applied to God, because it signifies estrangement and non-being[17] and because it has fallen from essence. Tillich's concept of essence involves

[14] *De Ente et Essentia*, 1; Mascall, 65. See K. Foster, 'Paul Tillich and St. Thomas', *PTCT*, 100 f.

[15] See Gilson, *The Christian Philosophy of Thomas Aquinas*, 30.

[16] *De Ente et Essentia*, 5.3 (tr. Maurer, 16).

[17] C. Kiesling ('A Translation of Tillich's Idea of God', *Journal of Ecumenical Studies*, iv (1967), 704) rightly argues that Tillich's notion of existence is thoroughly Kierkegaardian.

far more than mere definition. It is more akin to Platonic form.[18] The meanings of essence and existence in Tillich are so distinct that it is probably misleading even to compare them with their meanings in Thomas. Thomas could not have predicated Tillich's notion of existence of God—such a notion would have been entirely foreign to him. Curiously though, what Thomas meant by existence is largely preserved in what Tillich has to say about power of being. That is why we have suggested that the difference between them is at least partly terminological rather than theological. There is little ontological difference between the power of being which gives beings their power to be, and the pure act which gives to existents their 'acts of existing'. The difference is largely one of nomenclature; the same ontological reality stands behind each. The reason why God does not 'exist' (as Tillich understands the term) is that existence is synonymous with estrangement. Tillich is right not to predicate such a term of God, and by not doing so, he still has the ear of interested inquirers who are surprised at the novelty of a theologian vigorously denying God's existence. What Tillich however has overlooked is that when Thomists, theists, and ordinary Christians alike say 'God exists', 'exists' is not meant in an 'existential' sense, parallel with the term estrangement. 'Exists' is used in a primary and unique sense, similar to what Tillich himself means when he says 'God is'.

Charles Hartshorne (who was in frequent dialogue with Tillich from the standpoint of process philosophy) attacks the ontology at this point by asking how, if we cannot say 'God exists', is it possible to say 'God lives'? Hartshorne comments

To exist *as we exist* of course means to owe our whole reality to accidents, and our continuance to the favour of the environment. So if to exist means 'as we exist', then God exists not. But just so, if to live means to live as we do, having been born, destined to die, open to degeneration to any degree, then God lives not.[19]

Hartshorne asks whether Tillich's refusal of the statement 'God exists' and his acceptance of the statement 'God lives' or 'God is the living God' 'does . . . not show how arbitrary it is to

[18] See below, pp. 100 and 108.
[19] 'Tillich's Doctrine of God', *TPT*, 188 f. Hartshorne's argument is reaffirmed and developed by B. L. Clarke in 'God and the Symbolic', *Anglican Theological Review*, xliii (1961), 307 f.

try to make "live" more general and ultimate than "exist" '.
Tillich's answer to this must be that the assertion 'God is the
living God' is symbolic. This would follow naturally, he claims,
since 'Life is the actuality of being . . . Therefore, we cannot
speak of God in the proper or non-symbolic sense of the word
"life". We must speak of God as living in symbolic terms'
(*ST* 1.268). Why then, we must ask, can we not equally
speak of God as existing, albeit in symbolic terms? Presumably
Tillich will answer, because the negative connotations of the
word 'existence' make it an inappropriate symbol. But is the
word 'life' any more appropriate? If life is the 'actuality of
being' and a ' "mixture" of essential and existential elements'
(*ST* 3.12), then life is as inappropriate as existence to symbolise
God, since actuality includes all the distortions and conditions
of existence.

We are not of course suggesting that Tillich should abandon
any mention of God as the living God, but that by his symbolic
use of 'life' he has also enabled himself to speak of God as existing. In his reply to Hartshorne's criticism he makes a notable
admission: 'If existence in God is thought of as united with his
essence, I could apply this concept to the divine life. I should do
so however, analogically or symbolically.'[20] But when most
people say God exists they mean exactly what Tillich has in
mind. His existence is not distorted or subjected to finitude; he
exists, essentially or eminently, in a manner unique to him
alone. And Tillich should not be troubled by the analogical or
symbolic character of such a statement—indeed he takes great
pains to establish that God-statements *are* symbolic. Strictly
speaking, if 'exists' is inapplicable to God, so is 'is'. For 'is',
like 'exists', is normally used in a spatio-temporal sense, not
in a unique ontological sense, so that to say God 'is' does not
guarantee his ontological supremacy over beings as being-itself.

The question of God's non-existence might appear to be
resolvable by contrasting two complementary senses of existence,
both of which are necessary for Tillich's ontology, if God's
existence is to be differentiated from creatures. In one, the
literal concept, creatures can be said to exist but God cannot.
In the other, the analogical or symbolic concept, God can be
said to exist but creatures cannot. But on this new double use

[20] 'Reply', 339.

of the concept existence, the problems are as great as the Thomistic ontology it could replace. In Tillich's attack on Aquinas' concept of existence[21] he accuses him of wrongly postulating 'two kinds of divine existence'. Tillich is right to say Thomas has combined two different traditions, the Augustinian and the Aristotelian, but he entirely fails to see that he himself has also combined two different traditions, the Augustinian and the existentialist. According to one, existence is a property God has more fully than any created being: according to the other, existence is the realm of estrangement which is scarcely appropriate to attribute to God even symbolically. Our criticism of the doctrine of existence and its implications for theology and Christology are developed in chapters VI and VII.

(b) The Ontological Argument

Tillich's attitude to the ontological argument is ambiguous. He rejects it as an argument, while all the time leaning heavily on the revised version of it which appeared in Hegel and Schelling. While he rejects the traditional argument, he fails to acknowledge his tacit acceptance of it as it appears in German idealism. The version he finds there shapes his treatment of the subject.

First Tillich predictably disavows the concept of existence which all the arguments for the existence of God presuppose (ST 1.227). As God does not exist, it is pointless trying to prove that he does. Existence is not a concept to be applied to God. Second, Tillich disapproves of *arguing* for the existence of God. Any 'argumentative rationality' removes God from the immediacy of experience (TTP, 15), and derives his existence from the existence of the world. It is another feature of the 'Thomistic dissolution' of religion. But this does not mean that Tillich has no use for the arguments for God's existence. He writes: 'The arguments for the existence of God neither are arguments nor are they proof of the existence of God. They are expressions of the *question* of God which is implied in human finitude. This question is their truth; every answer they give is untrue' (ST 1.228). As for the ontological argument, it 'gives a description of the way in which potential infinity is present in actual finitude' (ST 1.229).

[21] See above, p. 72.

Tillich attempts to ground his claims for the ontological argument with references to Augustine, Anselm, and Kant. He accepts as valid the use of the ontological argument by all three authors, in so far as they all point to 'the presence of something unconditional' in man's encounter with reality. But he rejects any attempt to go beyond the 'something unconditional' in order to prove the existence of the God of the Church (Augustine), a 'highest being' (Anselm), or a 'lawgiver' and 'guarantor of the co-ordination between morality and happiness' (Kant) (*ST* 1.230). His objection to the traditional ontological argument is *not* the one that is usually voiced against it, viz. that the argument as Anselm (and Descartes[22]) states it requires an impossible leap from thought to existence.[23] His disagreement with Anselm is only that Anselm makes God into a highest existent being. Anselm's statement, he writes, 'is not valid if this unconditional element is understood as a highest being called God' (*ST* 1.230). We must stress that he is not troubled by the ontological argument's passage from thinking to existing. He accepts that 'that than which a greater cannot be conceived'[24] must stand outside the mind. In his criticism of Aquinas he favours the Augustinian tradition in which 'the divine existence is included in his essence'.[25] God's essence is the guarantor of his existence provided of course we do not understand by 'God' anything more than 'something unconditional', not the Supreme Being of orthodox theism. He accepts as valid the reasoning of the ontological argument which a majority of theologians and philosophers dismiss as faulty, yet rejects the kind of God the existence of which the ontological argument claims to demonstrate. Why is this?

The answer lies partly in the influence of Hegel and Schelling. In his lecture on Anselm,[26] Hegel speaks of the opposition

[22] 'Third Meditation'.
[23] So, Gaunilo, *On Behalf of the Fool*, 1.127.25–128.13 in J. Hick and A. McGill, *The Many-Faced Argument*: Kant, *Critique of Pure Reason*, 3.4.
[24] Anselm, *Proslogion*, 2, in Hick and McGill.
[25] But in sharp contrast Tillich elsewhere claims 'whether a thing is real or not is not implied in its essence: we do not know whether there is such a thing by knowing its "essence" alone' ('Existential Philosophy: Its Historical Meaning', *TC*, 81).
[26] Hegel expounds the ontological argument in three places: *Lectures on the Philosophy of Religion*, Appendix, iii. 360–7: *Logic* 51: *Lectures on the History of Philosophy*, iii. 61–7.

between being and thought, corresponding to Anselm's distinction between that which exists in reality and that which exists in the understanding only. According to Hegel, through Anselm 'the ontological proof . . . came to mean that God as the Idea of existence which unites all reality in itself, also has the reality of existence within Himself; *this proof follows from the Notion of God*, that He is the universal essence of all essence.'[27] For Hegel the ontological argument can be affirmed because within the terms of his system, *Notion* cannot be separated from *Being*, or divine essence from divine existence: 'The Notion is actual being . . . the Notion makes itself objective, turns itself into reality, and is thus the truth, the unity of subject and object.'[28] Tillich's concept of Being operates like Hegel's notion. It carries itself out of pure thought into actuality. Tillich never doubts whether his term Being really refers to anything. It has its referent in that which thinking presupposes, which he calls 'the unity of subject and object', or 'the unity of thinking and being', prior to their separation in existence. As Tillich says, 'the ontological argument relies on the sound principle of the identity of being and thinking, which all thinking presupposes'.[29] Thinking presupposes being as the essential unity between the thinker and what is thought. Being transcends the distinction or separation between them. Being, or the Unconditioned, is 'the *prius* of subject and object' (*TTP*, 25). And being has already been identified with God. This is how Tillich uses the ontological argument. While he is correct to say that he does not use the ontological argument as an explicit argument for God's existence, he clearly relies very heavily on the use of the argument as it appears in German idealism. In Tillich we may say the argument runs: thinking presupposes being; being is God; therefore God is the *sine qua non* of thought. While he never states this as an explicit argument, he would have to readily accept each of its three stages as integral to his thought.

Schelling in similar vein had spoken of *das Unvordenkliche* ('that which is prior to thought'),[30] or alternatively the *unvordenkliche Dass* or the *unvordenkliche Sein*,[31] and by each of

---

[27] *Lectures on the History of Philosophy*, iii. 63.
[28] *Lectures on the Philosophy of Religion*, iii. 365.
[29] Ibid., n. 25.　　　　　　　　　　　[30] Ibid.
[31] See Sommer, 30.

these expressions he had meant God. His use of the ontological argument is best illustrated in his Berlin Lectures of 1841–2, in which his 'positive philosophy' is outlined against the 'negative philosophy' of Hegelianism. In his later period of critical reaction to idealism he denied that any passage lay from thinking to existing. One cannot think the idea of God, and then argue from such an idea to the affirmation that God is because the idea of God includes the idea of existence within itself. This was what Hegel sought to do. One must begin with existence and work from existence back to the essence or idea of what exists. So Schelling's God is first of all an existent God, whose existence is prior to his essence and prior to the existence of anything else. Schelling writes

To be sure I cannot start from the concept of God in order to prove God's existence, but I can start from the concept of the mere unquestionably existing and vice-versa prove the godhood of the unquestionably existing. Now if the godhood is the what, the essence, the potency, then I do not go here from potency to being, but vice-versa, from being to essence. Here being is *prius* and essence *posterius*. This transition, however, is not possible without a reversal, without changing the entire direction of the science of being, and without breaking away from it and beginning entirely anew, in other words, beginning a new science, and this is what positive philosophy is.[32]

Schelling chose what he called 'the unquestionably existing' (*das unzweifelhaft Existirende*) in order to remain true to the avowed aims of his positive philosophy, which were to begin with existence and to reverse the direction idealism had taken in beginning with God as 'the universal essence of all essence'. Schelling begins with existence or act and from thence he moves to the realm of essence or potency. Being, i.e. existence, comes before essence. Schelling starts with what 'unquestionably exists'. And what unquestionably exists is simply God who exists prior to all thought and awareness of him. 'The ontological argument', he writes, 'had it been understood in its proper meaning ... would have led to the starting-point of positive philosophy ... to Being, the Prius of all thought.'[33]

But Schelling's use of the ontological argument is as devious as any of the other authors whose use of the argument Tillich

[32] 'Berlin Lectures', in *The Search for Being* (eds. J. Wilde and W. Kimmel), 34.
[33] *Schellings Werke*, vii. 158.

rejects. Schelling is merely arguing that for something to exist contingently, something else must exist necessarily (i.e. unquestionably), an argument more usually associated with cosmology than with ontology. And this necessary existence is God. One begins with being or existence, and then one posits the divine essence of the unquestionably existing. But this procedure is unsatisfactory for several reasons. For Schelling starts *not*, as he says, with the unquestionably existing, but with the *concept* of the unquestionably existing. But how, we must ask, does he proceed from the *concept* of the unquestionably existing to what actually exists? For while we may at least be able to think of the unquestionably exising, our thinking does not by itself guarantee either that there is that which exists unquestionably or that this is somehow divine. There is no reason why anything should exist unquestionably, or as we are accustomed to say, necessarily. Why should the phrase 'unquestionably existing' have a referent at all? If there is a God then his existence is arguably necessary. It follows from what he must be if he is God. But such an argument presupposes God's existence; it does not establish it. The 'unquestionably existing' or the ' "That" of existence' or 'that beyond which thought cannot penetrate' is still an essence or concept, however strenuously Schelling would deny it. It need not of course be pointless to call God 'the unquestionably existing', but it is certainly pointless to assume that by doing so, one has established the existence of what one has named. Schelling's attempt to distinguish his procedure from his philosophical antagonist, Hegel, fails.

Tillich is right to say he does not use the argument as an *argument*. But he draws upon the important contention contained in the idealist account of the argument that the gap between thought and reality or subject and object is overcome in the idea of God which precedes any such separation. This is the *prius* of thought and is very obviously identified by Tillich with the God of the Christian faith, even though the identity is assumed and not argued or proved. As we have seen Hegel simply said that 'this proof thus follows from the Notion of God': Schelling that the 'unquestionably existing' and 'godhood' are the same conceptually and actually. But this is to confuse logical with ontological necessity, i.e. the concept of God must include his existence, but the existence of God is not demonstrated by the concept. According to Schelling it is unthinkable that God should not exist, but this unfortunately tells us more about Schelling's thought than it does about God's existence. It is the same with Tillich. It is always implicit that the 'something unconditional' which Tillich says is drawn out by the classical ontological argument is, in fact, the God of the Christian revelation. The 'unconditional' is not an indefinite something. When we inquire more closely into it, the unconditional is the structure of being which all thinking presupposes. And this structure of being is also the philosophical expression of 'God' and is identical with it.[34] On this basis Tillich's use of the ontological argument makes it much more important than a mere expression of the 'question of God'. His disclaimer of the ontological argument is disingenuous— his dependence upon one particular version of it is greater than he admits.

(c) The God above God

Tillich speaks of the God above God, or the God beyond God, in the final section of CTB.[35] The term is a revival of der Gott über Gott which appeared for the first time in 1915 as a criticism of the God of supranaturalism which was dubbed 'the God below God'.[36] Tillich says his use of the idea of the God above God belongs to apologetic, not dogmatic, theology (ST 2.13). It is born out of an apologetic need to transcend the various forms of theism. The forms of theism he has in mind are threefold: the 'unspecified affirmation of God' where the word God is reduced to an empty slogan; the personalism of the Jewish-Christian tradition; and the 'theological theism' which tries to prove God's existence (CTB, 176–9).

The idea of the God above God is most effective in the situation of existential anxiety and doubt. It is the source of the

---

34 W. Rowe has rightly contended that Tillich uses the ontological argument in an attempt to prove there is an ultimate 'ground of thought' which is then identified with God, Religious Symbols and God, 88 f.

35 CTB, 176–83. For 'the God beyond God', CTB, 182: 'Theology and Symbolism', Religious Symbolism (ed. F. E. Johnson), 114: 'Religious Symbols and our Knowledge of God', Christian Scholar, xxxviii (1955), 14 (revised in TC).

36 Der Begriff des Übernaturlichen . . . , 44. See also GW i. 369.

courage by which the three main types of anxiety inflicting man are overcome.

It gives one the courage of self-affirmation even in the extreme situation of radical doubt. In such a state the God of both religious and theological language disappears. But something remains, namely the seriousness of that doubt in which meaning within meaninglessness is affirmed. The source of this affirmation of meaning within meaninglessness, of certitude within doubt, is not the God of traditional theism but the 'God above God', the power of being, which works through those who have no name for it, not even the name God. (*ST* 2.13–14)

It may be that the God above God has high apologetic value for those in the predicament Tillich describes. But if the price of apologetic relevance is the transcending of theism itself, is it too great a price to pay? The ontological implication of the question is clear. If the God who is being-itself is 'the god above the god of theism', is he also beyond being? If the God of classical theism is being-itself, what is the ontological status of the God above God? To answer this question, the thinking which underlies the phrase 'God above God' must be examined further.

Within the context of the experience of doubt (in the Cartesian sense), the idea of the God above God is made to express the insight contained in Augustine's statement 'For if I doubt, I am'.[37] Augustine pointed to the presence of truth even in the state of radical doubt. God is Truth.[38] If a person doubts, that he doubts is true. He cannot doubt that he doubts, and if it is true that he doubts, there is truth even in the presence of radical doubt. (This is a solution certain to commend itself to Tillich. It presupposes the immediate religious certainty (*TTP*, 16) which is the key feature of the Augustinian type of philosophy of religion.) Just as truth reappears when all trace of truth was thought lost, so God reappears as the God above the God of theism when all belief in God is lost.

But the phrase 'God above God' implies more than the inward presence of God in the experience of existential doubt. Augustine did not need to 'transcend theism' in order to express the same insight. Tillich means something more provocative than this. He intends to challenge the whole idea of

[37] 'Si enim fallor sum': *De Civitate Dei*, 11.26.
[38] See above, p. 29.

theism as it is commonly understood.[39] He suggests in his
lectures on the History of Christian Thought that his source for
the idea of the God above God may have been Pseudo-
Dionysius the Areopagite. He certainly leans heavily on the so-
called *via negativa* or *via negationis* in his approach to the God
above God, in the manner of the Areopagite. He says: 'God is
beyond even the highest names which theology has given to
him . . . He is supra-divinity, beyond God, if we speak of God
as a divine being.[40] This is exactly the position of the Areopagite
on which Tillich was commenting, and the motive for the Areopagite's *magnum opus On the Divine Names*. So anxious is Dionysius
to protect the transcendence of God that he even refuses to
predicate deity of God. His work *The Mystical Theology* begins
'O Trinity, which exceedeth all Being, Deity, and Goodness'.[41]

There are other attempts in historical theology to go beyond
God in order to discover him. Eckhart, for example, drove a
distinction between God and Godhead, regarding the latter as
inaccessible to description.[42] But it is doubtful whether any
of these negative theologies, Tillich's among them, wholly
succeed in their attempt to safeguard the transcendence of
God and prevent any objectification of the divine being. First
it is difficult to see how theism can be transcended by the God
above God, for even the God above God is a theistic concept.
Moreover there is a type of theism, the Augustinian-Fran-
ciscan type, which Tillich accepts and which does not need to
be transcended. It posits God as immediately present to the
human soul without going 'beyond God' to do this. In any case
God scarcely needs to be transcended in order to be understood
as other than all finite existents and conceptions. Orthodox
theism equally, has a place for the radical otherness of God.

Second, a God above or beyond God is, according to the
spatial connotations of 'above' and 'beyond', further removed
from, not nearer to, man in his existential predicament than
the God of Christian theism. Third, the phrase does not, as a
matter of course, obviate the difficulty of speaking of God as

[39] Tillich is reported to have said of *CTB* that he let the conclusion 'come to a
point like a needle' which was 'meant to prick' (C. Rhein, *Paul Tillich, Philosoph
und Theologe, Ein Einführung in sein Denken*, 111 n. 27).
[40] *A History of Christian Thought*, 192.
[41] *The Mystical Theology*, 1 (tr. C. E. Rolt, *Dionysius the Areopagite*, 191).
[42] *Sermons*, 16.

an existent being. All the questions about the existence and causality of the God of theism, are transferable to the God above that same conception. It does not avoid the difficulties— it intensifies them. Fourth, the God above God is an attempt to conceptualize that very aspect of the term 'God' which by the very nature of the case cannot be conceptualized. 'God is symbol for God'.[43] Beyond the symbol 'God' we cannot go. The word 'God' is a primary word (*Ur-Wort*) that cannot be replaced,[44] and which has a partly literal, partly symbolic character. With the God above God Tillich tries to do what he has elsewhere deemed impossible. He tries to express the *symbolizandum* of the symbol 'God' by another more explicit less symbolic term 'God above God'. The attempt fails.

But the God above God (which, it must be admitted plays only a small part in Tillich's writings) raises a deep implication for the understanding of the concept of being. The God above God is, within its context, ineffable, removed from the world, the Areopagite's super-transcendent deity which 'is not in the likeness of any created thing, and we cannot comprehend Its super-essential, invisible, and ineffable Infinity'.[45] This is not the immanent, involved God of the earlier chapters of *CTB* who affirms meaning in the individuals' courage to take meaninglessness upon himself in a courageous self-affirming act. This is Augustinian, not Plotinian. Is there here not one God but two? One is the super-transcendent deity, beyond any predication whatsoever, the other the involved God whose life is strictly analogous to earthly life-processes and which in Jesus Christ became identical with them. The distinction between the transcendence and the immanence of God becomes so attenuated that a danger arises of forming two separate ideas of God. When the problem receives an *ontological* for-mulation, it raises the question how everything finite can participate in being-itself if being-itself is utterly remote from finitude. How can the finite be essentially included

---

[43] *Dynamics of Faith*, 45.

[44] 'Martin Buber and Christian Thought', *Commentary*, v–vi (1948), 515 (revised in *TC*), and 'Martin Buber, 1878–1965', *Pastoral Psychology*, xvi (1965), 52. Tillich says he learned from Buber the impossibility of any attempt to replace the word 'God'. Written in 1948 he reaffirmed this position in 1965. But is 'God above God' an attempt to replace 'God'?

[45] *The Celestial Hierarchies* (tr. The Shrine of Wisdom), 2.

within being-itself, how can being-itself posit its opposite non-being within itself in a dialectical process, if being-itself is at the same time ineffable and beyond characterization? How can that which is utterly beyond any life-processes also be the supporting ground and moving power of them all? Two different concepts of God and of Being seem to be required if both God's transcendence and his immanence are to be forced so far apart in some contexts and held so close together in others.

The ontology cannot in fact cope with the radical immanence of God and his radical transcendence together. On the one hand being-itself is beyond infinity (*ST* 1.212), beyond essence and existence,[46] in fact beyond any 'special qualification' (*BR*, 16). On the other hand, everything finite participates in being-itself (*ST* 1.263) and being-itself is said to have the character of becoming or process (*ST* 3.344). God as the 'creative ground of everything that has being' is said to be nearer to things than they are to themselves (*ST* 2.8). The ambiguity is reflected when the experience of the God above God ('absolute faith') is described as the 'power of being-itself' (*CTB*, 179 : *ST* 2.14). But on Tillich's own terms, *everything that is* participates in the power of being-itself. He cannot distinguish ontologically between the extraordinary experience of absolute faith and the ordinary experience of every being as it participates in the power of being, i.e., he cannot differentiate ontologically between transcendence and immanence—the power of being embraces both.

Tillich cannot be blamed for this fundamental ambiguity because it seems to have been inherent in the tradition in which he stands, going right back as far as Plato. The Areopagite for example, had no apparent difficulty in maintaining his super-transcendent deity as the cause and creator of all things, 'the substantial Cause and Creator of Being, Existence, Substance and Nature'.[47] Dorothy Emmet has noticed that the Areopagite is here ambiguous.[48] It is a tension of any kind of genuine theism that the God who is strictly uncharacterizable must be ascribed, however inadequately, certain characteristics appropriate to him (the Hindu Brahman is still more susceptible

[46] *ST* 1.262: 'Afterword', *PTCT*, 308.
[47] *On the Divine Names* (tr. Rolt), 5.4.   [48] 'The Ground of Being', 290.

to the same extremes). In Berdyaev's terms, it is the difference between apophatic and cataphatic theology.[49] It is better to live within the tensions than to emphasize either at the expense of the other. The result is usually pantheism or atheism, and not surprisingly Tillich has been accused of both.

The tension between the immanent and transcendent interpretations of the concept of *being* (i.e. the ontological version of the same problem) is probably unresolvable. The problem is more hidden in ontology than theology, for theology has to do with the relation between God and the world, whereas the same contrast ontologically takes place within the unifying concept of being. Whatever is said about God, man or world takes place within the 'frame of being'—it *is*.[50] The tension between the two concepts of God has been analysed by A. O. Lovejoy in his famous work *The Great Chain of Being*. He claims: 'The most noteworthy consequence of the persistent influence of Platonism was ... that throughout the greater part of its history Western religion, in its more philosophic forms, has had two Gods.'[51] If Lovejoy is right in his claim about the history ot philosophical theism in the West, we ought not to single ouf Tillich for special blame in the matter. Interestingly though, Lovejoy singles out Schelling as an outstanding example of a modern author in whom both concepts of God are uneasily combined. His middle period Lovejoy claims has two gods and two religions, 'the religion of a time-transcending and eternally complete Absolute, an 'Identity of Identities', the One of Neoplatonism—and the religion of a struggling, temporally limited, gradually self-realising World-Spirit or Life-Force'.[52] Later in Schelling, Lovejoy observes, the latter conception overcomes the former and the combination of the two becomes incompatible. Tillich deliberately places himself in the Schellingian tradition and is open to the same accusation. The unifying language of being has enabled him to combine two widely differing theological concepts of God and to move readily from one to the other. So successful has been the effect of the language of being that Tillich seems to have been unaware of Lovejoy's distinction!

[49] 'Unground and Freedom', 2.
[50] 'Philosophy and Theology', *PE*, 86.
[51] *The Great Chain of Being*, 315.   [52] Op. cit. 315.

(d) The Holy Trinity

One feature only of the doctrine of the Trinity is here discussed, viz. its dialectical character. This has a direct bearing on the ontology. The dialectical account of the doctrine of the Trinity is an imaginative and constructive attempt to restate a notoriously difficult Christian belief but it runs into many problems. We shall show how Tillich so allows dialectical thinking to shape his doctrine of the Trinity that the orthodox conception of it and his revised dialectical account of it are almost incompatible. There is of course another major difficulty which should not be missed, i.e. what account of the relationship is possible between the dialectical doctrine of the Trinity and the God above God of the previous section? The God who is dialectically related to himself in the manner of the terms of an Hegelian synthesis is not the 'God above God' who is far above any opposition or contrary within himself. Both accounts perhaps have their limited value as separate philosophical models for the concept of God, but they plainly cannot support each other if they are taken together as complementary symbolic descriptions. The problem here is yet more evidence for our charge against Tillich of almost unrestrained eclecticism. But having drawn attention to the point, our main task is to trace out how the traditional doctrine is affected when it is presented in a dialectical framework.

Tillich repeatedly says that the doctrine of the Trinity is to be understood dialectically. This is his 'main contention' about the Trinity (*ST* 3.302) which must be stated 'with great emphasis' (*ST* 2.105). The dialectical interpretation of the doctrine is to be carefully distinguished from other possible interpretations which may be irrational or paradoxical. God is the living God. And as life itself is dialectical then God as the living God must be spoken of dialectically if we are to take seriously that he is himself Life (*ST* 2.105). The over-all character of life, Tillich claims, is a 'going beyond itself' and a 'returning to itself'. This is what the Trinitarian symbols express. The doctrine stands for the 'outgoing of God from himself and the reunion of God with himself'.[53] Alternatively, 'The doctrine of the Trinity . . . describes in dialectical

[53] 'The Word of God', 123: see 'Being and Love', 671.

terms the inner movement of the divine life as an eternal separation from itself and return to itself' (*ST* 1.63). The language of separation and reunion is partly drawn from Tillich's understanding of the divine love as *eros*,[54] partly from Schelling's description of the life processes within God and outside him,[55] and partly from the Hegelian dialectic. It is important to determine whether the dialectical interpretation of the Trinity that Tillich proposes does in fact safeguard the character of God as the *living* God. We shall suggest that it does not.

The term 'dialectic' needs clarification. Tillich uses the term widely and not always precisely. It is derived from the classical Greek verb *dialegesthai*, 'discourse' or argue', and suggests the picture of two opponents engaged in philosophical argument, each maintaining opposite positions, but moving together as the argument proceeds. Through the process of the argument the opposites lose their opposing character, and the argument ends in a higher 'synthesis', Tillich calls dialectic 'the way of seeking for truth by talking with others from differing points of view, through "Yes" and "No", until a "Yes" has been reached which is hardened in the fire of many "No-s" and which unites the elements of truth promoted in the discussion'.[56] To Hegel however, the greatest exponent of dialectical thinking, something far exceeding a mutual seeking for truth by discussion is intended. Dialectic embraces literally everything we find in reality. 'Dialectic is the principle of all the movement and of all the activity we find in reality . . . Everything that surrounds us is an instance of Dialectic.'[57] In Hegel's mature thought the dialectic determines everything else— even Tillich admits that it became a 'universal law' which ceases to mediate knowledge and instead 'presses reality into a mechanized scheme' (*ST* 3. 350). The difficulty is that in the numerous contexts where Tillich uses the word 'dialectical', he gives no indication how rigorously the dialectic is to be applied. In its systematic use, it usually has something of the uncompromising necessity that it contains in Hegel.

[54] See above, pp. 44–8.   [55] e.g. *The Ages of the World*, 97.
[56] 'Author's Introduction', *PE*, xiii. See also 'What is Wrong with the Dialectical Theology', *Journal of Religion*, xv (1935), 127: *BR*, 18: *ST* 1.259–60.
[57] *The Science of Logic*, 150.

Kenan Osborne has analysed Tillich's use of dialectic and rightly located it in almost every sphere of theological thought that Tillich's writings encompass.[58] Of particular importance is Tillich's claim that 'it transforms the static ontology behind the logical system of Aristotle and his followers into a dynamic ontology' (*ST* 1.63). Few people would deny that dialectics is a type of thinking which may enrich the interpretation of certain theological concepts. But Tillich has fallen into the *error of confusing the triadic structure of dialectical thinking with the triadic structure of Trinitarian thinking*. But the two are very different. Tillich should not be faulted when he tries to arrange and to illuminate his ontological concepts dialectically. This is a legitimate technique even if it is not always desirable or fruitful. But when he regards the doctrine of the Trinity merely as an instance of the dialectic which he has already posited within God, then it is the dialectic itself (in the full Hegelian sense) not the Christian doctrine of God that calls the tune. Tillich tries to interpret the Holy Trinity through the Hegelian dialectic in order to safeguard the doctrine of God as 'living', i.e. in tension and movement with himself. When he does this the dialectic becomes much more than a method of argument or a seeking for truth—it itself determines the truth and shapes it in its dialectical mould.[59]

We have seen how Tillich has systematically depicted a dialectical tension within God or being-itself, expressed for the most part through the pairs of terms being and non-being, and ground and abyss of being. The doctrine of the Trinity will *not* sustain such an interpretation. There is one obvious objection. The dialectic within being-itself includes negation. Without negation (or non-being) it is claimed, God could not be God—he could not be living or dynamic. Tillich says that one of the motives for applying Trinitarian symbolism to God is that as 'Life' we are able to attribute an element of non-being to God's being (*ST* 3.302). But there is no negation in the doctrine of the Trinity. More precisely 'the element of non-being' Tillich locates within the Trinity is the non-being of *differentiation* (e.g. the Father *is not* the Son etc.), not dialectical

---

[58] *New Being*, 20–1, 80 f., 158 f.
[59] For the opposite view, W. Nicholls, *Systematic and Philosophical Theology*, 263. Nicholls thinks Tillich's doctrine of the Trinity is derived 'from revelation'.

non-being. If dialectical non-being is located with the Trinity, which of the three Persons corresponds to it? Which of the three Persons is negated, and which affirmed? Is the Son to be equated with non-being? Boehme's solution to the problem was to say that the person of the Father is negated—he is the abyss who generates the Son as a ground—but this is nothing to do with what most Christians recognize as traditional Trinitarianism. The doctrine of the Trinity does not admit of any dialectical negation in God. It admits only of *distinction* between the Persons, not negation. The three Persons are not in opposition or dialectical tension with each other— neither is one of them the unity of the other two. Tillich may be fairly accused of operating two distinct but irreconcilable dialectics in his doctrine of God. One is the interplay between being-itself and non-being within the higher unity of some third principle which is also sometimes called being-itself; the other is the interplay between Father and Son within the higher unity of Spirit (not Godhead). One is philosophical, the other theological.

There are other difficulties with the dialectical interpretation of the Holy Trinity on its own terms. Hegel identified the triune God with the Absolute Idea of *The Logic*,[60] an identification which raises as many problems for the philosophy of religion as it solves. But there are other more serious shortcomings in the nature of the dialectical thinking itself. A dialectical triad is formed as soon as the mind posits an inadequate or incomplete idea. The other two 'moments' in the triad are then deduced *a priori*, i.e. the contrary of the idea and the higher synthesis of the idea and its contrary together. Within the dialectic itself the synthesis constitutes the reality or truth—the thesis and antithesis have no value outside pure thought, i.e. they are conceptual and not real. McTaggart made this damaging criticism of the dialectic in 1918, and its consequences are disastrous for the doctrine of the Trinity. He writes:

In every dialectical triad it is certain that the Synthesis contains all the truth which there is in the triad at all . . . The Thesis and Antithesis are transcended and reconciled in the Synthesis. In so far as they assert themselves to be anything more than moments in

[60] *Lectures on the Philosophy of Religion*, ii. 227.

the Synthesis, in so far as they claim to be independent terms, only externally connected with the Synthesis—they are false.[61]

The inescapable conclusion for the dialectical interpretation of the doctrine of the Trinity must be plain:

According to Hegel's exposition, the Father and the Son and the Thesis and Antithesis of a Triad of which the Holy Ghost is the Synthesis. It will follow from this that the Holy Ghost is the sole of reality of the Trinity. In so far as the Father and the Son are real, they are moments in the nature of the Holy Ghost. In so far as they are taken to be correlative with the Holy Ghost, as on the same level with the latter, the Father and the Son are simply abstractions which the thinker makes from the concrete reality of the Holy Spirit.[62]

So the dialectic on its own terms fails to do justice to the meaning of the doctrine of the Trinity. It safeguards only one of the three Persons. It respects neither the equality of the Persons nor their separateness within the unity of the Godhead. Although the ingredients of the dialectic always comprise a triad, the result of the dialectic is never a triad but 'a single truth in which two complementary moments can be distinguished'. Tillich would of course deny that the Persons of Father and Son exist only within pure thought. But such a conclusion is however an unhappy outcome of the application of the dialectic to the triune God. It is remarkable how close Tillich comes to the Hegelian view. For instance he says 'God's life is life as spirit, and the trinitarian principles are moments within the process of the divine life' (*ST* 1.277). Later in the same passage he wrires: 'As the actualisation of the other two principles, the Spirit is the third principle . . . The third principle is in a way the whole (God *is* Spirit), and in a way it is a special principle' (*ST* 1.278). In his maturest writings Tillich shows a marked preference for referring to God as Spirit. He avoids speaking of divine Persons and speaks instead in an Hegelian manner of principles or moments. Again the statement that the third principle is the actualization of the other two principles seems to owe more to dialectical thinking than to the orthodox Trinitarian view that each of the Persons is

[61] J. McTaggart, *Studies in Hegelian Cosmology*, 204.
[62] Ibid.

coequal with the other. It is possible to detect here a weakening of the actuality of the first two Persons of the Trinity—a consequence of the use of the dialectic against which McTaggart warns.

Dialectical thinking and Trinitarian thinking are similar in that both are triadic, but there the similarity ends. The two types of thought have little more than the number three in common. What happens then, when theological and ontological concepts are combined to produce a reinterpretation of the doctrine of the Trinity? Perhaps the conflict between the two should not be understood by contrasting theology with ontology, or religion with philosophy at all. Perhaps the resulting confusion between trinitarian and dialectical thinking simply arises out of the sincere but careless attempt to interpret one tradition of historical thinking through another more recent one, with the result that both are conflated and each loses its distinctiveness. We have already contended for the freedom of the theologian to borrow his concepts from where he likes and modify them as he pleases. The difficulty seems to lie somewhere between the fruitful borrowing of ideas from new and unexpected sources, and the wholesale incorporation of large chunks of philosophical thought into a systematic whole which already includes all kinds of disparate historical elements. Tillich is often guilty of the latter fault. We observed the same problem in comparing the dialectical and neoplatonic accounts of God.

We have now looked in some detail at the concept of being and its qualifiers, power of being and ground of being; at the different accounts of non-being; and the concepts of God. These are the most important concepts in Tillich's writings. Our historical method of approach has drawn attention to the widely divergent contexts from which key terms are drawn, often with the result that their whole sense is changed. We are now in a position to develop briefly our finding that much of the difficulty in understanding Tillich is due to the complex eclecticism of his writings, sometimes heightened by a lack of familiarity with his German intellectual background. For convenience we shall refer to five separate strands of thought which undergird the concept of being, all of which are of the utmost importance for understanding it.

1. *The Platonic-Augustinian tradition*

We have seen how for Augustine God is *esse ipsum*, being-itself or fullness of being. Only God is being-itself, for being-itself is alone eternal and changeless. Creatures come both from God and non-being, with the result that they are subject to transience and change. Being-itself operates like Plato's Form of the Good on which every entity depends for its continuing existence. Being-itself is the primary transcendental principle, and as such the presupposition of all existence whatsoever. The other transcendental principles Truth Itself and Goodness Itself, are immediately present to the mind in the awareness of anything true or good, and are immediately knowable by intuition. Knowledge of the principles, the *transcendentalia*, provides Tillich with the basis for his doctrine of the 'ontological principle', which is the immediate awareness of the divine, or the communion of the soul with God. The tradition is preserved in Eckhart and the Franciscans. The concept of being derives its most characteristically theological use from this tradition.

2. *Neoplatonism*

Closely linked with the Augustinian tradition is the neoplatonism of Plotinus, whose doctrine of the 'One' as the remote, unknowable, transcendent principle we have already outlined. We had particular occasion to refer to the influence of neoplatonism in our discussion of the God above God.

3. *Protestant mysticism*

We have emphasized the influence of Boehme and Schelling on the development of Tillich's thought, and drawn out some of the characteristics of their writings. These include a monistic God whose life consists of a violent interaction between two poles, and a dualism internal to God himself. Non-being in this tradition is the originating principle in God himself and the source of all change and potentiality in the created world. The terms ground and abyss vividly reflect Boehme's dialectic.

Leaving aside the question of the orthodoxy of internal dualism a simpler question should be raised which has never been adequately debated. What is the relationship between the *transcendental* concepts of the Augustinian tradition, and the *di-polar* or *dialectical* concepts of the Protestant mystical tradition? In the earlier tradition, Being, Truth, and Goodness operate like Platonic forms, particularly the Form of the Good. They instantiate particulars and they are presupposed by all entities, acts of knowledge and all value-judgements whatsoever. The forms or essences constitute the real world, and the existent world is real insofar as it is upheld by the eternal forms. Clearly the latter tradition interprets the concept of being dialectically. On this view particulars participate in being-itself *and* non-being: they have an abyss as well as a ground, and their existence is a tension between the two fundamental ontological poles. So is being-itself dialectical or not? This is a crucially important question for Tillich does not ever seem to have addressed himself to it. The answer must be that sometimes being-itself is dialectical and sometimes not, according to which tradition is dominant at the time. But clearly this is an unsatisfactory answer for the dialectical and undialectical concepts of being are incompatible. If however being-itself is predominantly dialectical, what about the other *transcendentalia*, the true and the good? Clearly these cannot be dialectical. At any rate no kind of dialectical engagement with their contraries, falsehood and evil, has ever been suggested. So dialectical and undialectical concepts are indiscriminately combined. Like rolling stones gathering moss, Tillich's ontological concepts gather successive layers of meaning, according to their loci in philosophical history. Again, we have seen how the impossibly wide spread of the concept non-being has covered over several subsidiary but incompatible uses of the term, reinforcing our charge of radical eclecticism against the system. The two main traditions, the Augustinian and the Schellingian are indiscriminately combined, producing an amalgam which is needlessly perplexing and obscure. Plainly either tradition may be of service to Christian theology, but it is doubtful if they can serve theology if they are uncritically brought together into a single whole.

4. *Hegelian idealism*

We chose the doctrine of the Trinity, perhaps predictably, as the best example of the influence of dialectical philosophy on Tillich's thought, and we concluded that the Persons of the Trinity are not helpfully re-expressed as 'moments' in an Hegelian synthesis of Spirit. We also suggested in our discussion of the ontological argument that the Hegelian version of it is valid only if one accepts the Hegelian system itself as a valid, all-embracing understanding of reality. If a 'notion' embraces thinking and being, then without doubt the notion of God *includes* his necessary being, as Anselm and Descartes would readily agree. But very few philosophers would defend either the idealist account of the world (and God), or the implicit reference theory of language which seems to be involved in making the notion of God necessarily refer to anything at all. Our objection is to the absorption of wholesale Hegelian elements into the understanding of God, not to a selective and critical use of the legacy of Hegel's thought. In the ontological argument God is presupposed as the ground of thought. The problem however is whether in theology today we *need* a ground of thought, and whether if we assert that there is such a thing we are saying anything sensible. Hegel's comprehensive system of thought is likely to be accepted or rejected *in toto*. But to combine part of it with other philosophical and theological traditions in the formation of a new system is a procedure fraught with complications.

5. *Existentialism*

Existentialism has a powerful influence on Tillich's thought which was traced in chapter I and will be met again in the discussion of estrangement and anxiety in chapter VI. Tillich regards the universal experience of anxiety, so distinctive a feature of existential philosophy, as a concrete and empirical approach to the ontological generalities of being and non-being, and as a justification for bothering with ontology at all. But existentialism arose in the nineteenth century as a *reaction against* Hegelian idealism as Kierkegaard, Schelling, and Marx all demonstrate in their different ways. But in Tillich's thought Hegelian idealism and Kierkegaardian existentialism actually *complement* each other despite their contrary approaches to philosophy, and as we shall see, the existential or ontological question 'Why is there something, why not nothing?' receives, in the form of the *ST*, a thoroughly idealist answer. We also suggested that the inability to speak of God as existing was less to do with inconsistencies in Aquinas's thought and much more a consequence of adopting a negative existential concept of existence. The problem of the meaning of 'existence' is partly solved when we separate out the backgrounds of the different concepts which lurk beneath the English word 'existence', for here again we met the fallacy of assuming that because two concepts share the same form, they share the same meaning. The interpreter of Tillich has a partly exasperating, partly exhilarating task in unravelling the different stands of thought. When he has made the effort, the problem he then has on his hands is, was it worth it? In our final chapter we still hope to answer that question affirmatively.

V

ESSENCE

THE concept of essence has already been encountered in the doctrines of God and non-being. We have seen how God has been placed beyond the essence-existence distinction (*ST* 1.262, 283), and how the term 'potentiality' links together both essence and non-being in obvious incompatibility. The subject of the next three chapters is the transition from essence to existence and the return to essence which is made possible through the New Being mediated through Jesus the Christ. This subject is dealt with in part 3 of the *ST*, and reverberates throughout parts 4 and 5. The transition is said to take place on what Tillich calls 'the third level of ontological concepts', the level which is said to explore 'the power of being to exist and the difference between essential and existential being' (*ST* 1.183). (The first two levels are the ontological structure itself, and the elements (i.e. polarities) which constitute it (*ST* 1.182).)

When essence is regarded as an ontological concept on the so-called third level, its meaning is always ontological. It is, however, used almost as commonly in an *ethical* context, where men confront their *essential being* through the categorical demand to act morally. In this neglected area of Tillich's writings, conscience is interpreted as the call of the *essential self* to the distorted existential self, and the 'essential structure of being' is the source of all moral values. For reasons of space we shall confine our remarks to the ontological concept of essence without developing the fascinating question of its value for ethics. In this chapter we shall look, in accordance with our stated historical approach, at the historical background of the term in order to assess its role in the system. We shall inquire into the ontological and epistemological status of the realm of essence, and note the relationship between essence and other key terms like power of being and form, in the system. In chapter VI we examine the account of the transition from essence to existence; in chapter VII we examine how Jesus as the 'bearer of New Being' is said to restore existence to its essential pre-transitional state: we also suggest in chapter VII that the account of the power of the New Being to overcome the split between essence and existence describes the same ontological process as the later account in *ST* 3 of the Divine Spirit overcoming the 'ambiguities of life'.

The term 'essence' has a long and distinguished tradition in Western philosophical and theological thought, and several of its varied uses from Plato onwards are echoed and reaffirmed in Tillich's writings. One of the most important influences on his concept of essence is Plato's *eidos*, 'idea' or 'form'. Several characteristics of Platonic form apply equally to Tillich's essences. Plato's forms, like Tillich's essences, transcend the empirical world; they constitute a higher level of being which is realized only imperfectly within the realm of existence; and they instantiate or participate in informed objects, just as essences participate in finite existents. The forms are as certain as the world of existents.[1] They are 'abstract terms', they are also 'the causes of things', and they are even regarded as the spirits with whose help God made the world. Equally the forms are abstract ideals, e.g. justice, temperance, and knowledge, or the images or ideas of sensible objects (e.g. a bed).[2] They are not only many but one, inhering together in the Form of the Good which is their unity.[3]

It would be wrong to attempt to press too closely any particular account of the doctrine of forms. Their relevance however, to Tillich's doctrine of essence is very considerable. As he says 'our word "essence" is what Plato called *eidos*, or Idea'.[4] The main features then of the Platonic doctrine of forms or ideas are important as a mythological and philosophical background to what Tillich says about ontological essences. He says so explicitly. Hegel's doctrine of essence also shows obvious affinities with that of Tillich. For Hegel essence is a substitute term for the notion of Being or Spirit in the 'Logic'.[5] It is commonly known that the major dialectical triad in the 'Logic' comprises the notions of being, nothing and becoming.

---

[1] *Meno*, 100 a. See Jowett, i. 259.   [2] *Phaedrus*, 247: *Republic*, x. 596–8.
[3] *Republic*, vi, vii.   [4] *My Search for Absolutes*, 72–3.
[5] *The Science of Logic*, 389.

Being and nothing are identical! They are purely indeterminate, and have reality only as moments in the synthesis of becoming. This particular instance of dialectic is of course universal in its application, for as Hegel says 'nowhere in heaven or on earth is there anything which does not contain within itself being and nothing'.[6] Now the triad of being-nothing-becoming has an alternative formulation in the 'Logic'. It can be expressed in the form essence–appearance–actuality. Just as pure being has only conceptual meaning and no actuality in itself, the same is said of essence, whose 'character is to lack all determinate character, to be inherently lifelesss and empty'. Nevertheless essence in its indeterminateness goes over into actuality by giving determinations their determinate being. 'Its movement consists in positing within itself the negation or determination, thereby giving itself determinate being.' Essence then, together with its antithesis, appearance, constitutes actuality. Only the synthesis actuality can be said to have any concrete existence. Essences realize themselves in the appearance of actual entities, and our conceptual grasp of actuality is not completed unless our minds first posit essences and see their embodiments in concrete existence.

But the dialectic essence–appearance–actuality is uncomfortably similar to the triad essence–existence–life, which appears in Tillich's theology. This similarity is developed below.[7] Within the present context however, we may understand essence to be a 'moment' in everything 'in heaven or on earth', for it is an element of everything living. It is indeterminate, but it issues out into actuality where it realises itself in determinateness, or takes determinateness into itself. Determinateness is the *limit* or *non-being* which together with being or essence, constitutes actuality. Aside from the dialectical scheme in which we encounter the Hegelian doctrine of essence, these characteristics of essence blend well with what we find in Tillich. In Tillich too, essence stands behind existence and everything within it. Everything that is is a manifestation of essence. Essences actualize themselves in existence and in doing so they do not remain what they essentially are. They become distorted within existence, and what emerges is the ambiguous actuality called 'life'.

[6] Op. cit. 82–5.   [7] p. 153f. See Hegel, op. cit., 389–90.

When we speak of essences we have a wide variety of accounts of essence both within Tillich's writings and in the history of philosophy generally. Of the philosophers who have had recourse to the concept of essence, we refer particularly to Plato and Hegel, because Tillich is much nearer to them, and to the traditions which they represent, i.e. realism and idealism, than to nominalism, and the nominalistic understanding of essences. His indebtedness to Plato and Hegel will become clearer as the analysis of essence proceeds.

In the *ST* Tillich lists six possible meanings of essence and classifies them into two types. He writes:

Essence can mean the nature of a thing without any valuation of it, it can mean the universals which characterize a thing, it can mean the ideas in which existing things participate, it can mean the norm by which a thing must be judged, it can mean the original goodness of everything created and it can mean the patterns of all things in the divine mind. (*ST* 1.225)

The two predominant types of essence are the 'logical' or 'empirical' type and the 'valuational' type. When essence is understood as 'the nature of a thing, or as the quality in which a thing participates, or as a universal', then essence 'is a logical ideal to be reached by abstraction or intuition without the interference of valuation'. When essence is understood as 'that from which being has "fallen", the true and undistorted nature of things', essence is 'the basis of value judgements'.[8] The two different types of essence lead to a basic 'ambiguity' in the concept of essence, and this ambiguity, says Tillich, is the product of another ambiguity, viz. 'the ambiguous character of existence'. Existence 'expresses and at the same time contradicts it—essence as that which makes a thing *what* it is (*ousia*) has a purely logical character; essence as that which appears in an imperfect and distorted way in a thing carries the stamp of value' (*ST* 1.225).

A number of difficulties immediately present themselves. First, the list of possible meanings of essence does not correspond to Tillich's use of them. The pasage reads very like an entry in a dictionary of philosophy than a helpful guide to the behaviour of the word essence in the system. Sometimes its meaning is

[8] See 'Schelling und die Anfänge des Existentialistischen Protestes', *Zeitschrift für Philosophische Forschung*, ix (1955).

other than any of the six listed. Second, the distinction between 'logical' and 'valuational' is a pretty meaningless contrast. In what sense is 'logical' to be understood? In a Hegelian, or a more formal, analytic way? 'Valuational' essences are not simply bases for value-judgements either, for on the Platonic account of essences, they are more real than existents and thus have a higher ontological status. In practice no such distinction between 'empirical' and 'valuational' types of essences is acknowledged in the many contexts where essences are treated. 'Essence' is a blanket term, and our declared historical approach is once again necessary to separate out the nuances of meaning it contains. The result of our inquiry should show that, as in the case of non-being, an ancient philosophical term has acquired different meanings in its long history, which then get clumsily conflated and inconsistently put together in its modern use.

Essence belongs with the related terms potentiality, *ousia*, and power of being. In an early essay Tillich defined the essence of a thing or what a thing essentially is as its power of being.[9] The power of being of a thing, or more simply, the power of a thing, is the 'really real' of it, and the 'really real' of a thing is its *ousia*. In *ST* Tillich says the realm of essence is encountered in the mind's cognitive search for truth or true being (*ST* 1.112–13). It discovers that sense impressions provide it with only a surface appearance which must be penetrated so that the true or essential being of entities might be disclosed: 'the surface must be penetrated, the appearance undercut, the "depth" must be reached, namely, the *ousia*, the "essence" of things, that gives them the power of being. This is their truth, the "really real" in difference from the seemingly real.'

Essence is 'that which makes a thing *what* it is', and what it is is its *ousia* (*ST* 1.224–5). Both essence and *ousia* are identified with potentiality. Using the overworked example of 'treehood' Tillich illustrates what he means by potentiality:

Treehood does not exist, although it has being, namely, potential being. But the tree in my back yard does exist. It stands out of the mere potentiality of treehood, But it stands out and exists only because it participates in that power of being which is treehood, that power which makes every tree a tree and nothing else. (*ST* 2.23–4)

[9] 'Seinsmächtigkeit', 'Glaubiger Realismus' (1927): tr. as 'Realism and Faith', *PE*, see 69. The phrase 'powerfulness of being' would be a more accurate rendering.

Elsewhere potentiality is defined as

that kind of being which has the power, the dynamic, to become actual (for example, the potentiality of every tree is treehood). There are other essences which do not have this power (for example, the triangle). Those which become actual, however, subject themselves to the conditions of existence, such as finitude, estrangement, and so on. This does not mean that they lose their essential character (trees remain trees), but it does mean they fall under the structures of existence and are open to growth, distortion and death. (*ST* 3.12)

Other examples of essences are given to qualify the term 'potentiality'. The essence 'redness' is said to be 'the transtemporal potentiality of all red things in the universe', and the essence 'man' is said to have been a potentiality of being 'for perhaps billions of years' before 'what we know as "man" became actual'.

In the first citation above, essence is the 'underlying' depth of existence into which the mind penetrates by what could be called a process of induction. It accords well with the famous sermon 'The Depth of Existence' which considerably influenced the author of *Honest to God*.[10] In this sermon the exhortation is given to penetrate the realms of 'surface' and 'appearance' 'in order to learn what things really are'. *Ousia* and the Latin equivalent *substantia* (lit. 'what stands under') are terms well fitted for this particular interpretation of essence as the depth of existence. The essence of a thing is encountered when the mind goes beyond the sense impressions of a thing or 'beneath its surface' to the level of its true being. Immediately there are difficulties. Of course the description of our discovery of essences is metaphorical and cannot be understood as a precise phenomenological account of what happens in an actual cognitive process. Tillich cannot be blamed for this, but we for our part cannot therefore inquire into the meaning of the 'depth' of things too closely. Secondly, Tillich here has more in mind than our ability to form class words or *genera* in order to tidy up our apprehension of encountered reality. Thirdly, our own experience of 'depth-encounter' or 'surface-exposure' is not as

[10] In *The Shaking of the Foundations*, 59–70, see especially 60: cit. J. A. T. Robinson, 46 f.

straightforward as he assumes. A chair is after all what it seems to be, viz. a chair. There is little more to be divulged about the ontological reality of a chair that is not already known through its surface appearance. But if we take more complex examples of entities, we discover that a person, or a government, or an art form, or a symbol, or a civilization may very well deliver up to closer scrutiny a deeper level of itself. This deeper level of reality might then be called its essence, and the objects which have thus yielded up their true being may be said to have been grasped in their 'essential natures'.

However, is there any point in using ambiguous language about the essences of things in order to account for a deeper understanding or a heightened appreciation of their reality? If we study a particular problem for long enough, we might say we have acquired a 'deeper' understanding of the issues involved. But use of 'deeper' in this context is metaphorical and does not mean we have literally penetrated to another level of understanding, any more than one penetrates to the deeper level of being of an orange simply by peeling it. We have simply learned more about the problem. Wittgenstein used the con-trast between 'surface' and 'depth' in speaking of our use of words, but he did not allow his use of the terms to suggest some sort of higher or deeper ontological plane behind the actual world as we experience it. 'Surface' and 'depth' refer to the grammar of language-games, to the ways language gets used in 'forms of life'. To understand the depth-grammar of a word in a language-game is to apprehend it in its significance for the people who play the game.[11] We might in this regard take the highly topical and controversial example of the word 'God'. To examine the 'grammar of "God" ' a Wittgensteinian looks at the many different ways in which believers *use* the word. He does not assume that the word necessarily has a referent in a higher, transcendental being or Source of being. In the same way, there does not seem to be any reason why talking about the essence of a thing should necessarily take on a kind of supra-empirical dimension or *ousia* that gives to the things its power of being.

[11] e.g. *Philosophical Investigations*, §23, 90. For the influence of Wittgenstein on the philosophy of religion, see W. D. Hudson, *Wittgenstein and Religious Belief*, and A. Keightley, *Wittgenstein, Grammar and God*.

Having sounded a note of warning against a too facile tendency to 'reify' the purely conceptual properties of things, we must pursue further the question of the relationship between essence and potentiality. The answer must be given in terms of a contrast between Plato and Aristotle. When Tillich speaks of the *ousia* of a thing, he contrasts what he calls the 'really real' with the 'seemingly real' (*ST* 1.113). The imagery is Platonic. When he speaks of potentiality, he contrasts the actual with the non-actual. Here the imagery is Aristotelian. But essence in Plato is what is eternal, unchanging, immutable, while in Aristotle it is a principle producing change. Tillich admits that the function of Platonic essence was 'to describe the eternally true within the flux of reality' (*ST* 1.283). Aristotle's 'potentiality' (*dunamis*), which he himself described as 'a principle producing change',[12] cannot be the same as Platonic essence. For Plato it is the realm of essence which is 'real'; for Aristotle it is actuality. Tillich however, is happy to equate essence with potentiality and potentiality with essence. He does not use either with much precision, and this very lack of precision makes any attempt to come to grips with the meaning of his philosophical terms extremely difficult.

We need to trace three different meanings of the concept 'potentiality' in order to understand the difference between two highly important contrasts, essence–existence and potentiality–actuality. Treehood, Tillich writes, does not exist as a potentiality, yet trees participate 'in that power of being which is treehood, that power which makes every tree a tree and nothing else'.[13] Let us take treehood as an example of potentiality or power of being (it is with few exceptions the only such example in Tillich's writings), and ask how it helps to understand Tillich's concept of potentiality. What is treehood? There are at least three possibilities. It can be (1) the antecedent conditions which make actual trees possible; (2) a general property of every tree and therefore a universal and an abstraction; and (3) the ideal or essential tree which is embodied in particular trees. In fact treehood demonstrably means all three of these quite distinct possibilities. Let us take each example in turn;

---

[12] *Metaphysics*, Λ 1020ᵃ 5–7 (Loeb tr. v. 12.12).
[13] *ST* 2.20.

(1) *Treehood as the antecedent conditions of actual trees*

On this first view the potentiality of treehood is, or is contained in, the complete set of organic conditions which make actual trees possible. Such an interpretation harmonizes well with Tillich's statement that 'the dimension of the organic is *essentially* present on the inorganic' (*ST* 3.21) or that 'man never would have appeared if the essence "man" had not belonged to the potentialities of being'.[14] Here potentiality is already some kind of actuality which has yet to develop into what it can become. It is a process of change within actuality which can be described in both physical and metaphysical terms. This account of potentiality confirms that of Aristotle already referred to. Aristotle says: 'The authoritative definition of "potency" in the primary sense will be "a principle producing change, which is in something other than that in which the change takes place, or in the same thing *qua* other"'.[15] 'Aristotle's' 'potency', like Tillich's 'potentiality' is thus a principle which produces change in things which is both in things themselves, yet not identical with them. If we translate this particular thought pattern into language about essence and existence, then the existence of things is a development or realization of their essence. The existence of a thing is its actuality as opposed to its potency or not-yet-being. Potentiality is both the actual and the non-actual together, because it is already something and it has the power to become something else.

(2) *Treehood as a general property*

In this second sense treehood is an abstraction from individual trees. It is a 'universal', as the etymology of the term (*unum versus alia*, one against many) indicates. As such treehood belongs to the phenomenon of human language, to man's cognitive approach to reality. The term indicates that certain entities display a sufficient number of similar characteristics which enable us to call these entities 'trees'. This is a legitimate (and classical) use of the term 'essence', but it must be pointed out that it has *nothing whatever to do with potentiality*. There is

[14] *My Search for Absolutes*, 73.
[15] As n. 12. The Loeb translation here is an expanded paraphrase.

nothing potential about class names. Other examples of the use of essence as a class name are not hard to find, and we cite one of them here. Having spoken of essence as 'quality' Tillich observes:

> We find another type of essence in species and genera. In every pine tree we experience, first, this particular tree in our back yard, second, the species 'pine' which enables us to produce a word 'pine' and to plant a pine tree instead of an oak tree, and third, the genus 'tree' which gives us this word and enables us to grow a tree instead of a shrub . . .[16]

As the words 'species' and '*genera*' are plainly meant to indicate, this type of essence belongs to the cognitive, classifying attempt of the human mind to order what it encounters. It is a linguistic universal. As in the example, one begins with the phenomenon of a particular concrete existent, and by comparing its similarities and dissimilarities with other existents, one labels it by 'what it is', i.e. in this case a pine or a tree. Once the 'thatness' of an entity is established, its 'whatness' can be determined. Its 'thatness' is its existence, its 'whatness' its essence. This kind of essence, answering the question 'What is a thing?' is a classification or definition. It is a universal.

(3) *Treehood as an ideal*

If essence as potentiality is Aristotelian, then essence as a universal is 'nominalistic'. Against these two broad classifications we say that the third type of essence under consideration is Platonic. The actual, individual tree says Tillich, 'participates in that power of being which is treehood, that power of being which makes every tree a tree and nothing else.' Now for Tillich potentiality can be the same as power of being, and he here verges on the Platonic error of the duplication of forms or ideas and existents. He is explicit that essence is to be understood as Platonic form.[17] While he rejects the doctrine that every individual thing has its essential or ideal duplicate (*ST* 1.183), a reference to 'that power of being which makes every tree a tree and nothing else' certainly implies some kind of ontological power which is above existence, and which is *quite other than a purely linguistic understanding of essence*. In another

[16] *My Search for Absolutes*, 73-4.   [17] *My Search for Absolutes*, 72-3.

tiresome example of a tree Tillich says: 'we compare its actual
state with an image, an *eidos* or an idea that we have of its
essential nature. We call it a poor or sick or mutilated exemplar
of what, for instance, a pine tree could be.'[18] Here the mind is
able to both to attain an image or an archetypal idea of the
essential nature of a thing and also to judge whether the thing
in question is a good or a distorted realisation of the intuited
essence. Judgements of value, however, are not made in quite
this way. A pine tree can be judged a sick or a healthy specimen
by a comparison with other members of its class, without
reference to an essential or ideal pine. This was the error of
Aquinas who in his Fourth Way of demonstrating the existence
of God assumed that to affirm degrees of more or less requires
an absolute standard of value to make relative judgement
possible.[19] Leaving aside this difficulty, we ask instead what
kind of ontological status must be given to these essential
objects, known by intuition? Are they Platonic forms, more
'real' than existents and having some kind of independent
supra-existent character which can be intuited but never fully
known? Or are they universals in the nominalistic sense,
products of the cognitive consciousness with no ontological
validity in themselves? Essences in Tillich are capable of all
three interpretations we have considered, but a thorough
examination of the system indicates that the Platonic interpretation is dominant.

A Platonic account of 'powers of being' certainly seems
necessary to make anything of the following passage: 'The
essential powers of being belong to the divine life in which they
are rooted, created by him who is everything he is "through
himself" ' (*ST* 1.283). In addition to the use of power of being
which played a large part in the earlier analysis of being-itself,
we encountered another use of power or powers of being as a
virtual synonym for essence(s). This is perhaps somewhat
surprising since being-itself, which is first of all qualified by
power of being, is repeatedly said to be above the split between
essence and existence. In this passage though the 'essential
powers of being' are not something ontologically equal with

---

[18] 'Is a Science of Human Values Possible?', *New Knowledge in Human Values*
(ed. A. H. Maslow), 193.
[19] *Summa Theologica*, i, q. 2, art. 3.

being-itself or God, but something created by God, standing between the creator and the created, or between being-itself and finite being. (The difficulty which this account of essence presents for the Christian doctrine of creation is dealt with below.[20]) Essence functions here as a single realm of being which is created by God but which is not actual. The essences have a kind of intermediate range between God and creatures (a factor which is reminiscent not only of Platonism but also of Philo of Alexandria). Perhaps we need to differentiate between the singular and the plural uses of each term. There are *individual* essences of things (every person, according to Tillich, has his own individual and unique essence[21]), and there are *individual* powers of being which give being to each thing. But essence, like existence, is also a realm of being, which underlies not only individual existents but existence generally. Just as the single concept 'existence' embraces all finite existents, so the single concept 'essence' covers all individual essences.

Tillich is certainly aware that some distinction needs to be made between essences and universals. He sees this distinction as 'one of the most difficult problems connected with the ontology of essences, namely, how essences are related to universals on the one hand, and to individuals on the other hand' (*ST* 1.283). Ontological essences are intuited directly from the mind's encounter with reality, whereas universal concepts are the creation of language and enable the mind to transcend the particular object. In so far as man has language, says Tillich, 'he has universals which liberate him from bondage to the concrete situation to which even the highest animals are subjected' (*ST* 2.36). In the passage on p. 109 above, about the essence of a pine tree, species or genera of beings are classified as a type of essence, although strictly speaking, they are universals. It seems to have been well-known philosophic practice to conflate essences and universals and to call one by the other. The examples of Eckhart and Aquinas quickly come to mind. Eckhart taught that the essence of a thing was discoverable by asking the simple question what a thing is (*quaestio quid est*[22]). The answer to the question yields up the thing's *quiddity* or

---

[20] See below, p. 154f.   [21] *My Search for Absolutes*, 74–5.
[22] 'Commentary on the Book of Exodus', *Meister Eckhart: Selected Treatises and Sermons*, 218.

essence. The term has the same meaning in Aquinas. It is that
which the name of a thing signifies 'and which is indicated by
its idea or definition'.[23] But this understanding of essence is
markedly un-Platonic, and Tillich rejects it. In fact he is
obliged to do so, for to reduce ontological essences to the status
of linguistic universals would be to adopt a nominalist position
with respect to essences. Tillich repeatedly criticizes such a
stance and calls it the final 'outcome' of the Thomistic dissolution (*TTP*, 19). What then is the distinction between essences
on the one hand and universals on the other?

The question is grounded in a long historical debate.
Porphyry (234–*c*. 301) asked 'whether genera or species really
exist or are in bare notions only; and if they exist whether
they are corporeal things, or incorporeal; and whether they
are separated or exist in things perceived by the senses and in
relation to them'.[24] Boethius (490–*c*. 524) claimed that 'universals subsist in sensibles, although they are understood apart
from bodies'.[25] Abelard (1079–1142) adopted the moderate
position that the reality of universals consists in their status
as words only, though even as words they could be assigned
considerable power in signifying states of being. Aquinas
taught similarly that 'universals are not subsisting things, but
have existence only in singulars'.[26] Ockham (*c*. 1285–1347)
however dismissed universals as mere figments of imagination
(*ficta*),[27] while Hobbes (1588–1679) called them 'the name
of some word or name'.[28] Modern positivism and linguisitic
analysis stand in this tradition. German idealism saw the philosophical revival of essences. As the English speaking world
has been deeply influenced by nominalism, there is little sensitivity to the ontological problem of universals, and scarcely much
of an awareness that any such problem exists.

The solution of the problem for Tillich lies in the ontological priority of the essence over against the universal, making
the creation of universals possible. Ontological essences are not
the creation of language. They belong rather to the structure

---

[23] *De Ente et Essentia*, 1. See above, p. 75.

[24] Porphyry, *Commentaria in Aristotelem Graeca*, cit. R. I. Aaron, *The Theory of
Universals*, 1.

[25] In *Isagogen Porph.* 1.11. This and the following references are taken from the
article 'Universals' in the *New Catholic Encyclopaedia*, xiv. 453.

[26] *Contra Gentiles*, 1.65.   [27] *Sent.* 2.8.   [28] *De Corpore*, 2.9.

of being-itself, and the essential structure of being is what makes language possible. Language creates universals, or more precisely, language expresses the object of the mind's abstraction, but it is only able to do so because there is a prior, essential, ontological structure which makes language possible:

Abstraction gives us the power of language, language gives us free-dom of choice, and freedom of choice gives us the possibility of infinite technical production . . . all this would be impossible without the absolutes we call 'essences', *through which language can come into existence.*[29]

In an article written in 1956, the problem is succinctly stated in terms of the power of universals to express both ontological essences on the one hand and *existentialia*, i.e. concepts used in existential descriptions on the other.[30] From the point of view of linguistic analysis, Tillich says, a word which expresses an ontological essence *and* a word which expresses an abtract concept, whether ontological or not, can be given the label 'universal'. But within the domain of universals so labelled, there is no logical way of knowing whether a universal is an abstract concept or an ontological essence.

This solution was forced upon Tillich by the question, 'Does not a description of existence transform itself into an essence?' Here he tries to face openly the charge that terms such as 'finitude, non-being, freedom, self, anxiety, estrangement, guilt, courage', which belong to virtually any existential philosophy, in fact essentialize existence by reducing it to an elaborate conceptual framework, thereby losing the intensity of the experience of existence which lies at the root of all existentialist thought. Tillich successfully answers the charge by saying:

The argument (that a description of existence transforms it into essence) does not annihilate the difference between universals rep-resenting essences and universals representing existentialia. Logically both have the same character, ontologically they are separated by the gap which separates the potential (the what) from that which constitutes the actual (the that).

[29] *My Search for Absolutes,* 74. My italics.
[30] 'The Nature and Significance of Existentialist Thought', *Journal of Philosophy,* liii (1956), 742.

All universals then fulfil certain logical criteria which separate
universals from other words: some universals, while still
recognizably universals in the logical sense, express ontological
essences which are intuitions of the way the world essentially is,
not descriptions of the way the world existentially is. Essences
belong to the structure of being while language is subject to
man's estrangement from his world under the conditions of
existence. Essences and universals therefore, belong on two
different levels of being or within two different aspects or
accounts of being while their logical form remains the same.
Within the essential structure of being the split between essence
and existence does not occur, while under the conditions of
existence the essential structure of being is lost. Thought, however, by its power of intuiting essences, is able partially to
rediscover the essential structure of being. Our grasp of existence is the product of universals: our grasp of essence is the
product of our direct intuition. Essences then are best understood as approximations to Platonic forms. They are certainly
more than universals and more than definitions. They are
more than creations of thought, more than mere notional or
conceptual entities, and they have a *fundamentum in rebus* as
well as *in verbis*. In expressing the essential structure of being,
they represent within existence the original goodness of the
created world prior to its distortion in existence.

We have seen how the idea of form has been related to what
Tillich understands as *actus purus*,[31] and we have developed
several criticisms of the polarity of dynamics and form. A
further clue towards the understanding of essences is to examine
their relationship with the concepts of form and non-being.
Tillich says of form

Whatever loses its form loses its being. Form should not be contrasted
with content. The form which makes a thing what it is is its content,
its *essentia*, its definite power of being. The form of a tree is what
makes it a tree, what gives it the general character of treehood as
well as the special and unique form of an individual tree.[32]

Here form is explicitly associated with power of being and *essentia*,
but to apprehend only the form of a thing is to understand
that thing incompletely, from the point of view of a single side

[31] See above, p. 72 f.   [32] See above, p. 65. *ST* 1.197.

of the polar structure which is manifest in everything. 'Every form forms something', writes Tillich (*ST* 1.198), and that something is 'dynamics'. In practice when we look at entities through the polar structure of being we isolate certain characteristics of the entity and then apprehend that entity as the fusion of them both. We have seen how the dynamics–form polarity represents the dialectic between becoming and being, and between motion and rest. We suggest that the form or essence of any existent thus apprehended is something fixed, eternal, trans-empirical, and 'supremely real', modelled along the lines of Plato's forms: the dynamics side is its contingent, temporal, finite aspect, its ability to grow or change into something else, and its inevitable ceasing to be. Both sides of the polarity only make sense when understood in tension with their opposites. Form then, in the structure of being, approximates to Plato's use of the same term. The similarity between the two terms is more than a terminological accident, and supports our contention that Tillich's account of essence owes more to Plato than anyone else.

We have spoken of essence by way of the Platonic contrast between essence and existence. An alternative way of expressing the same thing is the Aristotelian pair of contrasts potentiality–actuality. Potentiality in the system is 'the "not yet" of being' (*ST* 2.23), or simply 'not-yet-being', and in order for something to become actual 'it must overcome relative non-being, the state of *me on*'. As we shall see, two accounts of existence result from the Platonic and Aristotelian contrasts: in the Platonic account, existence is a 'falling' from essence; in the Aristotelian account, existence is an emerging out of potentiality. Now these two accounts simply will not harmonize. Each of them by itself is difficult enough, together they contradict each other. In the Platonic account *me on* is the negative principle which limits and conditions the eternal forms: in the Aristotelian account, *me on* is the source of existence, the created potentiality from which things emerge in order to be. We develop the consequences of this antimony in chapter VII.

The potentiality–actuality contrast dispenses with the need for the Platonic essence–existence contrast. However, both contrasts are plainly at work in the system, and we have argued that, in so far as essences appear, a Platonic account of them is the most adequate and normative we can find. This conclusion would seem to be confirmed by a brief discussion of the sort of epistemological account that Platonic forms require.

In speaking of essences, reference has been made to intuition and abstraction as the means whereby knowledge of essences is obtained. Another word for the same cognitive act is *ideation*,[33] but Tillich prefers 'abstraction'. He says our knowledge of essences is both intuitive and 'experiential'. He learned his intuitive method of discerning from Husserl, noted its use in Otto, Scheler, and Schultz,[34] and in 1922 he developed what he called the 'critical-intuitive' method[35] which was a little later given the name 'metalogic'.[36] By this method, i.e. 'the metalogical intuition of essences', Tillich sought to perceive 'the inner dynamic in the structure of meaning-reality'. He tried to combine the methods of Kantian criticism and Husserlian intuition into a single method for the philosophy of religion. He claimed that by themselves each method failed, but together a workable knowledge of essences could be discovered. He writes: 'The critical method cannot grasp the "whatness" of things; the intuitive method cannot grasp their "thatness".'[37] Nevertheless the final perception of 'that which is the "real" of all things' is the product of intuition. Intuition perceives the 'unconditionally real' beyond the point where the critical method by itself reaches its boundaries of thought:

That which is the 'real' in all things is not itself a reality, nor is it the totality or even the infinity of the real. The perception of this however, is no longer a matter of criticism but of intuition. Where criticism establishes its boundary concepts (which are testimony to its own limitedness), there intuition perceives the unconditionally real that constitutes the root of reality from which all criticism lives. Indeed, it intuits this root not beyond those boundaries set by criticism, but precisely in the midst of the critically defined realm.

One could give the name 'abstraction' to the critical method. If we do this we see criticism or abstraction giving us the forms of pure thought, and the method of intuition taking

[33] 'Is a Science of Human Values Possible?', 193: *My Search for Absolutes*, 72.
[34] *What is Religion?* 136 f. From 'Die Überwindung des Religionsbegriffs in der Religionsphilosophie'. German in *GW* 1.313.
[35] *What is Religion?* 149 f. (*GW* 1.385).
[36] *What is Religion?* 50. From 'Religionsphilosophie' (*GW* 1.313).
[37] *What is Religion?* 149. (*GW* 1.385).

over as the mind penetrates the forms of thought and perceives a meaning-reality that cannot be expressed in any thought form. Tillich's early doctrine of our knowledge of the 'really real' or of the 'Unconditioned' is substantially the same as the later doctrine of our knowledge of essences. Abstraction gives us universals which are a product of human thought and reflection. Intuition brings us to the reality of essences, for intuition penetrates beyond the bounds of thought and therefore furnishes us with knowledge of a pre-critical or pre-conceptual type. The *Unvordenkliche* which we intuit is God, or ground of being, or essence, or the 'really real', or the 'depth of reality', etc.

We have devoted a good deal of space to the concept of essence because it is the all-important contrast against which the account of the realm of existence stands out. Essences are the conditions of the possibility of language and are prior to thought and to language itself which is a creation of thought. They constitute a realm which our cognition can never entirely penetrate. The realm of essence is the source of existence, and has a higher ontological status. Now we have drawn attention to some of the problems inhering in the concept of essence, the all-important relationship between essence and existence will be examined.

VI

THE TRANSITION FROM ESSENCE TO EXISTENCE

THE transition from essence to existence is called a ' "half-way demythologisation" of the myth of the Fall' (*ST* 2.33). The mythical character of the story of the Fall is not removed because it is retold in abstract philosophical and psychological terms. The language used is 'temporal' and therefore to that extent mythological (*ST* 2.33, also 38, 42). But what does it describe? The transition is not 'an event that happened "once upon a time" ', and 'the state of essential being' with which it begins 'is not an actual stage of human development which can be known directly or indirectly' (*ST* 2.38). The transition is said to have 'the character of a leap' from essence to existence (*ST* 2.50). It is 'a universal quality of finite being. It is not an event of the past; for it ontologically precedes everything that happens in time and space. It sets the conditions of spatial and temporal existence' (*ST* 2.42). The transition is called the 'original fact',[1] for everything that exists in time and space is affected in some way by it.

Unfortunately a hollow ring echoes through the description of the transition to existence because of a dire lack of direct experience of the state of affairs which is being described. Essential being never was, before the 'fall'. We cannot know it 'directly or indirectly'.[2] In so far as it is appropriate to speak of it as an object of knowledge at all, the transition to existence is, like the realm of essence, a matter of intuition, the contents of which can only be described in a mythological or metaphorical manner.[3] D. J. Keefe aptly calls the essential being of man 'a mythical reflex from existence'.[4] The task of description is made

---

[1] *ST* 2.41, 50. But this is in contrast to *ST* 1.122 where the original fact is that there is something and not nothing.

[2] 'A Reinterpretation of the Doctrine of the Incarnation', *Church Quarterly Review*, cxlvii (1949), 141.

[3] See also *ST* 3.421.

[4] D. J. Keefe, *Thomism and the Ontological Theology of Paul Tillich*, 216.

still more difficult because the transition is not just inaccessible to thought; it is downright 'irrational' (*ST* 2.14; 3.302). The transition then, is a 'universal quality of finite being' which must never be construed literally as a transition because it never actually happened. To some extent the difficulties encountered here can be anticipated in any reinterpretation of the doctrine of the fall which does not posit a historical 'perfect' world prior to the supposed event of Adam's sin. However the use of the term 'transition' unavoidably gives the impression that some kind of 'before' and 'after' in a spatio-temporal sense is meant. The word 'transition' ('going across') implies the crossing from one realm to another. It is a spatial term which cannot be understood without the categories of space and time. Moreover the stages involved in the description of the transition, all of them interconnected, make it impossible to escape the conclusion that what is referred to is to be understood, in part at least, as a happening, a process, or a going across from one state of things to another.

Perhaps it was these difficulties which led Tillich to admit how his colleague Reinhold Niebuhr disliked the phrase 'transition from essence to existence universally', and then surprisingly to add, 'I do not like it either, and forbid my students all the time to use it in their sermons. But nevertheless, I think as an analytic term it is quite adequate to the situation and not different from what Neibuhr means.'[5] Unfortunately a majority of theologians would flatly deny that the phrase is 'analytic' at all. It is certainly not analytic in the sense that it is true by definition in a manner similar to logical or mathematical statements. We return to the meaning of the phrase later, for as Tillich admits, it is one of the most important in his entire work. He even says of it

A complete discussion of the realm of essence is identical with the entire theological system. The distinction between essence and the existence, which religiously speaking is the distinction between the created and the actual world, is the backbone of the whole body of theological thought' (*ST* 1.226–7).

The description of the transition to existence and the resultant existential state is given in a number of stages. We indicate

[5] 'Reinhold Niebuhr: A Prophetic Voice in our Time', 37.

briefly what the stages are, before examining each of them in turn and then suggesting a number of criticisms in the latter part of this chapter. First, the transition is possible because of the structure of finite freedom (ST 2.35–8). While finite freedom is unactualized, essential being is symbolized as 'dreaming innocence'. Dreaming innocence is in turn exposed to temptation (ST 2.39). Finite freedom then becomes 'aroused freedom' and aroused freedom becomes actualized freedom' (ST 2.40–1). Actualized freedom is both loss of innocence and loss of freedom itself, and with the loss of dreaming innocence the transition to existence has become actual. The actuality of existence has both a moral element in that man is personally responsible for it, and a tragic element in that it is unavoidable (ST 2.41–3). Although the description is, at least in part, drawn from psychology, the transition is nevertheless both 'a cosmic event' and 'the universal transition from essential goodness to existential estrangement' (ST 2.45).

The description continues with an account of the transition, not just to the realm of existence generally, but to existence in its ever more extreme and desperate forms. Existence is estrangement (ST 2.51), and the 'marks of estrangement' are detectable in the three theological ideas of unbelief, concupiscence, and *hubris* or pride (ST 2.54). The self–world structure of being becomes disrupted (ST 2.69–72), followed by the disruption of the three pairs of ontological elements (ST 2.72–6). Other consequences follow. The fact of having to die becomes a 'horror of death'; guilt is induced by the awareness that estrangement is one's personal responsibility (ST 2.78). In the categories, time becomes transitoriness; space becomes 'spatial contingency' (ST 2.80). Similarly man reacts to the categories of causality and substance under the conditions of existence by attempting 'to make himself into an absolute cause in resistance to the endless chain of causes in which he is one among others', and 'to give to himself an absolute substance in resistance to the vanishing of the substance along with the accidents'. His resistance against the non-being which confronts him through the categorical features of existence may break down, and the breakdown is an element in the complex phenomenon of 'despair' (ST 2.79: CTB, 61–3). Suffering and solitude under the conditions of existence become destructive (ST 2.81–3).

Lack of security and certainty under the same conditions also lead to despair (*ST* 2.83–6), which is 'the final index of man's predicament'. The pain of despair in turn causes the longing to escape from one's self by destroying one's self (*ST* 2.87). The doctrine of the 'bondage of the will' describes 'the inability of man to break through his estrangement' (*ST* 2.92). This inability leads him to the 'quest for the New Being' (*ST* 2.100).

A further step towards the understanding of the transition to existence lies in an analysis of 'finite freedom' which makes the transition possible (*ST* 2.35). The concept is a conflation of two others, finitude, which belongs to a discussion of the contrast with infinity, and freedom, which belongs to a discussion of the polarity between freedom and destiny. The analysis of finite freedom begins our discussion of the stages of the transition from essence to existence.

Finitude is widely misunderstood as a synonym for existence, but any simple identification of the two terms should be avoided. It is important to realize that finitude belongs to essence, while existence is the *contradiction* of essence. Tillich sometimes refers to 'essential finitude' (*ST* 2.78, 84). Essential finitude provides the possibility of the transition to existence but it is not an agent in the transition itself. Finitude is created being. It is 'conditioned' (*ST* 2.108). It is *not* a polar opposite to infinity. Infinity, according to Tillich, is a 'directing concept' which 'directs the mind to experience its own unlimited potentialities, but it does not establish the existence of an infinite being' (*ST* 1.212).

Tillich's understanding of the infinite and its relation to the finite is again broadly Hegelian. Hegel taught that the infinite cannot be infinite if it is regarded as a realm set over against the finite. Such an infinite would then be limited by the finite because the finite would be excluded from it, and a limited infinite would be self-contradictory. Hegel dismisses it, calling it the 'spurious infinite' or the 'infinitised finite'.[6] In opposition to the 'spurious infinite' Hegel spoke of the 'good infinite'. The good infinite is that notion of infinity which is inseparable from finitude, which receives finitude into itself, overcoming the negation that belongs to finitude, and which makes the distinction between the infinite and the finite possible. Tillich accepts

[6] *The Science of Logic*, 137, 140.

Hegel's understanding of the infinite. He writes: 'that which is infinite would not be infinite if it were limited by the finite. God is infinite because he has the finite (and with it that element of non-being which belongs to finitude) within himself united with his infinity' (*ST* 1.279). Infinity then, is not a realm above finitude but a realm which includes finitude within itself. It generates an awareness of itself in finite being, an awareness which reminds man that he belongs to being-itself, i.e., to that which is beyond the limits of his finitude (*ST* 1.212). Tillich defines finitude as 'being, limited by non-being' (*ST* 1.210).

Everything which participates in the power of being is 'mixed' with non-being. It is being in process of coming from and going toward non-being. It is finite. Both the basic ontological structure and the ontological elements imply finitude . . . To be here and now in the process of becoming is not to be there and then. To be something is to be finite (*ST* 1.211).

Nothing in these definitions contradicts the view that finitude is unambiguously good. To be 'limited by non-being' is not to have fallen into existence or estrangement. The non-being referred to is the nothing out of which anything that is created must proceed, and to which it must return. There is nothing 'fallen' about any entity qualified in this way, since to come from and return to nothing is characteristic of everything created. And as we have seen, non-being is also a principle within God as being-itself, so the limitation of finitude by non-being is no evidence for the transition from essence to existence. Hegel called finitude 'determinate being' and as such, it is determined by 'limit'. Limit acts negatively upon it, giving to the finite entity its determinateness as some particular qualitative being.[7] When man begins to 'transcend himself' he realizes the limits which finitude imposes upon him, and makes him aware of his nature as finite (*ST* 1.211). Since for Tillich being and non-being are firmly anchored within the divine life, a negative principle may easily be located within finitude which does not compromise its essential character. The negativity of finitude is not the same as the negativity of existence.

Finitude is systematically expressed by the ontological categories which are called 'forms of finitude'. They 'unite an

[7] Op. cit., 115, 126–30.

affirmative and a negative element', seeing that 'they express being, but at the same time they express the non-being to which everything that is is subject' (*ST* 1.214). They have an essential, ontological validity which however only changes under the conditions of existence (*ST* 2.79). Not only is non-being an element of essential finitude but also anxiety, the experience of non-being, can be located on the *essence* side of the transition. There can be an 'essential anxiety' about estrangement which is not part of estrangement itself (*ST* 2.78). 'Occasions in which anxiety is aroused' must be distinguished from 'anxiety itself' (*ST* 1.212). Like freedom, anxiety can be 'aroused' from its latency, in which it belongs to the pre-transitional, essential realm. In another context Tillich says finitude and anxiety are the same. Anxiety is the awareness of our finitude.[8] Finite being even includes the phenomenon of doubt, in that the limitations of any finite human being do not enable it to see 'the whole' of truth (again in an Hegelian sense) (*ST* 2.85). Therefore a finite being 'accepts the fact that doubt belongs to his essential being'. Finitude also includes the phenomena of uncertainty, insecurity, and contingency—terms which we cannot yet label 'existential' because they do not yet apply within the realm of existence after the transition from essence. All these are said to belong to 'man's essential finitude', to 'the goodness of the creative', to 'the state of mere potentiality'. On the essence side of the transition they can be accepted in an 'unbroken courage' which accepts the limitations of finitude in the power of 'the eternal'.

There is then, nothing in the concept of finitude which implies fallenness. The state of finitude is compatible, mythologically speaking, with man's original perfection in the garden of Eden. His 'essential freedom' likewise is a characteristic of his original created goodness. In *ST* 1 and in several other contexts Tillich makes it clear that to speak about freedom is to speak of something far more basic than a discussion about the freedom of the *will*.[9] In an article in 1939 Tillich defined freedom as man's '*essential* nature'. He then contrasted it with man's 'servitude'

[8] *ST* 2.39: 'What is Basic in Human Nature', 19.

[9] *ST* 1.202 f., 223: *ST* 2.73: 'Freedom in the Period of Transformation', in *Freedom: Its Meaning* (ed. R. Anshen), 124: 'The Conception of Man in Existential Philosophy', *Journal of Religion*, xix (1939), 207: 'The Nature of Man', *Journal of Philosophy*, xliii (1946), 676: 'What is Basic in Human Nature', 17.

which he defined as man's *existential* nature': 'Since freedom is the characteristic which distinguishes man from all other beings and since all other human characteristics follow from this, the doctrine of human nature has its center in the doctrine of human freedom (the doctrine of man's essential nature).'[10] Here freedom and servitude do not balance each other as polar contrasts but represent man at the two different levels of his being, viz. essence and existence. The transition of man from his essence to his existence is interpreted as the predominance of his servitude over his freedom. His servitude is said to have a double character, that of tragedy and sin. Man's existence is tragic in that, *universally* and *inescapably*, he tries like Adam and Eve before him, to become like God: 'The servitude to which he is subjected is the law of tragedy. Human creativity when it is accompanied by the determination of the individual to be the ground of himself (or in classical terms "to be like God") is the tragic servitude of man.' *Tragic* servitude is a 'universal situation', a 'cosmic event'. *Sinful* servitude makes the cosmic event an individual event. The individual willingly affirms his independence from his ground of being or God. 'Tragic servitude exists in mutual dependence with the servitude of sin. Sin is the act in which the free self turns away from its essential being and surrenders itself to servitude'. The distinction between tragic and sinful servitude is re-expressed in *ST* 2, where Tillich speaks instead of 'the *moral* and the *tragic* element' in the transition from essential to existential being (*ST* 2.41, my italics). The 'moral' and the 'tragic' represent the personal and the universal transition to existence respectively.

Tillich often uses the single non-polar concept of *finite freedom* to express in an alternative manner the meaning of the freedom–destiny polarity. When applied to man it conveys exactly the same meaning as the application to man of the freedom–destiny polarity, but without using polar contrasts or ontological elements in the description. Tillich sometimes simply defines man *as* finite freedom: 'Man is essentially "finite freedom" ... Man, as finite freedom, is free within the contingencies of his finitude. But within these limits he is asked to

---

[10] 'The Conception of Man in Existential Philosophy', 202–3, 209. Despite the general title of the article, the philosophy Tillich expounds is unmistakably his own.

make of himself what he is to become, to fulfil his destiny' (*CTB*, 58–9). Finite freedom is identical with created goodness, but it is also, Tillich says 'the turning-point from being to existence' (*ST* 1.183), and 'anxiety'. All creatures, he writes

> are driven by anxiety; for finitude and anxiety are the same. But in man freedom is united with anxiety. One could call man's freedom 'freedom in anxiety' or anxious freedom' [in German, *sich ängstigende Freiheit*]. This anxiety is one of the driving forces towards the transition from essence to existence. (*ST* 2.39–40)

The extremities of the concepts of freedom and finitude are best illustrated by the description of the earthly life of our Lord, since here according to Tillich is the only actual, concrete manifestation of essential finitude under the conditions of existence. Jesus is subject to the contingency of everything that is 'thrown' into existence: he experiences the anxiety of having to die and the threat of the victory of non-being over being: he experiences 'the lack of a definite place'; he experiences bodily, social and mental insecurity; he is even 'subject to uncertainty in judgement and risks of error' which include 'his ancient conception of the world, his judgements about men, his interpretation of the historical moment, his eschatological imagination'. His experience of doubt leads him to 'his doubt about his own work, as in his hesitation to accept the messianic title, and, above all his feelings of having been left alone by God without God's expected interference on the Cross' (*ST* 2.150–1). Jesus is even said to be 'involved in the tragic element of guilt', because 'he made his enemies inescapably guilty' (*ST* 2.152). We do not propose to discuss the adequacy of this account of the person of Christ or the question whether Tillich has correctly interpreted some of the gospel reports on which the account is based. The description of the life of Christ is referred to in the present context only in order to show how far the range of essential finitude extends prior to its existential distortion. The life of Jesus is of course for Tillich the only case where the distortion does not occur. Nothing so far mentioned compromises the 'essential manhood' of Jesus.

Although it is important to emphasize the essential character of finitude and to distinguish the negative element of essential finitude, which is always overcome by the power of being-itself, from the negative element of existence, finite freedom should also be seen as the structure or the occasion which makes the transition to existence possible. The creation of finite freedom is described as 'the risk which the divine creativity accepts' (*ST* 1.299). Man's freedom is also his 'power of contradicting himself and his essential nature' (*ST* 2.36). The creation of finite freedom includes the possibility that man will lose his freedom:

finite freedom implies the possibility of contradicting man's essential nature.[11]

Finitude is the possibility of losing one's ontological structure and, with it, one's self. But this is a possibility not a necessity. To be finite is to be threatened. But a threat is possibility, not actuality. (*ST* 1.223-4)

The ambiguity of freedom, and the sinister possibility of the loss of freedom are best expressed by the term 'dreaming innocence' which appeared for the first time in *ST* 2 in 1957. The experience of innocence is only possible in relation to states of affairs which are not, or not yet, actual, and Tillich says he likes the term 'dreaming innocence' because it suggests something which 'precedes actual existence'. It is, he says, 'a state of mind which is real and non-real at the same time—just as is potentiality' (*ST* 2.38). Dreams, unlike wakeful experiences, are said to be restricted by neither place nor time. They precede 'temporality'. Dreaming innocence is 'an image of the state of essential being' (*ST* 2.38). The state of dreaming innocence and the consequential loss of innocence are both exemplified in the growth of a child's sexual consciousness. During puberty an 'awakening' takes place where experience, and subsequent responsibility and guilt are acquired, and the state of dreaming innocence is lost. The experience of temptation produces 'a desire to sin' or an 'aroused freedom' which is not yet sin but which is now no longer innocence. This situation is paralleled in the Genesis account of the 'fall' where divine prohibition is given not to eat from the tree of knowledge (*ST* 2.39-40). A desire is created which results in loss of

---

[11] 'Propositions'. These were produced for private circulation and never published. The passage is quoted by Reinhold Niebuhr, 'Biblical Thought and Ontological Speculation in Tillich's Theology', *TPT*, 222.

innocence even before sin is committed. Precisely at this point the ontological transition to existence occurs:

> In the state of dreaming innocence, freedom and destiny are in harmony, but neither of them is actualized. Their unity is essential or potential; it is finite and therefore open to tension and disruption —just like uncontested innocence. The tension occurs in the moment in which finite freedom becomes conscious of itself and tends to become actual . . . Man is caught between the desire to actualize his freedom and the demand to preserve his dreaming innocence. In the power of his finite freedom, he decides for actualization.[12]

He experiences the anxiety of losing himself both by actualizing or not actualizing his potentialities. He universally chooses the first way. By this act the transition to existence occurs. He actualizes himself by actualizing his freedom, thereby losing his innocence, and consequently his essential being. Nature and universal existence all share in man's guilt for having lost his innocence (*ST* 2.46–8). Nature and man interpenetrate: 'They participate in each other and cannot be separated from each other. This makes it possible and necessary to use the term "fallen world" and to apply the concept of existence (in contrast to essence) to the universe as well as to man' (*ST* 2.49).

With the loss of man's dreaming innocence, both he and his world are 'fallen'. The transition from essence has already taken place. His loss of innocence brings him into existence, and consequently into existential estrangement. 'The state of existence is the state of estrangement. Man is estranged from the ground of his being, from other beings, and from himself. The transition from essence to existence results in personal guilt and universal tragedy' (*ST* 2.51). Tillich defends his doctrine of existence by an etymological appeal to the Latin *existere*, to 'stand out' (*ex-sistere*) (*ST* 2.21–3). To exist, he says, means to 'stand out', but to stand out of what? Both absolute and relative non-being. To exist *means* to stand out of the realm of non-being. But, he continues, to 'stand out' logically implies to 'stand in' at the same time, since 'only that which in some respects stands in can stand out'. Existence then, both as finitude and as actuality, stands in and stands out of non-being.

---

[12] *ST* 2.40. See also 'Paul Tillich and Carl Rogers: A Dialogue', *Pastoral Psychology*, xix (1968), 58.

But the matter is more complex than Tillich allows. Existence must stand *out* of non-being in two senses. First it stands out of non-being because it is *not* nothing, but *is* something. It 'can be found, directly or indirectly, within the corpus of reality. It stands out of the emptiness of absolute non-being' (*ST* 2.22). But not only is existence not *nothing*, it is not *potentiality* either. This is the second type of non-being out of which existence stands. Any thing that exists is an actuality and is no longer purely a potency or possibility. How then can existence also stand *in* non-being at the same time? It is very difficult to see how existence can stand in absolute nothing, whatever Tillich says—absolute nothing cannot provide a basis in which anything can stand. But he not only thinks existence somehow stands in absolute nothing, he thinks it *stands in potentiality too*, for 'An actual thing stands out of mere potentiality; but it also remains in it. It never pours its power of being completely into its state of existence. It never fully exhausts its potentialities' (*ST* 2.23). Existents are always changing, becoming something else. However Tillich makes it plain that the non-being in which existence stands is the full blown dialectical concept of being which is as much a feature of creaturely life as it is of the divine life. In God, non-being is eternally overcome by being: in existence being and non-being are mixed, with all the resultant effects of world loss, anxiety, and estrangement. This kind of non-being is dialectical. It has to be balanced by the opposite pole of power of being, and then it issues in a dialectical synthesis, existence, or life.

According to Tillich we cannot speak of existence without speaking of estrangement. Nothing that exists is as it 'ought to be', i.e., its essence. Creation and fall are identical, or at any rate, there is a point at which they coincide. 'Actualized creation and estranged existence are identical' (*ST* 2.50). The myth of the immanent fall (i.e. Genesis 3) describes the transition in psychological terms, while the myth of the transcendent fall (*ST* 2.43) describes the transition in universal or ontological terms.[13] The fall is for mankind both 'fact and act' (*ST* 2.63–6). It is a fact because he knows of no other existence which does not include estrangement. It is an act because he himself is personally responsible for his own estrangement, from

[13] 'Propositions': cit. B. Martin, *Paul Tillich's Doctrine of Man*, 136.

himself, from other beings, and from God. 'Sin as an individual act actualizes the universal fact of estrangement' (*ST* 2.64). The actualization of freedom takes place in polar union with destiny, and man experiences both tragedy at the universality of estrangement and guilt for his personal responsibility for it. He has two natures, his 'true', 'essential', or 'created' nature, and his 'existential', 'temporal', or 'historical' nature. The existential nature has 'a characteristic of being estranged from his true nature'.[14]

Surprisingly Tillich does not follow the general trend of the existentialists in reserving the word 'existence' for the being of that unique entity, man. It is instead a realm of being which covers everything finite, and leads to estrangement. The term 'estrangement' largely replaces 'sin', though Tillich admits that 'sin', despite the moralistic abuse of the term, expresses something that is not implied in 'estrangement', i.e. 'the personal act of turning away from that to which one belongs' (*ST* 2.52–3). The 'marks of estrangement' are said to be un-belief, *hubris*, or self-elevation and concupiscence. Unbelief is 'man's estrangement from God in the centre of his self'. In *hubris* 'he elevates himself beyond the limits of his finite being and provokes the divine wrath which destroys him' (*ST* 2.57). Concupiscence is 'the unlimited desire to draw the whole of reality into one's self' (*ST* 2.59).

One of the ontological consequences of the doctrine of estrangement is that, under its impact, the basic self–world polarity and the ontological elements which depend upon it are lost. In the essential structure of being tension can still develop between each side of the polarities, but the tension is 'essential' and the polar character of the elements is not broken. But within 'essential finitude' the breaking of the polar unity is a 'possibility' (*ST* 1.220). In estrangement the threat of a break is fulfilled: the possibility becomes an actuality, and the tension becomes conflict (*ST* 2.72). Like the transition to existence, estrangement is not something that happens. Man 'finds himself' in it (*ST* 2.68). Under the drives of unbelief, *hubris*, and concupiscence, he loses his determining centre, and the unity he has as a person begins to disintegrate. The world too is lost— 'it ceases to be a world, in the sense of a meaningful whole'

14 'P. Tillich and Carl Rogers: A Dialogue', 56.

(ST 2.71). As a result, within the ontological elements, freedom becomes arbitrariness (ST 2.72), and destiny becomes necessity. Dynamics becomes 'a formless urge for self-transcendence' and form becomes 'external law' (ST 2.74). Individualization becomes isolation or loneliness and participation becomes 'submergence in the collective' (ST 2.76).

The description of the ontological polarities in the state of estrangement is perhaps one of the most evocative parts of the ontological system. Here the system reads more like a sensitive phenomenological description of human existence such as modern existentialism has provided, and less like the abstract speculations of the Hegelian type. It is an interesting combination of existential, psychological, theological, and sociological description. The state of affairs it describes gives rise to the quest for the New Being. Before we examine the account of New Being in chapter VII, a number of difficulties which arise in connection with the transition to existence must first be looked at.

A key feature of the transition to existence is the state of dreaming innocence. Dreaming innocence is a somewhat puzzling feature of the description, especially since so much importance is attached to the 'non-actual' state it refers to. The account is similar in several respects to Kierkegaard's psychological account of man's prelapsarian innocence in *The Concept of Dread*. Kierkegaard writes that in the state of innocence 'spirit is dreaming in man'. He uses the dream metaphor to try to account for the unrealized non-actual possibilities which are present potentially in the state of innocence. Tillich thinks the value of the term consists in the characteristic of dream states that they are both actual and yet non-actual at the same time. But there are both psychological and ontological difficulties to be overcome before its use can be allowed to stand. First, it must be doubtful whether, as Tillich thinks, dreams are innocent. He says 'the metaphor "dreaming" is adequate in describing the state of essential being' (ST 2.38). But the dream state is simply not innocent. A dispassionate recollection of what we dream about ought to dispel any question about whether the dreamer is innocent in relation to his dream contents. Freud explicitly affirms that the individual is responsible for the contents or 'evil impulses' of his dreams, which are to be

regarded as part of the ego.[15] The Hindu philosopher Radhakrishnan recalls a passage in the Hindu *Chandogya Upanisad*
where the question is raised whether the true self is the same as
the 'dream self' or 'dream consciousness'.[16] Radhakrishnan
notes Indra's reply: 'though it is true that this dreaming self
is not affected by the changes of the body, yet in dreams we feel
that we are struck or chased, we experience pain or tears. We
rage in dreams, storm with indignation, do things perverted,
mean and malicious.'[17] Quite so. But perhaps Tillich would
counter that he has in mind only those dream states where the
subject *is* innocent, and that his term 'dreaming innocence'
clearly implies this. If this is the case, the term is still subject
to a number of ontological difficulties. One wonders whether
the notion is sufficiently bold or expressive to amplify the
'distinction between essence and existence', since this distinction
is 'the backbone of the whole system of theological thought'
(*ST* 1.226–7). Granted that it is to be understood as a 'motif' or
an 'image' (*ST* 2.38), a 'psychological symbol' which is used in
an 'analogical' and not a 'proper' sense, the state of dreaming
innocence does seem to be a flimsy analogy with which to
bring into focus the 'backbone' of the system.

But there are other more serious difficulties since the metaphor 'dreaming' stands in a misleading relation to potentiality.
Potentiality implies the power of something to become actual,
whereas dreams are always dreams, and apart from being
dreams, they have no power to become actual at all. Even
Kierkegaard saw that the state of innocence as qualified by
dreaming, is anxiety-producing in that what is represented to
us in our dreaming is fleeting and ungraspable. 'Dread is a
qualification of the dreaming spirit',[18] so that even in the state
of innocence, man is the subject of an anxiety which is compounded by its own indefiniteness. Dream consciousness does
then seem a poor way of elucidating what is meant by the state
of essence or potentiality. If existence is that which has fallen
from essence, then the realm of essence must have a fullness of
being, a richness, a created goodness, and an ontological

[15] *S. Freud: Collected Papers*, v (1950), 156–7, cit. H. M. Tiebout, Jr., 'Tillich and
Freud on Sin', *Religion in Life*, xxviii (1958–9), 224–5.
[16] *Chandogya Upanisad* 8.10.1–4: *The Principal Upanisads*, Radhakrishnan, 506–7.
[17] *The Principal Upanisads*, 74.
[18] Op. cit., 38.

priority which is incompatible with the symbol 'dreaming'.[19] Our consideration of essence in the previous chapter indicates that the realm the term signifies is of much greater importance than the metaphor 'dreaming innocence' suggests. If existence is alternatively that which emerges from potentiality, then the metaphor of the dream-state does not reflect the process whereby potentialities become actual, simply because dream-contents do *not* become actual. Our knowledge of dreams comes to us through a blurred recollection of equally blurred, and often absurd, experiences. If we allow this kind of experience to form the material of an analogy which gives us the clue to understanding essential being, then the significance of essential being in the ontology is in danger of being lost.

Is it the case that the actualization of freedom *must* result in the loss of dreaming innocence? In the state of 'aroused freedom' which is no longer innocence, but not yet sin, Tillich says man is confronted with two possibilities. He is 'caught between the desire to actualize his freedom and the demand to preserve his dreaming innocence. In the power of his freedom, he decides for actualization' (*ST* 2.40). Consequently he loses his innocence, and with it his essential being. Now there are two contexts in which such talk can be understood, in the mythological context where the factors involved in Adam's free decision to disobey God are regarded as paradigmatic for the human race as a whole: and in the psychological context of the sexual awakening of a person where the experience of sexual arousal acts as a kind of model for understanding the general and inevitable tendency of all human beings to misuse their freedom. The problem here is whether these two particular instances of loss of innocence adequately account for the universal state of human estrangement, and the supposed free choice of all men to fall into it. However, leaving this major difficulty aside, the paradigm or model is in any case misleadingly constructed. The choice that Adam is given (and with him all human kind) is between 'the desire to actualize his freedom' and 'the demand to preserve his dreaming innocence'. Now clearly *whatever* Adam decides to do he will actualize his freedom by doing it, and a decision to preserve his innocence

<hr />

[19] Thus D. D. Williams, 'Review of *ST* 2', *Review of Religion*, xxii (1958), 3–4: repr. *Journal of Religion*, xlvi (1966), 216.

is as much an actualization of freedom as the decision not to preserve it. He cannot 'decide for actualization' because he actualizes his freedom whatever he decides, even if he decides not to do anything. There is here a rather serious misrepresentation of what is involved in moral choice. Also, what can be made of the 'demand to preserve his innocence'? If the preservation of Adam's essential nature is possible only at the cost of his *never making decisions at all* (which is only possible in a mythological sense) then it is difficult to see how freedom can be part of his essential nature.

Part of the problem here of course lies in the broader scheme of Christian doctrine whereby man's *original* sin is compounded by his *actual* sin so that he becomes responsible for a state of affairs he cannot help. We ought not to treat a difficulty in Augustinian theology as if it were of Tillich's own making. But must we admit, even within the context of the myth of the fall, that man's wrong actualization of his freedom is the cause of the estrangement of the realm of existence generally? Does man's 'fall' bring about the 'fall' of the world? Our modern view of the relation between man and the rest of nature gives us insights into the problem which were denied to earlier generations. We now take for granted that what we call nature existed for hundreds of millions of years before *homo sapiens* appeared within it. We also know that his biological pre-history indicates his solid continuity with earlier species which preceded him. The world is not fallen because man has fallen; it was a fallen world long before mankind had a place in it. If we continue to speak mythologically of mankind as fallen, then his fallenness is one with the rest of nature and not a prelude to it. The problem here is that of attempting to reconcile the Augustinian account of the fall of Adam in the garden of Eden with the modern biological account of the rise of man from earlier more primitive biological species. Tillich, however, is at fault, we suggest, in that his account of the consequences of the fall, as they affect the basic self–world polarity, seem to have repercussions for the self side of the polarity, whereas the world side is actually *effective* in the fall of the self side. When the state of estrangement is described as the loss of the self–world polarity (*ST* 2.72), the description is unevenly confined to the self side of polarity. The world is lost from the point of view of man's relation to it. He sees it through his own 'determining centre', through 'the disintegration of the unity of the person' (*ST* 2.71). But the world is not only fallen from the point of view of our distorted relationship to it, it is also fallen in itself. The destructive flaws in the natural world, the suffering and disorder which continue even without human apprehension of them, furnish us with evidence that estrangement from essence is a brute characteristic of the existence of the world itself, independently of the cognizance of the self. The world's relation to us, as well as our's to the world, is distorted under the conditions of existence. Tillich's position admits this, but does not develop it.

One of the most common criticisms of this part of Tillich's system is the charge that he has insufficiently distinguished between the created and the fallen world, or between finitude and sin.[20] But the impression cannot be avoided that such objections simply do not match up to our recent scientific knowledge of the origins of the human race, and that their validity rests on a literalizing of the myth of the fall at least in so far as it implies a perfect world before the fall and a fallen world afterwards. Some theologians tend to face both ways at this juncture, optimistically assuming that the new post-evolutionary scientific world-view of the late twentieth century is compatible with the old literal, chronological view of the fall in Genesis. But the latter is precisely what a modern view excludes. There is much to be said for the almost solitary defence of Tillich by W. N. Pittenger at this point, who argues that any theological talk of the fall as an historical event, with the several implications of a 'before' and 'after' and a 'divinely intended condition' prior to the fall taking place is 'disingenuous'.[21] He says: 'His point is not that these are the same; rather, it is that wherever we happen to see man or created

[20] e.g. J. Heywood Thomas, *Paul Tillich: an Appraisal*, 132: D. E. Roberts, 'Tillich's Doctrine of Man', R. H. Daubney, 'Some Structural Concepts in Tillich's Thought', Re. Niebuhr, 'Biblical Thought and Ontological Speculation in Tillich's Theology', all in *TPT*, 126, 277, 218: B. Loomer, 'Tillich's Theology of Correlation', *Journal of Religion*, xxxvi (1956), 156: B. Martin, *Paul Tillich's Doctrine of Man*, 135: Rowe, 204: Killen, 187: G. B. Hammond, *Man in Estrangement*, 158: etc.

[21] W. Norman Pittenger, 'Paul Tillich as a Theologian: An Appreciation', *Anglican Theological Review*, xliii (1961), 281.

existence, there we find estrangement. This is a description of a fact, not ontological identification of creature and sin.'

If, however, we tend to exculpate Tillich from the charge that he has insufficiently distinguished between creation and fall, we cannot acquit him of another related charge, that he distinguishes too sharply between the created and the *essential* world, with the result that God creates only essences, and the realm of existence somehow emerges out of essence independently. He claims: 'Creation is good in its essential character. If actualised, it falls into universal estrangement through freedom and destiny' (*ST* 2.50). Now clearly creation is here something unactualized, something that has yet to become what it can become. *If* creation is actualized (and this is a genuine conditional), then it becomes estrangement. Whereas creation is good, the same cannot be said for existence. Existence is not created. The essential goodness of creation never extends beyond pure potentiality, since 'there is no point in time and space in which created goodness was actualised and had existence' (*ST* 2.50). So whatever God creates, it certainly is not *actual*. But in accordance with any normal understanding of the term 'creation' it must refer to some kind of actuality, i.e. in traditional terms, to what is no longer in potency, but has been brought forth into act. But for Tillich creation, at least in its character of essential goodness, is never actual. It is purely potential. Consequently it is difficult to see how creation cannot but be regarded as some sort of *tertium quid* between Creator and creature. God creates: what he creates is 'essential goodness'. But essential goodness is not the same as existence. It has to be actualized before it can be recognized as existence, and as existence, it is estranged existence.

There are of course dangerous implications in such a position. The identity of creation with potentiality is consistent with the beliefs that (a) the object of creation is confined to the realm of essence, or (b) that existence itself resists and distorts the created essences which instantiate existents, implying some kind of gnostic dualism. Neither view seems consistent with the Christian doctrine of creation, but both are consistent with the equation of creation with potentiality.[22] God does not create

<hr />

[22] A. McKelway differentiates between essential and actual creation, *The Systematic Theology of Paul Tillich*, 150.

the realm of existence. Existence is a transition from essence which takes place, inscrutably and irrationally, only after the creation of essence has first occurred.

As we shall see, Tillich provides two complementary accounts of the realm of existence: in one existence is a transition from essence; in the other it is an emerging from non-being. According to the etymological account of existence we have just considered, existence stands both inside and outside non-being, an account which combines unsatisfactorily several distinct meanings of non-being. A more convincing etymological account of existence was once given by the Franciscan Richard of St. Victor (d. 1173),[23] followed by Alexander of Hales (c. 1170–1245).[24] Richard derived the noun *existentia* from the verb *existere* and then made a further distinction between the verbs *sistere* and *existere*. *Sistere*, so he claims, means to be as an uncreated essence, whereas when the same verb is compounded with the prefix *ex-* into the resulting *existere*, it means 'to have one's being from another'. *Ex-* denotes origin, and *sistere* denotes essence. Therefore, concludes Richard, *existere* means *to have one's being from essence*. Such a view is compatible with Tillich's own account of the functions of essences, and indicates how close he is to the ontology of the Franciscans (he includes them in his 'Augustinian solution'). What has happened though is that the Franciscan account of existence has been combined with the view of Marx and the anti-Hegelians that existence is estranged, with the consequence that it cannot be regarded as the direct object of God's creative act.

The transition from essence to existence can also be described as the transition from potentiality to actuality: this in turn means a movement from supreme created goodness to the state of universal estrangement. Now what brings about this partial and distorted realization of potentiality or essence within existence? Is it some kind of sinister stuff or matter (Platonic *hulē*?) which inhibits and resists the realization of essences in their corresponding existents? Or possibly there is another *tertium quid* which lurks between essence and existence and

[23] *De Trinitate*, iv. 11, 12: see *Textes phil. du moyen âge* (ed. Ribaillier), 1958.
[24] Alexander quotes Richard in *Summa Theologica*, 'Inquisitio Secunda', 2 (ed. Quarrachi).

frustrates the transfusion or implantation of essential goodness into existence. Such conjecture is incompatible with the Christian doctrine of *creatio ex nihilo*, but any modern contender for such a conjecture would find it strangely compatible with Tillich's ontology.

The transition from essence to existence presupposes that the fall takes place within the realm of essence. This presents a further difficulty. If the transition to existence replaces the traditional doctrine of the fall, how, one must ask, can essences fall? In order to be involved in a fall (even mythologically speaking) a thing must first *exist*. Essences cannot fall. As one critic put it, 'Man's fall is due to his choice and choice is an act; now nothing can act unless it exists. Therefore in falling, man does not fall into existence; he exists already. And, inasmuch as he acts, he is an individual existent, not an essence'.[25] Another commentator, W. O. Cross, makes the interesting suggestion that a distinction should be made between the essences from which things have 'split' and the essences which are the forms or definitions of things themselves.[26] He calls the former 'ur-essences', a term which well evokes a sense of their ontological primacy over existence. Cross asks what is the difference between the essence of a squirrel, a telephone pole and an atom of hydrogen, and these actual entities themselves. He also wants to know what difference it makes for a telephone pole to have been involved in a cosmic fall. Cross intends the questions seriously because he thinks them both unanswerable, thereby indicating that any meaning of essence other than the Platonic 'ur-essence' is vacuous. At any rate he agrees with our conclusion that there is more than one concept of essence to be found in the ontology, the most important of which is the Platonic.

There is one more problem which arises out of the transition from essence to existence, perhaps the most intractable one of all. If God as being-itself creates ur-essences he clearly 'participates' in them since he bestows on them his own being and goodness. To say that God as being-itself or power of being

---

[25] Demos, 'Tillich's Philosophical Theology', *Philosophy and Phenomenological Research*, xix (1958).

[26] W. O. Cross, 'Some Notes on the Ontology of Paul Tillich', *Anglican Theological Review*, xxxix (1957), 307.

participates in finite beings is one of the theological advantages of using ontological language, for it articulates the relationship between God and the world in such a way as to emphasize both the continuity and the discontinuity between them. And since finitude has an essential character God can be said to participate in finitude. But what about existence? If existence is first of all estrangement, can God be said to participate in estranged existence, or not? If man is 'estranged from the ground of his being, from other beings, and from himself', how can he at the same time participate in the being of his divine ground?

This dilemma constitutes an intractable problem for the ontology because the system seems to require both (a) that God cannot participate in estrangement because estrangement is by definition separation from God, and (b) that God must participate in estrangement since even what is estranged has being, and God is the ground of *all* being, whether it is reconciled to him or not. And both answers are present side by side in the ontology. On the one hand Tillich firmly insists that God can only participate in estrangement by overcoming it and bringing about 'new being'. He writes

When that which is beyond essence and existence participates in existence, it can only participate in the form in which it overcomes the conflict between essence and existence. The nature of divine participation in existence is the conquest of estrangement, the creation of New Being . . . Possible participation in existence is creation of a New Being. God cannot participate in it in any other way, because he cannot participate in estrangement.[27]

On the other hand the same passage continues with an implacable contradiction, for God 'cannot not participate in existence because he is the Ground which first makes existence possible. When we say of God that he is the Ground of Being, we say equally that he is as the Power of New Being which creates the new as restoration of the old'.

Now this plainly will not do. If estranged existence is any real state of affairs at all which is not absolute nothing, then on Tillich's own terms it clearly needs a ground of being in which to stand. But the presence of the ground of being does *not* in fact produce new being since estranged unrenewed being continues

[27] 'Das neue Sein als Zentralbegriff einer christlichen Theologie', *Eranos-Jahrbuch*, xxiii (1955), 263.

to exist independently from it. If the participation of being-itself in finite being takes place only in the form of new being, then God can have no part in estrangement, and 'old' being is entirely separate from God or being-itself. But this is clearly impossible since all beings participate in the divine ground of being, at least to some degree. The difference then between new being and estranged being is not that being-itself participates in one and not in the other. It is rather that in new being God's participation is present as restoration of old being. Estranged being must still participate in God, if for no other reason than that the primary example of estrangement, man, has an immediate ontological awareness of him. The term 'estrangement' in any case implies 'that one belongs essentially to that from which one is estranged'. And the passage continues 'Man's hostility to God proves indisputably that he belongs to him' (*ST* 2.22).

We might attempt to solve the participation of being-itself in estrangement by speaking of the general presence of God in the world and his special presence in Jesus Christ and the work of redemption. This would correspond to God's continuous undergirding of the realm of existence, supplemented by his 'gracious' or particular presence in revelation (which need not of course be confined to Christianity). The di-polar doctrine of God might also help to render the position less unsatisfactory, since it holds that there is within God an active principle of non-being. Even in the ground of being there is a contrary abyss. Being and non-being are in polar tension in God, but God's being differs from creatures in that in creatures the tension causes disruption and non-being becomes dominant. But what is needed most of all to render the ontology less self-contradictory is a thorough recasting of the doctrine of existence which is the source of our present dilemma. We have seen that existence is not the object of God's creative activity and therefore not essentially good: also that, according to one version, God cannot participate in it because it is evil. This is in fact a striking deficiency in the ontology. In chapter VII we examine how he came to hold his extraordinary doctrine of existence and how it might be resolved.

VII

NEW BEING

NEW Being is the 'restorative principle' of the theological system (*ST* 2.137), overcoming the cleavage between essential and existential being'. 'New Being is essential being under the conditions of existence, conquering the gap between essence and existence.'[1] Clearly then, no understanding of what new being is, is possible without a detailed look at the concepts of essence, existence, and estrangement. The time we have already spent on these concepts is justified as a preparatory study for the all-important concept of new being. In this chapter we shall examine the concept of new being as it arises out of the ontology, reserving most of the criticisms we may wish to make for the second part of the chapter.

New being appears in a 'personal life' (*ST* 2.138), the life of Jesus of Nazareth. It appears in the form of a personal life for this is the domain where the transition to existence is most acute: 'Only where existence is most radically existence—in him who is finite freedom—can existence be conquered' (*ST* 2.139). Jesus is the new being 'in the totality of his being', and not merely in one particular aspect of his being, such as his words, deeds, sufferings, or inner life. When applied to Jesus as the Christ, the concept new being

points to the power in him which conquers existential estrangement or, negatively expressed, to the power of resisting the forces of estrangement. (*ST* 2.144)

It is the Christ who brings the new Being, who saves men from the old being, that is, from existential estrangement and its self-destructive consequences. (*ST* 2.174)

The 'biblical picture' of Jesus as the Christ is said to confirm his character as 'the bearer of the New Being or as the one in whom the essential unity of God and man and man's existential

[1] *ST* 2.136: see also 'Das neue Sein . . .', 251; and 'Reply to Gustave Weigel', *Theological Studies*, xi (1950), 201–2.

estrangement is overcome' (ST 2.144). Although Jesus fully participates in finitude, he alone among men 'is not estranged from the ground of his being' (ST 2.145) for 'the conquest of existential estrangement in the New Being, which is the being of the Christ, does not remove finitude and anxiety, ambiguity and tragedy; but it does have the character of taking the negativities of existence into unbroken unity with God' (ST 2.153–4).

Tillich claims that the doctrine of the new being is fully in accord with the traditional Christological symbols and teaching. He thinks the 'Christological symbols' found in the New Testament were used 'by those to whom they had become alive as expressions of their self-interpretation and as answers to the questions implied in their existential predicament' (ST 2.125). Christology is 'existential' in that it contains the answers to the questions prompted by the existential situation. Thus the meaning of the term 'Son of Man', when applied to Jesus is the expectation that he 'will conquer the forces of estrangement and re-establish the unity between God and man' (ST 2.126). Similarly, 'Son of God' becomes the title of the one 'in whom the essential unity of God and man has appeared under the conditions of existence'. The symbol 'Christ' or 'Messiah' means 'he who brings the new state of things, the New Being' (ST 2.112). And within the Christian tradition, 'Logos' is said to have gained the meaning that 'the universal principle of divine self-manifestation is, in its essential character, qualitatively present in an individual human being. He subjects himself to the conditions of existence and conquers existential estrangement within estranged existence' (ST 2.129). Tillich reads the titles 'Saviour', Mediator', and 'Redeemer' in a like manner (ST 2.291 f.). The doctrine of atonement is to be understood existentially as 'the description of the effect of the New Being in Jesus as the Christ on those who are grasped by it in their state of estrangement' (ST 2.196). It 'must be understood' as Christ's own 'participation in existential estrangement and its self-destructive consequences' (ST 2.201).

The doctrine of salvation too is described as 'participation in the New Being (Regeneration)': as 'acceptance of the New Being (Justification)': and as 'transformation by the New Being (Sanctification)' (ST 2.203–7). Elsewhere the same theological terms regeneration, justification, and sanctification are defined respectively as the experience of the New Being as creation, paradox, and process (*ST* 3.235–58). The 'newness' (*Neuheit*) of new being is understood in terms of creation (*Schöpfung*), restoration (*Wiederherstellung*), and fulfilment (*Erfüllung*).[2] Alternatively we may speak of new being in terms of 'the Being of Love', since love, according to Tillich's ontological definition is 'the drive toward the reunion of that which is estranged'.[3] We can now see, through this otherwise compressed and inadequate sketch of new being, how central a concept it becomes. It is used to reinterpret philosophically and apologetically many of the very central doctrines of Christian faith.

A philosophical difficulty for the formulation of the doctrine of new being is its paradoxical character. Paradox is defined as that which is 'against man's self-understanding and expectation'.[4]

That is paradoxical which contradicts the *doxa*, the opinion which is based on the whole of ordinary human experience, including the empirical and the rational. The Christian paradox contradicts the opinion derived from man's existential predicament and all expectations imaginable on the basis of this predicament. (*ST* 2.106)

But paradox is not contrary to reason as such. It is rather, contrary to expectation. Neither is it irrational, absurd, or 'a logical riddle'.[5] Now the one basic paradox of the Christian faith is said to be the doctrine of the new being (*ST* 1.168). 'There is, in the last analysis, only *one* genuine paradox in the Christian message—the appearance of that which conquers existence under the conditions of existence' (*ST* 1.64). All other genuine paradoxes in Christianity are 'variations and applications' of the basic paradox of 'the appearance of the eternal or essential unity of God and man under the conditions of their existential separation' (*ST* 3.302). The nature of the paradox must now be examined more closely.

[2] 'Das neue Sein . . .', 256.

[3] '. . . . der Drang nach Wiedervereinigung des Entfremdeten', op. cit. 268.

[4] *ST* 2.107. For a critical survey of Tillich's use of paradox, see H. Schröer, *Der Denkform der Paradoxalität als theologische Problem*, 158 f: Scharlemann, *Reflection and Doubt in the Thought of Paul Tillich*, 37: L. S. Ford, 'The Three Strands of Tillich's Theory of Religious Symbols', *Journal of Religion*, xlvi (1966), 109.

[5] *ST* 2.107, see also 104 and 3; and 'A Reinterpretation . . .', 137.

Tillich says:

> The paradox of the Christian message is that in *one* personal life
> essential manhood has appeared under the conditions of existence
> without being conquered by them. One could also speak of essential
> God-manhood in order to indicate the divine presence in essential
> manhood; but this is redundant, and the clarity of thought is
> served best in speaking simply of essential manhood. (*ST* 2.108)

Now Tillich does not at all consider the term 'essential God-
manhood' entirely redundant, for he uses it again five pages
later (*ST* 2.113; 173). Elsewhere in a major paper on the
doctrine of incarnation, he describes the incarnation as 'the
manifestation of original and essential Godmanhood within and
under the conditions of existence'. 'Essential God-manhood' is
sometimes replaced by 'eternal God-Manhood' (*ST* 2.142, 6,
etc.). Alternatively 'eternal God-man-unity' (*ST* 2.170, 183,
196) is sometimes preferred. Whichever of the three compound
terms is used, the motive behind each is the desire to replace
the inadequate term 'nature' (a 'static essence') by concepts
expressing 'dynamic relation' (*ST* 2.170). The meaning of each
of the terms is to be found in the 'essential unity between God
and man' (*ST* 2.146) which, under the conditions of existence,
occurred in Jesus Christ and in the paradox of the new being.

But the paradox of the new being is not merely the fact of its
appearing within existence. It is also the *manner* of its appearance. The paradox of the new being is the same as the paradox
of justification by faith. It contributes a strong Lutheran
emphasis to Tillich's thought. Justification by faith is the
'Protestant principle'[6] whereby nothing at all, especially good
works, merits God's justification, except what God justifies
through Christ. In Tillich's typical language it is the principle
whereby nothing finite can ever become identified with the
infinite, and where human beings have to accept that they are
unacceptable to the finite and accepted by the infinite. *CTB*,
159f. But the principle is applied more widely than in the
theological controversy over justification. It includes a con-
demnation of everything finite which misguided believers

---

[6] A major theme of *PE*, especially ch. 14 'The End of the Protestant Era';
'Kairos and Logos', *The Interpretation of History*, 172: *Christianity and the Encounter of
the World Religions*, 47–8: *Morality and Beyond*, 30.

identify with the divine or claim even to represent it. A formidable list of subjects can be found throughout Tillich's writings which, in the history of the Christian religion have made the 'self-elevating claim to ultimacy' or 'unconditional validity'. They include religion itself, empires and emperors, holy objects, sacraments, personalities and movements, churches, theological traditions, religious leaders, and even the Christian message. Tillich calls this process 'demonization'.[7] The only corrective against it is the 'Protestant principle' whereby nothing which is less than ultimate is allowed to usurp the ultimacy which belongs to God alone.[8]

Now the Protestant principle is a constant feature of Tillich's early articles, particularly the collection 'The Protestant Era', and the concept comes into prominence again in ST 3 where it establishes itself as the corrective against the power of the demonic in finite things. But this same principle is evoked in ST 2 in a new context altogether, viz. in the interpretation of the life and death of Jesus. Of course in Lutheran and Pauline theology the sacrificial death of Jesus is the means of God's justifying the sinner, and is therefore the source of the Protestant principle, but in Tillich's Christology it does not bear this meaning at all. It means that for Jesus to be the bearer of the new being, even he has first to negate or at the very least subjugate everything finite in him in order to be completely transparent to the infinite ground of being of which he is the medium (ST 1.151). Tillich speaks of the 'continuous sacrifice' of Jesus, of himself 'as a particular individual under the conditions of existence to himself as the bearer of the New Being ... He proves and confirms his character as the Christ in the sacrifice of himself as Jesus to himself as the Christ' (ST 2.142). The position is more baldly stated in ST 1 where 'Jesus of Nazareth is the medium of the final revelation because he sacrifices himself completely to Jesus as the Christ (ST 1.151). For Jesus to be the bearer of final revelation, he has first to satisfy the criterion of final revelation. This criterion is whether

[7] 'The Conquest of the Concept of Religion in the Philosophy of Religion', in What is Religion? (German in GW, i. 365 f.): My Search for Absolutes, 132–4. 'Demonization' is a very common feature of ST 3, see 149, 153, 163, 195, 221, 230, 239, 259, 363, etc.

[8] The most recent statement of 'the Protestant principle' is in Morality and Beyond, 30.

a revelation 'has the power of negating itself without losing itself' (*ST* 1.148). Christ is the 'medium' of revelation who 'became' the Christ by 'conquering the demonic forces which tried to make him demonic by tempting him to claim ultimacy for his finite nature'. Jesus negates himself on the cross as a finite person because 'the claim of anything finite to be final in its own right is demonic'.

As a consequence of our Lord's sacrifice of himself as Jesus to himself as the Christ, his followers are said to be 'liberated from the authority of everything finite in him, from his special traditions, from his rather conditioned world view, from any legalistic understanding of his ethics' (*ST* 1.149). Such a consideration, continues Tillich,

condemns a Jesus-centred religion and theology. Jesus is the religious and theological object as the Christ and only as the Christ. And he is the Christ as the one who sacrifices what is merely 'Jesus' in him. The decisive trait in his picture is the continuous self-surrender of Jesus who is Jesus to Jesus who is the Christ. (*ST* 1.150)

The crucifixion is rightly understood as a paradox in that Christians believe that God manifested his love for the world in a rejected, forsaken human being who is also God's 'beloved son'. But the paradox whereby a finite thing reveals its infinite ground only by negating all its finite qualities is quite another formulation, and it leads to some alarming conclusions, even though it is firmly based in reformation theology. According to this theology man is unacceptable (as a sinner), God accepts him none the less (through Christ), and his faith in God is his own acceptance that he is accepted despite his unacceptability. But there is an essential difference between the willing subjection of our Lord to the 'conditions of existence' (whatever these are) and the subjection of himself as a real individual to himself as the bearer of the new being. Tillich has done considerable service to Protestant theology in reinterpreting the doctrine of justification by faith through the notion of acceptance, linking it as he does to the individual's pastoral, social, psychological, and existential needs. But as a means of interpreting the paradox of the death of Jesus, the Protestant principle has its deficiencies to which we shall need to return.

New being differs from essential being in that it is actual, not merely potential, and it differs from existence in that it is actual yet unestranged.

The New Being is new in so far as it is the undistorted manifestation of essential being within and under the conditions of existence. It is new in two respects: it is new in contrast to the merely potential character of essential being; and it is new over against the estranged character of existential being. It is actual, conquering the estrangement of actual existence.[9]

New being is 'above' essential and existential being, above the former because it is 'actual and not merely potential', and above the latter 'because it brings essential being or essential God-manhood into existence'.[10] The conflict between essence and existence can raise the question of new being but cannot engender it.[11] The contrast between new being and essence is drawn out by a comparison between new being and Schleier-macher's term *Urbild* ('original image'), which Tillich describes as 'essential man'.[12] The *Urbild* remains above existence in an 'idealistic transcendence', while new being 'participates in existence and conquers it'.

Just as there is a transition from essence to existence, there is also a further transition from existence back to essence, or alternatively 'from the temporal to the eternal' (*ST* 3.421, 5). This transition occurs at 'the end of history' (*ST* 3.420), but as the end of history is 'ever present' (*ST* 3.423–4) the futuristic eschatological connotation of the transition is not to be adhered to too closely. The name of the transition is 'essentialization'.[13]

[9] *ST* 2.137: see 'A Reinterpretation . . .', 142.
[10] 'A Reinterpretation . . .', 142, and see *ST* 3. 148, 287.
[11] 'Discussion', following 'Sin and Grace', 52.
[12] *ST* 2.173. The participation of new being in existence has given rise to the interesting suggestion of D. A. Fox ('Eros and Logos', *Encounter*, xxix (1968), 176–7) that Tillich has *feminized* Christology! Fox, claiming to follow some insights of Jung, sees Logos-Christology, and all traditional language about the fatherhood of God as 'heavily masculine'. Tillich's Christology, he suggests, reflects important feminine elements. The Christ who calls us to participate in him, and through him in being-itself is a feminine symbol. Fox writes of participation in new being, 'This no longer is the masculine *logos* Christology of Barth but a consistently feminized thought in which salvation amounts largely to a re-entry into the Great Womb'.
[13] *ST* 3.427. On 'essentialization' see Osborne, 111 f.: C. Armbruster, *The Vision of Paul Tillich*, 271 f.: I. C. Henel, 'Paul Tillich's Begriff der Essentifikation und seine Bedeutung für die Ethik', *Neue Zeitschrift für systematische Theologie und Religionsphilosophie*, x (1968), 1–17.

Just as new being is more than essence, so essentialization is more than a return to essence. Tillich finds the idea of a return to essence in Schelling but quickly goes on to qualify his use of the term in a more concrete way. Essentialization, he says, means

that the new which has been actualized in time and space adds something to essential being, uniting it with the positive which is created within existence, thus producing the ultimately new, the 'New Being' not fragmentarily as in temporal life, but wholly as a contribution to the Kingdom of God in its fulfilment. (*ST* 3.427)

Here we have an interrelationship between several levels of ontological concepts: the essential or purely potential realm of being which is non-actual; the realm of existence, where the positive and the negative are ambiguously mixed; new being, where existential estrangement is overcome but where the experience of the conquest of estrangement is only 'fragmentary' and 'anticipatory' (*ST* 3.149–50); and the 'ultimately new' where the Kingdom of God is finally fulfilled and all being is new being. In the transition to the eternal 'the negative is defeated in its claim to be positive' (*ST* 3.425). Just as the transition from essence to existence was expressed by the rather flimsy metaphor 'dreaming innocence', so the transition from the temporal to the eternal is expressed by the equally flimsy metaphor 'eternal memory' (*ST* 3.426). Eternal memory is a metaphorical clue to the state of essentialization, for, from the standpoint of the eternal, only the positive elements of existence which stand out from estrangement in the power of the new being are remembered. The negative is not retained in eternal memory, but rather 'forgotten' and discarded as the nothingness which it is (the negative side of the symbol of ultimate judgement). All that is follows the process 'from essence through existential estrangement to essentialization' (*ST* 3.450–1). It is important that the single process here involved ('the world process') (*ST* 3.451) gains something on the way. Essences 'are creatively enriched in existence' (*ST* 3.429). More tentatively, though still affirmatively, Tillich says that because 'all things . . . participate in the Divine Life according to their essence' (i.e. since they are good by creation), then 'the conflicts and sufferings of nature under the conditions of existence and its longings for salvation, of which Paul speaks

(Romans, chapter 8), serve the enrichment of essential being after the negation of the negative in everything that has being, (*ST* 3.432). Essences then are 'enrichable'. Something positive can be added to them which they do not have in the realm of potential being. Their enrichment occurs by a threefold process of actualization (existence), restoration (new being), and finally the transition to the eternal from which they came (essentialization).

What consequences does essentialization have for a di-polar doctrine of God, since there is also a negative pole in the life of God as well as in the realm of existence, which must also be presumably affected by final essentialization? Tillich realizes the difficulty he has made for himself in negating the negative in eternity. If it is the negative element within the Divine Life which makes it a life, can God still be said to live in eternity if there is no negative element in eternity or eternal life? (*ST* 3.430). His answer is that 'the Divine Life *is* the eternal conquest of the negative; this is its blessedness' (*ST* 3.431). The negative pole in the di-polar account of life processes is still retained in eternity but it remains as something which is eternally overcome. Since all that is, is now 'in God', the negative pole of essentialized life can no longer be a source of disruption and estrangement. The Divine Life is a dialectical concept, and so is the concept of essentialization (*ST* 3.433). The essentialization of the individual person is a matter of degree. It consists basically of how much 'positive' there remains in him after the 'negative' in him is negated. Thus Tillich speaks of the 'degree of essentialization' (*ST* 3.444) or 'the amount of fulfilment or non-fulfilment which goes into the individual's essentialization' (*ST* 3.446). It may be an 'extreme poverty' or an 'extreme richness' (*ST* 3.433–4).

A theological appraisal of Tillich's Christology is beyond the scope of the present task. Some critics believe him to be orthodox in his Christology,[14] others that he is Nestorian,[15] Sabellian and

[14] Pittenger, 'Paul Tillich as a Theologian: An Appreciation': A. T. Mollegen, 'Christology and Biblical Criticism in Tillich', *TPT*, 230–42: D. Hill, D. D. Williams, T. F. Driver, and W. D. Davies in D. Hill, 'Paul's "Second Adam" and Tillich's Christology' (and ensuing discussion), *Union Seminary Quarterly Review*, xxi, (1965), 24 f.: D. J. Keefe, 257 f.

[15] G. Weigel, 'Contemporaneous Protestantism and Paul Tillich', *Theological Studies*, xi (1950), 194.

Monarchianistic,[16] Adoptionistic,[17] Docetic,[18] Dionysiac,[19] and Gnostic![20] The fact of the wide diversity of judgements about Tillich's Christology is probably more significant than any one of them by itself, because it demonstrates how difficult it is to judge a largely ontological vocabulary according to traditional theological norms. We do not wish to compare Tillich's Christology directly with any traditional theological norm, or to assess his orthodoxy (which would probably be impossible anyway). Instead we want to examine some problems for his Christology which arise mainly out of his choice of the onto-logical concepts which express it. The first two problems arise out of the use of the concepts essence and existence.

If Jesus was 'essential manhood', how could he be an actual human being as well? How could he become 'actualized' in existence without distortion and estrangement? Just as we were unable to see how essences became distorted during the transition to existence, we now have to ask, how did essential manhood, unlike all other essences, remain *undistorted* when it entered into existence as Jesus the Christ? How is it possible for the purely potential to become actual, and yet at the same time remain essential and unestranged? From the side of exist-ence, the problem can be put still more simply. If existence is estrangement, and Christ actually existed, then his existence is presumably impossible without his also being estranged. If actual existence is distorted, fallen existence, and if Jesus actually existed, then his being is distorted and fallen. One critic asks, 'How then can we avoid the conclusion that Jesus, like every-thing actual, was estranged rather than perfect? Can there be an essential existent?'[21] If the familiar phrase 'under the con-ditions of existence' means 'estrangement from God', how then could Jesus of Nazareth, who existed under these same condi-tions, have maintained an unbroken unity with God? Tillich

[16] H. D. McDonald, 'The Symbolic Theology of Paul Tillich', *Scottish Journal of Theology*, xvii (1964), 427–8.

[17] T. A. O'Meara, 'Paul Tillich and Ecumenism', *PTCT*, 295.

[18] G. Tavard, *Paul Tillich and the Christian Message*, 131: M. S. Sulzbach, 'The Place of Christology in Contemporary Protestantism', *Religion in Life*, xxiii (1954), 22.

[19] W. Taubes, 'On the Nature of the Theological Method, *Journal of Religion* xxxiv (1954), 22.

[20] W. F. Albright, quoted by G. Weigel, 'Myth, Symbol and Analogy', *Paul Tillich in Catholic Thought*, 190–1.

[21] E. H. Peters, 'Tillich's Doctrine of Essence, Existence and the Christ', *Journal of Religion*, xliii (1963), 300.

says that Protestantism demands 'a Christology of the participation of the Christ in sinful existence' (*ST* 2.172). If Jesus exists
he must participate in sinful existence. But is existence intrinsi-
cally sinful? According to Tillich it is. And if Jesus participates
in it, including its sinful aspects, how can he overcome it?[22]

It is difficult to see how Tillich can avoid the force of these
questions. It may be argued that the appearance of the new
being is a paradox and not therefore susceptible to such
rational criticism. But paradox is not contrary to reason. It is
only contrary to expectation. The main difficulty with Tillich's
position is that Jesus first has to exist before he is able to conquer
estrangement, and as existence is already a transition from
essence, it is not possible for Jesus to retain his 'essential nature'
under such conditions. The reality of the temptations of Christ,
which Tillich stresses, is superfluous unless it is regarded as the
point at which existential estrangement could become real. But
for Tillich existential estrangement is real at every point, for
existence and estrangement are one. There is probably no
alternative but to agree with N. Ferré that Tillich's ontology
has distorted his Christology because it has become controlled
by the relation of essence to existence.[23] However, as with the
doctrine of the fall, we must not accuse Tillich of ambiguities
in his thought when they merely reflect wider ambiguities
within the area of Christian doctrine. It is often rightly remarked
that Christians have readily affirmed the real humanity of Jesus
only to deny many of the consequences of such a view, e.g. his
dependence upon his cultural and sociological background, his
human psyche and sexuality, etc.[24] On this view, which we
shall not pursue, Jesus unavoidably participates in estrangement
for he cannot otherwise be human. Language about his 'sinless-
ness' says John Robinson, ought perhaps in any case to be

[22] D. J. Keefe puts forward the novel suggestion that the dogma of the Immaculate Conception and Assumption might solve the problem of the participation of
our Lord in estrangement. He regards the Virgin Mary as an example of unestranged, created goodness, and thinks that as Jesus the man had his being from
his mother, Jesus may be regarded as existent yet unestranged. The Immaculate
Conception, thinks Keefe, saves Tillich's system from 'a Platonic paganism'
(Keefe, 321 f., 326).

[23] 'Three Critical Issues in Tillich's Philosophical Theology', *Scottish Journal of
Theology*, x (1957), 236.

[24] e.g. N. Pittenger, *Christology Rediscovered*, ch. 2: J. Knox, *The Humanity and
Divinity of Christ*, b f.: J. A. T. Robinson, *The Human Face of God*, ch. 2.

primarily regarded as theological and evaluative rather than factual and historical.[25] Thus, in Tillich's terms, it might well be maintained that when essential being became actual under the conditions of existence, it *did* become estranged, at least in so far as it assumed real solidarity with the rest of existence. However, Tillich did not choose such a solution, probably because Christology generally was much less open about the humanity of Jesus even in 1957 when the second volume of *ST* was written, than it is today. So the problem remains. Either essential manhood remains what it is and does not become fully actual within existence; or, essential manhood does become fully actual in estranged existence, and loses its essential nature.

Another problem for Tillich's Christology is his account of the two natures of Christ, the essential and the existential. Once again the relation between essence and existence determines the account of their relationship. We have noted how he 'became' the Christ, how he is said to be a 'medium' of revelation and not the revelation itself, and how he sacrifices the 'Jesus as Jesus' to 'Jesus as the Christ'. This pair of terms merely raises in acute form the old problems of a two-nature Christology and some new ones besides. If there are two Jesuses, and one of them sacrifices himself to the other, there is at once a dichotomy within the unity of the person of Christ. On this interpretation of the work of Christ, the essential Jesus (Jesus as the Christ) can become manifest only when the existent Jesus (Jesus as Jesus) is negated. The appearance of the essential Jesus then, in the incarnation of our Lord, does not 'save' existence; it crushes it. We may say with Ferré, that in Jesus essence never became existence, but existence, by negating itself, became perfectly transparent for essence.[26] The arrival of essential manhood under the conditions of existence does not restore anything to existence after its fall or transition from essence. Essence does not fulfil existence, it rather negates it. In more traditional terms we could say that the divinity of our Lord causes him to destroy his humanity. What happened on the cross, according to another critic, is that 'Jesus consciously sacrificed all that was finite in himself in order that the divinity in himself might be manifested'.[27]

[25] Robinson, 117.   [26] Ibid.
[27] G. B. Hammond, *The Power of Self-Transcendence*, 116.

Another and more subtle ontological objection to Tillich's account of the person of Christ concerns the ontological polarity of individualization and participation. Jesus as the bearer of the new being ought to express the perfect balance of the ontological elements. In him the elements should be in harmony, undistorted and unseparated. But Jesus as the Christ cannot possibly harmonize the elements of individualization and participation, when as an individual he sacrifices himself completely to that in which he participates (i.e. the divine Ground of Being which is manifest in him).[28] Tillich seems unaware that at this point his ontology and his Christology flatly contradict each other. He says that 'life in unity with God' is 'determined by the polarity of dynamics and form' (*ST* 2.148), and that the reality of the temptations of Christ and his victory over them is determined by the 'polar unity of freedom and destiny' (*ST* 2.149). No reference is made to the determining factor of the other polarity, that of individualization and participation. Perhaps Tillich was uncomfortably aware that his account of the person of Christ was irreconcilable with his earlier account of the individualization—participation polarity. In a later part of the *ST* he discusses the ontological polarities in the state of essentialization or Eternal Life and says 'the element of individualization cannot be eliminated or the element of participation would also disappear' (*ST* 3.441). But when Jesus as Jesus constantly sacrifices himself to Jesus as the Christ, the element of individualization *does* disappear. The first ontological polarity must be applied to essential manhood as to anywhere else, yet here, at the heart of the 'restorative principle' of the entire theological system, one polar element is more distorted in its actualization than anywhere else in the whole of finite being. The individualization pole is annihilated for the sake of the pole of participation.

Unfortunately such a conclusion affects the doctrine of salvation. Jesus as the Christ is the new being in the totality of his being. He is the *locus* where alone new being in its undistorted actualization is to be found. But in Jesus as the Christ, Jesus as Jesus is sacrificed. The individuation pole is negated in order that the new being might be made manifest. But this is

---

[28] B. J. Cameron, 'Some Nineteenth Century Sources of the Historical Problem in Paul Tillich's Christology: Hegel to Schweitzer', 81: Osborne, 176.

the exact opposite of the doctrine of salvation. In the Christian experience of salvation, the individual is reaffirmed as he participates in divine grace. He is not negated as an individual and he does not sacrifice himself as an individual in order to enter into salvation. It is only what separates him from God, i.e. traditionally speaking his sin, which is negated. When Jesus is said to sacrifice 'what is merely "Jesus" in him' (*ST* 1.150), his humanity, and all humanity by implication, is disparaged. Such a Christology is made to look all the more alarming when it is compared with the doctrine of the presence of God in other beings. Even ordinary inanimate finite beings participate to some extent in the divine ground of being. There is something of God in them. Yet when Tillich deals with the one finite being in whom, according to the Christian faith, the ground of being is said to be completely manifest, i.e. in Jesus of Nazareth, that manifestation is only possible when his finitude is annihilated. This is the meaning of the central mystery of the Christian faith, the cross.

The reasons for this impasse in Tillich's Christology are twofold. First, what came to be known as the 'Protestant principle', which originally was a kind of shorthand reinterpretation of the doctrine of justification by faith, became a *systematic* principle according to which the claim of anything finite to rise beyond itself is condemned. The corollary of the large-scale use of the Protestant principle was the view that the infinite only reveals itself through the finite when the finite first negates itself. This principle, when mistakenly applied to the life of Jesus makes even he himself sacrifice his humanity in order to manifest his divinity. The principle whereby the infinite only reveals itself through the negation of the finite is also an important element in Tillich's much discussed doctrine of symbol (which, because of the exhaustive treatment it has received, we have omitted). But the second and less-discussed reason for Tillich's unsatisfying Christology is his negative doctrine of existence which we have already noted is identical with the state of estrangement. Now there is no compelling reason why Tillich should have remained committed to his negative doctrine of existence. The place existence is given in the ontology is the result of an unfortunate defect in the structure of the ontology, which, despite the flow of literature on it, does not seem to have been detected.

The flaw in the ontological structure can be uncovered by asking a relatively simple question 'Is existence actual?' Expanded, the question would read, 'What stands for actuality —existence or life?' Or again, more simply, 'What is the difference between existence and life?'[29]

If we refer to Part 3 of *ST*, 'Existence and the Christ', the question seems superfluous. That existence is actual is a firm presupposition of the argument. The fall of man is his transition from essence to existence. Man's existence is his estrangement 'from the ground of his being, from other beings, and from himself' (*ST* 2.51). Jesus Christ as the bearer of the new being, appears 'under the conditions of existence'. His appearing, i.e. the entry of essential manhood into the realm of existence, is the one major paradox of the Christian faith. In all this existence is actual, and the appearance of Jesus within existence is actual. From this point of view our question 'Is existence actual?' seems a rather pointless and unpromising line of inquiry.

It is all the more surprising then, to find that much of the evidence in *ST* leads inescapably to the conclusion that existence is *not* actual at all. In the first place *ST* 3 insists that life, and *not* existence, is actual. Actuality is qualified, not by the concept of existence, but *by the concept of life*. Life, is 'the actuality of being' (*ST* 3.12). Tillich explicitly states here that only life is actual:

This concept of life unites the two main qualifications of being which underlie this whole system; these two main qualifications are the essential and the existential ... We use the word 'life' in this sense of a 'mixture' of essential and existential elements. In terms of the history of philosophy we can say that we envisage the Aristotelian distinction between *dynamis* and *energeia*, between potentiality and actuality, from an existentialist viewpoint. (*ST* 3.12)

In all life processes an essential and an existential element, created goodness and estrangement, are merged in such a way that neither one nor the other is exclusively effective. Life always includes essential and existential elements; this is the root of its ambiguity. (*ST* 3.114)

---

[29] Much of what follows first appeared in my 'Existence and Life in Tillich', *Scottish Journal of Theology*, xxvii (1974).

Existence then, according to the account in *ST* 3, is plainly not the same as life. It is a qualification of life, an element in the ambiguous mixture which constitutes the single actuality 'life'. And as only life is actual, existence plainly is not. Existence and life then, overlap within the totality of the system. Yet perhaps we ought not to be too surprised about this, for in the first part of the system (written twelve years before Volume 3 in 1951) Tillich maintained that existence, like essence, was non-actual. In his early elaboration of the contents of the system, he writes: 'A third part is based on the fact that the essential as well as the existential characteristics are abstractions and that in reality they appear in the complex and dynamic unity which is called "life" ' (*ST* 1.74–5). Later in Volume 2 existence is equally non-actual:

From the point of view of systematic structure . . . the existential elements are only one part of the human predicament. They are always combined ambiguously with essential elements; otherwise they would have no being at all. Essential as well as existential elements are always abstractions from the concrete actuality of being, namely, 'Life'. (*ST* 2.32)

And in the very last paragraph of the book, after the theme of Christology has come to an end, Tillich adds:

This concludes the third part, 'Existence and the Christ'. Actually, however, neither the doctrine of man nor the doctrine of the Christ is brought to an end within this part. Man is not only determined by essential goodness and by existential estrangement; he is also determined by the ambiguities of life and history. Without an analysis of these characteristics of his being, *everything so far remains abstract* (*ST* 2.107, italics added).

Clearly then there are two concepts of existence in *ST*. In one, existence is actuality, the realm which has fallen from essence, the realm of estrangement into which the Christ comes, and paradoxically overcomes. In the other, existence is non-actual, and only *contributes* to life. As Tillich says 'existential characteristics are abstractions'. In this second concept, existence is only a contributory element to the one concrete actuality, 'life'.

If, however, existence is not actual, certain other conclusions inescapably follow. First, the transition from essence to existence becomes nonsense. It cannot be a transition from potentiality to actuality because existence is not actuality. The transition is reduced to a kind of imaginary transference from one mode of potentiality to another. Second, essences are not actualized within existence. Essence and existence are merged together. Each contributes equally to the actuality of life. Existence is not the realm where essences are actualized. Third, existence itself becomes an essence. Existence contributes to actuality, but is not the same as actuality. Like the realm of essence, it can be said to realize itself in actuality, just as essences are normally said to realize themselves in existence. Existence is only a potency, waiting to be brought into act as it realizes itself in the synthesis of life.

How has Tillich arrived at two distinct concepts of existence? There is a relatively simple answer to the problem. Plainly the definition of life as a mixture of essential and existential elements is an example of Hegelian dialectic. Life is the synthesis of the dialectic: essence and existence the thesis and antithesis. Tillich has got himself into trouble because he has pressed both Platonic and Aristotelian contrasts into an Hegelian mould. As the classical contrasts are *two-term*, (i.e. essence and existence, potentiality and actuality), and the Hegelian contrasts are *three-term* (i.e. essence, existence, and life) some kind of overlap in the structure of the *ST* might have been confidently expected. This is precisely what has happened.

The distinction between essence and existence is, of course, Platonic. In Plato, the unchanging, eternal world of essence instantiates the world of appearance and illusion (existence). The essence–existence distinction is *two-term*. The distinction between potentiality and actuality is, as Tillich acknowledges, Aristotelian. The Aristotelian *energeia* is 'actuality' or 'life'. This distinction is again *two-term*. But when these two two-term distinctions are fitted into a conspicuously dialectical mould, confusion and overlap take place. It is easy to see why. If one speaks of the distinction between the empirical and the transempirical world by invoking the Platonic contrast of essence and existence, one does not need the concept of life as a third reality. It is already implied in existence. If one speaks of the same distinction by invoking the Aristotelian contrast of potentiality and actuality, one does not need the concept of

essence. It is already implied in potentiality. But when each
of the four terms is pressed into an over-all dialectical framework, existence and life no longer refer to the same realm.
Essence and potentiality, however, *do* refer to the same realm,
i.e. the realm which might be called 'pre-existence'. They
provide the first term of the dialectic. But their contrasts are
separated. Existence, the contrast of essence, and actuality, the
contrast of potentiality, refer to *different* realms. Tillich needs
another term, in order to give his dialectic the three terms it
needs. What happens is that existence sacrifices the actuality
which it has in the *two-term* Platonic distinction, essence–
existence. It becomes the antithesis of an Hegelian triad, and in
doing so, it loses all its concreteness. Like essence, it becomes a
set of abstractions drawn from the one actuality 'life'.

Obviously, the student of Tillich is free to choose which
concept of existence he prefers, but he cannot have them both.
Which is the better alternative? If we regard existence as non-
actual, then our basic philosophical concept is that of 'life'.
Essence and existence are contributory 'moments' in life-
descriptions. We shall have to regard Parts 2 and 3 of the
system, which deal with being and existence, as wholly
abstract. Only when we get to discussing life (Part V), have we
come as far as actuality. If we accept the non-actual concept of
existence, we will presumably be untroubled by the Hegelian
idealism which in the last resort determines the arrangement of
the system. But if this option is adopted, what becomes of the
Christology? Unfortunately Tillich's Christology can only
make any sense if existence *is* actuality. The transition from
essence to existence is not followed by another transition from
existence to actuality. Existence is actual. So is estrangement.
Theologically speaking, the actual character of estrangement
constitutes the stark reality of the world in its separation from
God. What possible use can the markedly existential concept
'estrangement' have, if it is to be understood essentialistically as
a contributing element to life, and not life itself? If existence is
not actual, there is little point in talking about the existence of
Jesus and his conquest of existential estrangement in the power
of new being.

The other option is the obvious one to take. If we take this
option we can take the Platonic contrast, essence–existence, at

its face value, without bothering about the third term 'life'. Christology is saved, and the existential and the actual world are one and the same. If we take this option, what has to be abandoned? Does the whole of Volume 3 have to be jettisoned? Again the answer is a simple one. All that need be abandoned is the unnecessary dialectical mould which is largely responsible for the present difficulty. What is at fault is the structure of the *ST*, its pattern of development. The discussion in *ST 3* about life has to be interpreted as a continuation of the discussion about existence. Both existence and life are actual. There is only a terminological difference between 'existence and estrangement' on the one hand, and 'life and its ambiguities' on the other. And the answers given to each by Christian theology refer to the same basic reality. Christ as the bearer of new being is the answer to existential estrangement. The Divine Spirit is the answer to 'the ambiguities of life'. The Divine Spirit mediates the new being as it is manifest in Jesus Christ, who paradoxically entered into existential estrangement without being overcome by it.

According to this option then, existence *is* actual, and Christology is saved (although other Christological problems remain). The description of life in Volume 3 is a redescription of that realm of being which can be called either existence or actuality, depending upon whether we prefer Platonic or Aristotelian language. *Both* existence *and* life are actual. If of course we adopt this option, we shall need to abandon the Hegelian triad essence–existence–life. But as this triad is the cause of the trouble, its removal is a small price to pay, in order to achieve greater systematic clarity.

The discussion of the whether existence is actual brings this chapter, and the whole examination of the details of Tillich's ontology to an end. But no examination of the ontology would be complete unless it faced two wider questions, not yet attempted. First some balanced evaluation of Tillich's ontology must somehow be attempted from a standpoint which is both critical and yet sympathetic to his philosophical and theological position. Second, some consideration of the wider role of ontology in theology and philosophy is needed, for unless its role can in some way be defended, the whole of this study loses its point. Our final chapter is devoted to these issues.

VIII

THE WIDER ROLE OF ONTOLOGY

THE method used in the present study has been the simple combination of elucidation and criticism. In attempting to elucidate the ontology great importance was attached to grounding Tillich's complex thought in the historical traditions of theology and philosophy upon which he drew, in the belief that the neglected historical approach to his work would frequently uncover the unexpectedly subtle and sometimes long-forgotten meanings of basic concepts. The major criticism we have more than once launched against him is that of philosophical eclecticism, whereby basic ontological concepts and ideas have become almost indistinguishably merged together, sometimes with the result that quite incompatible meanings are fused together beneath single general terms. We need to ask how damaging his eclecticism is to his ontology before asking whether his ontology adds anything to his theology, or to theology generally. These two questions are quite separate, since to accuse an author of eclecticism is plainly not to accuse him of mystification or logical meaninglessness. Ontology may have a significance for theology which Tillich has simply failed to exploit. Finally we need to say something about the vexed question of the role ontology has to play in philosophy generally.

Two general comments first need to be made about the voluminous criticism to which Tillich's writings have been subjected. Many of the works on Tillich are unduly influenced by the particular theological viewpoints of their authors. Two of the major English writings on Tillich, Kenneth Hamilton's *The System and the Gospel* and J. Heywood Thomas' *Paul Tillich: An Appraisal* (both published in 1963 in the SCM Library of Philosophy and Theology) are both written from a standpoint unsympathetic to the kind of theology Tillich has produced. Hamilton has written about Tillich's 'system' from a markedly Kierkegaardian stance which frequently gets in the way of positive appreciation. Heywood Thomas too, stands firmly in the 'nominalist' tradition of theology as his cursory dismissal of the concept of being[1] makes all too clear. The upsurge of Catholic interest in Tillich inevitably reflects a strong preference for the metaphysics of St. Thomas. An earlier work on Tillich's ontology by R. A. Killen, *The Ontological Theology of Paul Tillich* was written from an extreme and dogmatic Calvinist position, and more recently a remarkably ungracious, and insensitive book from the standpoint of polemical fundamentalism has appeared, by L. F. Wheat, entitled *Paul Tillich's Dialectical Humanism*. The latest scholarly work on Tillich by A. Macleod, is written from an expressly Wittgenstenian point of view, with the inevitable result that the author, charged with compiling a volume in a Contemporary Religious Thinkers Series, finds little or nothing in Tillich's works to commend.

Second, much of the published writing on Tillich has come from theological students who have chosen to write about aspects of Tillich's work for periodical articles or research degrees. This is how the present study originated. But the very nature of this kind of work usually entails a somewhat over-critical stance in order to justify itself. One reviewer of the books of J. Heywood Thomas and Kenneth Hamilton could have cast his net rather wider when he remarked that there was in the attitude of both authors 'too much of the parlor game mentality, too much of the métier of the graduate student who thinks he has his master by the tail'.[2] The present writer is conscious that he too may be found guilty in this respect. To criticize another's thought is a necessary and healthy endeavour. But it is quite another matter to produce a theology worth criticizing. In any appraisal of the work of a man as justly renowned as Tillich, one dare not speak without humility and respect.

Our main charge against Tillich is that he often uses his ontological concepts carelessly and inconsistently. This of course is no new charge, but in a system of ontology it is serious and damaging, for whatever the deficiencies of a philosophical system, one at least is entitled to hope that it

[1] 36.
[2] H. J. Forstman, 'Paul Tillich and His Critics', *Encounter*, xxv (1964), 477.

will be internally self-consistent. Basic ontological concepts
attract a variety of different meanings, and it is not always
clear from the different contexts which is meant. The concept
of being for example, is a dialectical concept when it is used
in conjunction with non-being, but undialectical when it is
qualified by the Augustinian *esse ipsum*. Is it then dialectical
or undialectical? The only answer that can be given is that
it is both. But this of course is highly unsatisfactory. The
Augustinian-Scholastic concept of being, and that of German
idealism have the same name 'being', but there are wide
differences between them. That Tillich's concept of being is
both polar and non-polar at the same time indicates that his
account of it is not anything like sharply enough defined.

We noted with surprise Tillich's constant definition of the
term *actus purus* as 'pure actuality'. Because he has failed to
interpret the phrase as 'pure activity', an interpretation which,
it seems, is widely accepted by modern Thomists, he has
deprived himself of an idea most congenial to his own concept
'power of being', and needlessly widened the gulf between
himself and Thomism. God, understood as the pure activity
which activates every individual 'act of existing' is arguably a
richer idea for an ontology of power than Nietzsche's 'will to
power' and Spinoza's *conatus*. Other key concepts betray their
unclear, inconsistent use. 'Dynamics' came to mean both the
power of being against non-being, and the power of non-
being against being, at the same time. Non-being was seen to
operate in half-a-dozen different ways. 'Essence' was seen to
have different meanings, and to have been identified with
several other concepts, making its usage almost impossible to
elaborate. Potentiality too was found to be susceptible to
different definitions, and the corresponding term 'actuality' was
clearly seen to feature equally in the systematically separated
realms of 'existence' and 'life' with the result that in ST 2
existence is the same as actuality, whereas in ST 3 life is the
only actuality in the system, to which both essence and existence
contribute. The term 'Spirit' was found to owe more to
Schelling and Hegel than to Christian orthodoxy. The same
was said of the doctrine of the Holy Trinity. Great confusion
was detected over the issue whether any non-symbolic statement could be made about God, and if so, what the statement

was. The refusal to use 'existence' as a symbol in a symbol-system was also noted, and two quite separate concepts of existence were separated out. These are only some of the detailed inconsistencies. Even if generous allowances are made for the development of the meanings of key terms during the long maturation of Tillich's philosophical thought, the inconsistencies remain. If a comparison were to be made between Tillich's ontology and the idealist ontology of Hegel or the existentialist ontology of Heidegger, there can be no doubt who is the most careless in his use of terms.

But the confusions which undoubtedly exist in Tillich's ontology do not by themselves justify the full-scale rejection of ontology either as a branch of theology or of philosophy. Philosophical and theological attempts to do away with it abound, but not all of these are well placed. One quite unjust attempt to remove ontology from theology proceeds from a misunderstanding of how an account of the relationship between ontology and theology might be attempted. The very phrase 'relationship between ontology and theology' implies two clearly defined realms, exclusively marked off from each other, each with its own distinctive content. Describing the relationship between them then becomes a task rather like describing the juxtaposition of two points on a map. Ontology gets separated from theology, and once the separation is made the argument can proceed whether theology needs ontology or whether it is sufficient by itself. But this kind of argument starts from a basic misclassification of what the issue is. 'Ontology' and 'theology' are separate terms, but their subject matter is basically the same. The difference between them must not be understood primarily as a difference in subject matter, but as two different approaches to the same basic reality. How can this claim be justified?

Whatever way Tillich defines ontology he clearly intends his basic ontological concept 'being-itself' to have its referent in some primordial power or ground which gives to beings their existence. Without this primordial power the existence of anything at all would be inexplicable. The difficulties attaching to this view do not detract from what Tillich in fact is doing with his concept of being. Now what ontology calls 'being-itself', theology calls 'God'. The relation between ontology and

theology is to be elaborated in two separate approaches to the
same putative reality, being-itself or God. The one approach
draws on philosophers from Parmenides to Heidegger; the
other on the Judaeo-Christian traditions with their biblical
bases. But time and again as we have shown, the two approaches
come together when God and being-itself are identified. For
Tillich, ontology is theological, and theology is ontological.
The terms 'theonomous metaphysics' and 'theological ontology'
of his early period indicate this. To state such a view is not to
indulge in paradox but to state that two approaches are being
made to the same reality or field of inquiry.

Of course increasing numbers of theologians are at pains
to deny that 'God' and 'being-itself' have anything at all to
do with each other. The ghost of Ritschl is not yet laid to
rest. Moltmann thinks, from the influential standpoint of the
'Theology of Hope' that the 'coming God' of biblical faith
(and hope) can have no truck with the static God of Greek
metaphysics (which is what *he* means by 'being-itself').[3] Most
of the 'secular theologians' will not have metaphysics at any
price, either because (it is claimed) it is beyond the wit of
secular man to comprehend it, or because the philosophical
objections to it are simply regarded as conclusive.[4] Barthians
have never liked metaphysics because of its attempt to speak of
God apart from the outside of his revelation. Process theologians[5] are of course heavily dependent on metaphysics but
work instead with a system based on 'process' or 'becoming'
rather than one based on 'being'. But none of this detracts
from two basic facts about the use of ontology. First, other
theologians, from classical Thomists to Christian existentialists,
do make a sensitive and valuable use of ontology in their
theological writing, and in a climate of increasing theological
pluralism, the way of doing theology that *does* involve using
metaphysics or ontology is at the very least no *less* respectable

[3] e.g. *Hope and the Future of Man* (ed. E. H. Cousins), 58–9: *The Theology of Hope*,
17 f., 30 f., etc. For an elaboration of Moltmann's position, see my 'Three Theologies
of the Future', *Baptist Quarterly*, xxv (1974).
[4] e.g. Paul van Buren, *The Secular Meaning of the Gospel*; Harvey Cox, *The
Secular City*.
[5] e.g. W. N. Pittenger, *Process Thought and Christian Faith*. For a comprehensive
account of Tillich's relationship to process thought, see Tyron Inbody, 'Tillich and
Process Theology', *Theological Studies*, xxxvi. 3 (1975).

than the alternatives that reckon to manage without it. Second it is at least arguable that any theology whatever which regards belief in God as in some sense factual and cognitive, and which also takes seriously the doctrine of creation, needs an ontology to make any sense of its *own* account of the relationship between God and the world.

The Johannine prologue is just such an example of theological writing that requires an ontological interpretation. Tillich in fact overemphasized the role of the divine Logos in his own account of the relationship between philosophy and theology, and as a result he lost an opportunity for arguing for the necessity for ontology in theological interpretation. He believed that the writer of the fourth gospel was familiar with the *Hellenistic* concept of *logos*.[6] Tillich called the Hellenistic concept of *logos* 'the rational word that grasps being and in which being overcomes its hiddenness'.[7] The *logos* then becomes a point of identity between philosophy and theology since 'the *logos* who has become concrete in Jesus as the Christ is at the same time the universal *logos*'.[8] On a much less ambitious level we suggest the interpretation of the Johannine prologue needs ontology, for it already uses ontological concepts in order to achieve its effect. The author writes: 'The Word, then, was with God at the beginning, and through him all things came to be; no single thing was created without him. All that came to be was alive with his life, and that life was the light of men' (John 1 : 2–4). Now 'through him all things came to be' is clearly a statement so general that it is universal in its application. It is a totally inclusive statement because it refers directly to literally everything that is. The statement is ontological in the philosophical sense that it is about everything that is; and it is ontological in the theological sense that it is about *how* all that came to be, came to be.

But the ontological character of this passage goes beyond its identification as a statement with a universal frame of reference. The statement is intended to convey to the readers

---

[6] There is some doubt whether 'Logos' is used philosophically at all in the fourth gospel: see C. H. Dodd, *The Interpretation of the Fourth Gospel*, 278: McKelway, 198: J. H. Thomas, 96: H. Kraemer, *Religion and the Christian Faith*, 437.

[7] 'Philosophy and Theology', *PE*, 90: *BR*, 75.

[8] *ST* 1.32. See also *PE*, 90–1.

of the gospel something literally and factually significant about being or life itself, viz. that without the operation of the divine Word there would not be beings at all, and still less a world for them to inhabit. 'No single thing was created without him' is certainly intended as a factual assertion, so that philosophically speaking, it is in order to ask what state of affairs it denies. What the author is denying is that the world is self-sufficient or self-explanatory. But he is also affirming two other matters. He affirms that prior to and beyond the spatio-temporal world there is an infinite reality on whom that world continuously depends.

The passage of course offers the ontologist a good deal more than this. 'Life' is as broad and inclusive a concept as 'being' and the writer wants to say that the life of God himself which 'became flesh' (v. 14) was already in the world, albeit unrecognised (v. 10). His life in fact is to be construed as the animating power of 'all that came to be' (v. 3). But according to Christianity such a power cannot be the same as the life-power of all that is and no more, or God's transcendence (which if he exists he logically must possess) evaporates. Clearly then some kind of distinction needs to be made between the two concepts of life which are involved. This is best done by isolating the *biological* and the *ontological* concepts of life and attempting to trace out both the continuity and the discontinuity between them. Whatever we are to make of the striking phrase 'the light of men' (vv. 4, 9) the author again clearly intends some personal, moral influence which is independent of human life while at the same time dimly manifested in it. How such an influence can be accounted for without involving ontology is hard to comprehend.

It is no part of our purpose to develop the ontology of the Johannine prologue or to claim the *logos* concept it contains builds a convenient bridge between ontology and theology. We merely wish to point out ontology is already present in the biblical literature,[9] and an ontological sensitivity is needed to unpack the far-reaching implications of the passage just discussed. What has come to be known as 'panentheism' is in fact thoroughly biblical—only the term itself is recent. And it is difficult to see how any theology which affirms a belief in a

[9] See also Col. 1:16–17; Heb. 1:3.

transcendent God who exists and creates the world can avoid using ontology.

There are however other grounds for the use of ontology in theology which Tillich seems practically to ignore. The suggestion has been made that it is possible to regard ontology as an alternative kind of theological language, valid in its own right. Ontological concepts, despite their general unpopularity among philosophers and theologians alike, nevertheless display a certain character which, far from sentencing the theologian who uses them to an 'imprisonment in opaqueness',[10] is highly useful in the basic theological task of speaking about God. Ontological concepts, because of their general character, tend to lack descriptive content. They are, as R. N. Smart has said, 'non-perceptual' and 'non-visual'.[11] Whereas they cannot be entirely empty of content drawn from ordinary existence (even the term 'being' is unintelligible without some kind of awareness of our *own* being), ontological concepts are the most suitable kind of linguistic currency for speaking about what cannot be contained by any words at all. Smart speaks of their mystical character. Ontology is not mysticism in ontological guise, but when the religious mind probes behind the symbols of ordinary God-language to the God who transcends anything that is said about him, the very emptiness and colourlessness of ontological concepts is a distinct advantage. The less anchored ontological concepts are in straightforward empirical discourse, the more suited are they to express putative trans-empirical reality. It is perhaps surprising that Tillich has not developed a defence of ontological language along these lines.

But there is another important sense in which ontology may be regarded as providing an alternative theological language. Ontological statements, despite their descriptive neutrality, play an important role in theological interpretation. To assign to ontology such a role is not to make the wishful assumption that once theology appears in ontological language, the task of hermeneutics is done. In any theological hermeneutics tradition-al theological content is re-expressed in a different terminology. The new terminology does not necessarily express in a clear or more evident way the dogma which is interpreted, but the

10 Kraemer's phrase, 428.
11 'Being and the Bible', *Review of Metaphysics*, ix (1955–6), 599.

re-expression of it, its translation out of one set of word forms into another, itself may present the doctrine in a new light and afford new insights into it. When a doctrine of God is rewritten around the concept of being, or a Christology developed upon the doctrines of essence and existence, the ontological language is not intended as a substitute for language of faith, but it articulates the content of faith in an alternative manner. Ontology of course, has no monopoly in the field of hermeneutic translation, but it is a most appropriate discipline to assist in interpreting the basis of all theology, viz. the doctrine of God. Macquarrie locates in theological discourse the phenomenon of 'the possibility of expressing the same ideas in two or more modes of discourse, and so of providing a fresh interpretation'.[12] He lists as one of the prerequisites of the theological science of hermeneutics, that 'Interpretation becomes possible only when another mode of expression is available'.[13] Ontology, we suggest, is available as that 'other mode of expression'. We may take the ontological term 'existential estrangement' as an example of this procedure while not forgetting the criticisms made of it above.[14] 'Existential estrangement' approximates to the state of 'sin', to the mythological condition of 'Adam after the fall'. If 'existential estrangement' were to be whole-heartedly approved as an ontological reinterpretation of these two tradition-al doctrines, the traditional word 'sin' would not necessarily be removed from the language of liturgy or sermon. Merely by relating 'sin' and 'fall' to the ontological term 'existential estrangement', now light appears on old doctrines, and what the Christian tradition has to say about human nature under the heading of the state of 'sin' now appears in the wider context of human estrangement generally, giving the old doctrine a new relevance. Not every theological doctrine of course is capable of an ontological reproduction, and those that are may not be reproduced at all adequately. But whether the reproduction is successful or not, ontology is none the less at hand, offering itself in the service of theology as that 'other mode of expression'.

When ontology is regarded as an alternative theological language, the classical doctrine of God as being is included in its domain. But the ontology which the theologian is likely to

---

[12] *God Talk*, 146.   [13] Op. cit. 150.   [14] See above, p. 126 f.

use will be that of modern existentialism, rather than the ontology of rationalism or idealism. The use of existential ontology by the Christian interpreter is another advantage to theology which ontology provides. Tillich's ontology is grounded in human existence. The ontological question gets asked through the experience of non-being. Existential anxiety characterizes man's existence and courage is the power that overcomes it. Gustav Weigel, who sometimes severely criticizes Tillich, nevertheless admits that his 'existentialist ontology is vibrant, living, and immediately relevant to the anguish of existence.[15] The influence of existentialism on theology is now probably on the wane, and its value for theology and Christianity generally will doubtless be the subject of more vigorous debate. But whatever appraisal a theologian may make of existentialism, Tillich's ontology makes contact with it, and the contact produces valuable apologetic gains. If a point of contact is asserted, it is not of course thereby implied that Tillich is himself an 'existentialist' or that existentialism is the major influence on his theological writings.

Any acceptance of the classical doctrine of the 'analogy of being' (*analogia entis*) presupposes an ontology which is broad enough to encompass the relationship between God and his creatures. The word *ens* is an ontological word. In order to affirm the *analogia entis* an element of continuity and an element of discontinuity between the being of God and the being of creatures must be posited, which has its biblical counterpart in the doctrine of the *imago dei*. The *analogia entis* rests upon the belief that the being of creatures is conferred upon them by the infinite God whose essence is 'to be'. It takes an ontology to develop the doctrine of analogy.

If the task of defending the role of ontology within theology is not quite as difficult as it might have been supposed, the task of defending the role of ontology within *philosophy* is much more precarious. Tillich never fully appreciated the need to defend his use of ontology, especially in the face of the exasperation he caused those of his readers sympathetic to the tradition of British analytical philosophy. His lack of any compelling defence of ontology is unsatisfactory and has three main causes.

---

[15] Weigel, 'The Theological Significance of Paul Tillich', *PTCT*, 12.

He supposed (one has to add, naïvely) that all philosophy begins and ends in ontology, and that the classical metaphysical tradition is still entitled to be regarded as the dominant philosophical orthodoxy even today. Second he attacked logical positivism without ever having come to terms with it, with the result that his strictures against it often do not ring true because of his unfamiliarity with his philosophical opponents' positions. Third, despite his wide knowledge of historical theology and philosophy, he seemed quite unaware of other, contemporary, philosophical writers favourable towards ontology as an important branch of philosophy, but who were also acutely aware of its lack of philosophical popularity.

It simply will not do to affirm, as Tillich repeatedly does, that philosophy 'asks the question of reality as a whole' (ST 1.24) or that 'Ontology is the center of all philosophy' (BR, 6), because the great majority of modern philosophers do not understand their work in those terms. What is needed is an account, and there is no shortage of philosophers still prepared to take it up, of why metaphysics still has something important to say as one branch of philosophy among many. This, if successful, would be more valuable than the repetition of extravagant and unsubstantiated claims that ontology is 'first philosophy' or that every man 'is by nature a philosopher, because he inescapably asks the question of being' (BR, 9).

Positivism is singled out for attack because it eliminates almost all philosophical problems (ST 1.23) and because in any case its severely anti-ontological stance is itself based on hidden ontological assumptions (ST 1.256). Tillich sees positivism as devaluing the classical concepts of reason and knowledge. He distinguishes between the 'ontological' and 'technical' concepts of reason. Ontological reason 'is the structure of the mind which enables the mind to grasp and to transform reality. It is effective in the cognitive, aesthetic, practical and technical functions of the human mind' (ST 1.80). Technical reason by contrast is the capacity for 'reasoning' by itself. In technical reason 'only the cognitive side of the classical concept of reason remains, and within the cognitive realm only those cognitive acts which deal with the discovery of means for ends' (ST 1.81). Technical reason, because of its exclusive preoccupation with the observable, objective order produces a specific and limited kind of knowledge, 'controlling knowledge' (*ST* 1.108) which then

claims control of every level of reality. Life, spirit, personality, community, meanings, values, even one's ultimate concern should be treated in terms of detachment, analysis, calculation, technical use. The power behind this claim is the preciseness, verifiability, the public approachability of controlling knowledge . . . (*ST* 1.110).

Controlling knowledge is contrasted with a Platonic epistemology whereby one participates in, and is united with, what one knows. Such objects of knowledge are not features of the empirical world, but they are nonetheless the preconditions of the possibility of such a world, and of the possibility of cognitive processes within it. What for Tillich is ultimately knowable and ultimately worth knowing is by definition beyond the bounds of empirical verification.

Tillich's description of the different types of reason is a convincing theoretical construction of the wider processes of cognition, but it unfortunately does not provide an answer to the philosophical demand for verification of theological and metaphysical statements. The main passage where he deals with this demand is in a short section of *ST* 1, entitled 'Truth and Verification' (pp 112–17). Clearly he has in mind A. J. Ayer's *Language, Truth and Logic*, though he mentions neither by name. Unfortunately there is no genuine meeting of minds in this passage, for Tillich's counter to the verificationists rests largely on Platonic suppositions which his philosophical adversaries would not countenance for a single moment. His reply to Ayer rests on three observations, (i) to limit the use of the term 'truth' to empirically verifiable statements 'means a break with the whole Western tradition' of philosophy (*ST* 1.112): (ii) empirically verified judgements about things can still be false because of the nature of reality itself, i.e. 'Things hide their true being; it must be discovered under the surface of sense impressions, changing appearances, and unfounded opinions:' (iii) empirical verification, while containing an 'important truth', needlessly restricts the process of verification to sense-experience. 'It is not permissible to make the experimental method of verification the exclusive pattern of all verification' (*ST* 1.114). Tillich wants to widen 'experimental verification' to 'experiential verification' so that it includes the whole of a person's experience. Verification procedures are opened so wide by this move that it may take the experience of an entire lifetime to determine whether or not certain propositions are true. Most 'cognitive verification', argues Tillich, is 'experiential' and 'non-experimental', with the result that 'the verifying experiences of a non-experimental character are truer to life, though less exact and definite'.

Now if the challenge of anti-metaphysical philosophy is to be met, clearly this is hardly a satisfactory way of doing it. Statements such as 'Things hide their true being', only serve to convince the empiricist that Tillich is 'bewitched by language' into positing substantive referents for words which are only metaphorical descriptions of certain kinds of perception. There may indeed be a legitimate context for such statements, but in attempting to counter the verification principle, that principle must first be met on its own terms. 'Experiential verification' certainly takes the sting out of the demand that all synthetic statements should be confirmable in principle through sense-experience, but at the cost of rendering that demand completely innocuous. Such a move was gamely tried by an analytical philosopher, David Cox, in *Mind* in 1950. He proposed that the requirement that some sense-experience be relevant to the meaning of a synthetic statement could be modified by substituting *human* experience for *sense*-experience.[16] But such a procedure, however well intentioned, runs into the same difficulties as Tillich's 'experiential verification'. Which human, non-experimental experiences might be taken as verifying the truths of religious beliefs? How can one distinguish between conflicting religious truth-claims if such claims are experientially verified to the satisfaction of the people holding them? As Ferré shrewdly asks 'What is to prevent all manner of subjective delusion from masquerading as "verifying" experience?'[17] Experiential verification as a test for the truth of religious statements is a failure.

It is no part of our purpose to examine other more considered and worthwhile religious responses to the verificationist

---

[16] 'The Significance of Christianity', *Mind*, lix (1950), 210.
[17] *Language, Logic and God*, 68: see T. McPherson, 'The Existence of God', *Mind*, lix (1950), 547.

(and falsificationist) challenges to the truth-claims of religious statements.[18] We merely note that Tillich did not meet the challenge at all satisfactorily, and there is no trace at all in his writings after 1951 that he was even aware of the second phase of the debate over the demand for falsifiability, or the influence which the publication of Wittgenstein's *Philosophical Investigations* was to have on the philosophy of religion. He did however use his idea of 'experiential verification' again in 1952, when its use in justifying the content of *LPJ* is more judicious. In his second lecture he asks

Is there a way of verifying ontological judgements? There is certainly not an experimental way, but there is an experiential way. It is the way of an intelligent recognition of the basic ontological structures within the encountered reality, including the process of encountering itself. The only answer, but a sufficient answer, which can be given to the question of ontological verification is the appeal to intelligent recognition. For the following analysis this appeal is made. (*LPJ*, 24)

Here no attempt is made to contribute directly to the verification debate, but to directly defend the 'ontology of love' he was about to outline. Experiential verification amounts in this context to the 'intelligent recognition of the basic ontological structures'. More simply put, this procedure amounts to the ontologist's producing a kind of sketch or construct of some area of human experience, in this case the experience of love. The reader, instead of finding some relevant sense-experience to verify each constituent fact-asserting proposition of the ontological sketch, is asked to reflect on the whole of his life-experience to date, and to ask himself whether he recognizes his experience in the picture. Whether he accepts the picture as true depends on whether it confirms his experience. Confirmation need not take the form of a disposition to accept it. He might feel condemned or ashamed or even angered by it. Or his experience might take on a deeper, added dimension as a result of it. But its power to elicit any reaction from him at all would be due to his 'intelligent recognition' of his own life-experience in it, so that it cuts into his own individual

[18] e.g. B. Mitchell and I. Crombie, 'Theology and Falsification', in *New Essays in Philosophical Theology* (eds. A. Flew and A. McIntyre), and repr. in *Philosophy of Religion* (ed. Mitchell): J. Hick, 'Theology and Verification', in Mitchell (ed.).

domain, so to speak, and relates his own experience to wider, more general descriptions or structures of existence.

Other contemporary defenders of the metaphysical enterprise have begun in the same place with what Tillich called in the above passage 'ontological verification'. Macquarrie, whose theology is perhaps nearer than any other well-known theologian to Tillich's, has convincingly defended existentialist metaphysics as a valid philosophical endeavour which contributes vitally to human self-understanding. Existentialist metaphysics, he points out, unlike earlier varieties of metaphysics, is not speculative, but *descriptive*. These 'more modest' kinds of metaphysics 'set out to describe the most general categories under which we have an understanding of our world and they explore the most general conditions of experience'.[19] No ontological description, he continues, is to be regarded as 'final or adequate', and its truth cannot be established objectively. Its truth is that 'it yields a fuller interpretation of the existence of the persons who adhere to it . . . It supplies a basis for an ever-widening structure of intelligibility and meaning; and with every widening of this structure, the ontology itself gets confirmation'.[20] Macquarrie in fact provides the sort of account of ontology towards which Tillich was striving. The 'confirmation' of an ontology in the existence of the persons who adhere to it is identical with what Tillich had in mind when he spoke of 'intelligent recognition' or 'experiential verification'.

What sort of knowledge then does metaphysics provide? Is it factual? If so, why will straightforward empirical description not suffice? If it is not factual, how can it provide us with cognitive knowledge at all? These are amongst the hardest questions any metaphysician has to face. One counter-charge against the demand for the empirical verification of religious statements is the objection that the verificationists narrow down unacceptably what are admissible as facts, disallowing any class of statement not confirmable by actual or possible sense-experience.[21] The verification principle gives us accordingly a criterion of *empiricality*, but not a criterion of logical meaningfulness, for what is to be counted as meaningful need not be restricted to what is in principle empirical. But there is a sense

[19] *Existentialism*, 190.   [20] Op. cit. 199.   [21] Ferré, 71.

in which metaphysics does have factual significance. A vision of the world *as a whole* such as metaphysics provides certainly has factual implications in that it may help to shape the kind of person one becomes, or the kind of goals one strives for, or the quality of the life one leads. Indeed a poor, or outmoded or unbalanced metaphysic is able to produce prejudice or spiritual impoverishment in those who hold it. Whether metaphysical knowledge deserves to be called 'knowledge' depends largely on where one draws the limits of what can be known and what is regarded as in principle knowable. If knowledge of other persons, especially loved ones, is to count as knowledge, it is the most valuable form of knowledge we have, and it involves a mutual sharing in the being of others. Existentialists, and Tillich too, stress that knowing is in its richest form a matter of participation, or union of the subject with the object. If such an understanding of knowledge is admissible, then certainly an existentialist ontology is in principle knowable, for one knows the truth of ontological descriptions by recognizing their features in one's own existence, illuminating and interpreting it. One participates in the structures to which existentialist analysis draws attention. Macquarrie calls this 'ontological insight' and reckons it 'the most precious knowledge that we have'.[22]

There is another sense, almost entirely overlooked by philosophers in which existential metaphysics can justly be regarded as factual. Existentialism is widely influential in psychology and psychiatry. Existential analyses of specific psychological illnesses and psychotic conditions are used in the diagnoses of mental patients and the prescription of therapies. A wide reading of ontology (including Tillich's) influenced R. D. Laing's famous book on schizophrenia *The Divided Self*. The same kind of ontology lies behind Viktor Frankl's psychiatric technique of 'logotherapy'. 'Logotherapy' is a branch of existential psychiatry which supplements existential analyses ('ontoanalysis') with the therapeutic attempt to relate the patients' conditions to specific 'structures of meaning'.[23] Structures of *meaning* complement structures of being or existence in this school of psychiatry, and the word *logos* in 'logotherapy' is intended to make the emphasis on meaning

---

[22] Macquarrie, loc. cit.   [23] V. Frankl, *Psychotherapy and Existentialism*, 22.

clear. Ontoanalysis defines the condition: logotherapy effects the cure. Now it simply will not do to object that such analyses and methods are contentious, highly controversial, or professionally disputed. Theology is not the only discipline where pluralism flourishes! Psychiatrists and psychologists sympathetic to existentialist analyses are entitled to defend their position on the grounds that such analyses illuminate the condition of their patients and relate that condition to the wider more 'normal' forms of existence. This would seem to satisfy the most stringent demand for experimental verification! It is not simply that words such as 'anxiety', 'despair', 'fallenness', 'guilt', etc. overlap between two separate disciplines so that they have both separate philosophical and clinical uses. Rather it is the case that existential descriptions are recognizable in human existence generally and can be particularly apposite in analysing the specific human condition of patients clinically adjudged to be mentally 'ill'. Verification of this type of analysis is achieved every time it is successfully used in clinical treatment.

We hold that metaphysics has its place in philosophy, just as we have argued it has a place in theology, and that the verification principle, while happily effective against much that is purely speculative and logically meaningless in theology, and a welcome tool to be used alongside Occam's razor, does not succeed in imposing a linguistic veto on all metaphysical statements. Metaphysics can still be literally significant, and its significance lies in its communication of facts, which while not empirically straightforward in a scientific sense, impart to human existence a meaning or set of meanings underivable from the observation of particulars. In 1929, as the Vienna circle was bringing about a revolution in European philosophy, A. N. Whitehead wrote: 'Metaphysical categories are not dogmatic statements of the obvious; they are tentative formulations of the ultimate generalities'.[24] He went on (in the opening chapter of *Process and Reality*) to contrast the primary methods of mathematics and philosophy. The primary method of mathematics, he wrote (and fewer philosophers could pronounce about it with greater authority than he), is 'deduction; the primary method of philosophy is descriptive generalization'. Contrasting the methods of deduction and generalization he

[24] *Process and Reality*, 11.

continued: 'Under the influence of mathematics, deduction has been foisted onto philosophy as its standard method, instead of taking its true place as an essential auxiliary mode of verification whereby to test the scope of generalities.' Whitehead offered his vast system of speculative philosophy as a background against which particulars and observables might be understood. 'Every definite entity', he wrote, 'requires a systematic universe to supply its requisite status. Thus every proposition proposing a fact must, in its complete analysis, propose the general character of the universe required for that fact'.[25] His optimism in preparing a 'systematic universe' is now seen to be unfounded, but his philosophical starting point is one that metaphysicians may still justifiably take. Even Kant, who did as much as Hume to destroy traditional rational metaphysics, retained the term in order to speak of the principles of the possibility of experience,[26] given in any experiencing whatsoever.

Defenders of metaphysics are likely to begin here. Donald Mackinnon, in a recent work 'The Problem of Metaphysics', argues, as Aristotle and Kant had done before him, for the philosophical presentation of 'our ultimate conceptual scheme', which gives an 'inventory of the fundamental structural features of our world' and which '*must* be exemplified in any objective world'.[27] We hold that philosophical attempts to build rational constructions or 'visions of the world as a whole'[28] are valid ways of doing philosophy. Another recent restatement of metaphysics relies on the observation that 'there are various "points of view", those of common sense, science, economics, aesthetics and morality, and that there is also a metaphysical point of view which, if attained, would include and harmonize the rest'.[29]

James Richmond, in a well-argued defence of the use of metaphysics in theology defines the metaphysical enterprise as the construction of 'a model, pattern, grid or framework upon which we rationally arrange and structure our worldly experience *taken as a whole*, into some meaningful, organic unity'.[30]

[25] Op. cit. 13-14.   [26] See above, p. 2   [27] 1-2.
[28] J. Richmond's phrase, *Theology and Metaphysics*, 2.
[29] From H. B. Acton's 'Foreword' to P. Bowes, *Is Metaphysics Possible?*, 9.
[30] Richmond, 51.

With this we agree. Metaphysics does construct patterns according to which we see ourselves and our world in a particular light, but it does so in the knowledge that there is an ontological reality which gives itself to the pattern and upon which even the pattern itself depends. Of course the models and patterns will vary and so will the extent of the claims made for them. We have drawn material for this chapter from philosophers sympathetic to metaphysics but who would sharply disagree with each other about the method and scope of the metaphysical enterprise. Tillich managed to combine metaphysics of very different types in his works, to his own and his readers' confusion. But what the metaphysician seeks to describe is in principle amenable to more than one method or type of description (and so are most scientific facts). The variety of metaphysical maps available may be taken as an indication of the current healthy state of the subject! Two different maps of the same area, but of different scales and pointing out different features, can helpfully complement one another provided they are read separately and carefully compared. But read them together like two photographs on a single film and they will confuse and exasperate. Our claim in support of the philosophical relevance of metaphysics is in fact so modest, that in any other century it would have been considered unnecessary even to argue for such a mild and uncontroversial point of view.

In conclusion we urge that ontology has a rightful place both in theology and philosophy and that much of the criticism of its role in either discipline simply fails to take account of the possibilities that legitimately exist in the present day for doing either in a variety of different ways. True, our charge developed throughout this book against Tillich of eclecticism and needless confusion weakens the effectiveness of the ontology. But there remain many positive things to be said of his theological and philosophical work. Being written in continuous correlation with Christian theology his ontology relates that theology to human existence and sometimes illuminates theological ideas by expressing them in a non-traditional, non-biblical way. The ontology provides a welcome link with past philosophical and theological traditions which is regrettably absent in much recent theology. The ontology fruitfully links Christian theology with modern existentialism, and Tillich uses it effectively in his apologetic concern for the practical application of the historic Christian faith beyond the realm of the individual to the wider domain of universal being.

Of course, he represents only one way of practising philosophy and theology and bringing them together, and any attempt to do the same today would probably have to start with a very different understanding of the nature of each. It would be a great pity if Tillich were remembered mainly for the volume of unfriendly criticism his writings have attracted, for it is perhaps a measure of the greatness of his writing that he provoked his readers into reflections and responses that lesser writers fail to achieve. Many of his students and readers (including this one), whose thought has developed in ways that diverge sharply from Tillich's own, still have good reason to acknowledge gratefully the stimulation they received from his writings.

BIBLIOGRAPHY

(*i*) WORKS OF TILLICH

'Afterword: Appreciation and Reply', *PTCT*, 1965.

'Author's Introduction', *PE*, 1948.

'Autobiographical Reflections', *TPT*, 1952: repr. in *My Search for Absolutes*.

'*Der Begriff des Übernaturlichen, sein dialektischer Character und das Prinzip der Identität*, Königsberg Neumark, 1915.

'Being and Love', *Moral Principles of Action*, ed. R. N. Anshen, Harper & Bros., New York, 1952: repr. *Four Existentialist Theologians*, ed. W. Herberg, Doubleday Anchor Books, Garden City, New York, 1958.

Biblical Religion and the Search for Ultimate Reality, University of Chicago Press, Chicago, and Nisbet, London, 1955.

Biblische Religion und die Frage nach dem Sein, GW 5.

Christianity and the Encounter of the World Religions, Columbia University Press, New York, 1963.

'The Concept and Nature of Philosophy', *Twentieth Century Theology in the Making*, ii (ed. J. Pelikan): tr. of 'Philosophie: Begriff und Wesen', *Die Religion in Geschichte und Gegenwart*, iv, 1930.

'The Conception of Man in Existential Philosophy', *Journal of Religion*, xix, 1939.

'The Conquest of the Concept of Religion in the Philosophy of Religion', *What is Religion?* (tr. J. L. Adams). Tr. of 'Die Überwindung des Religionsbegriffs in der Religionsphilosophie', 1922: in *GW* 1.

The Courage To Be, Collins, Fontana, London, 1952.

'The Demonic', *The Interpretation of History*. Tr. of 'Das Dämonische; ein Beitrag zur Sinndeutung der Geschichte', 1926.

Dynamics of Faith, Harper Torch Books, New York, 1958.

'Eschatology and History', *The Interpretation of History*. Tr. of 'Eschatologie und Geschichte', 1927.

'Existential Philosophy: Its Historical Meaning', *Journal of the History of Ideas*, v, 1944. Revised in *TC*.

'The Formative Power of Protestantism', *PE*. Tr of 'Protestantische Gestaltung', 1929.

'Freedom in the Period of Transformation', *Freedom: Its Meaning*, ed. R. N. Anshen, Harcourt Brace, New York, 1940.

Gesammelte Werke, i, f., Evangelisches Verlagswerk, Stuttgart, 1959, f.

A History of Christian Thought, ed. C. E. Braaten, S.C.M., London, 1968.

'The Idea and the Ideal Personality', *PE*. Tr. of 'Die Überwindung des Persönlichkeitsideals', 1927.

'Is a Science of Human Values Possible?', *New Knowledge in Human Values*, ed. A. H. Maslow, Harper & Bros., New York, 1959.

The Interpretation of History (tr. of articles, N. A. Rasetzki and E. L. Tabney), C. Scribner's Sons, New York, 1936.

'Kairos and Logos: A Study in the Metaphysics of Knowledge', *The Interpretation of History*. Tr. of 'Kairos und Logos: Eine Untersuchung zur Metaphysik der Erkenntnis', 1926.

Love, Power and Justice, Oxford University Press, 1954.

'Martin Buber: 1878–1965', *Pastoral Psychology*, xvi, 1965.

'Martin Buber and Christian Thought', *Commentary*, v–vi, 1948. Revised in *TC*.

'The Meaning and Justification of Religious Symbols', *Religious Experience and Truth*, ed. S. Hook, Oliver & Boyd, New York, 1962.

Morality and Beyond, Collins, Fontana, London and Glasgow, 1969. First pub. 1964.

My Search for Absolutes, Simon & Schuster, New York, 1967.

'Mystik und Schuldbewusstsein in Schellings philosophischer Entwicklung', 1910. *GW* 1.

'The Nature and Significance of Existentialist Thought', *Journal of Philosophy*, liii, 1956.

'The Nature of Man', *Journal of Philosophy*, xliii, 1946.

'Das neue Sein als Zentralbegriff einer christlichen Theologie', Eranos-Jahrbuch, xxiii, 1955.

The New Being, S.C.M., London, repr. 1959.

On the Boundary, Collins, London, 1967. From *The Interpretation of History*.

'Participation and Knowledge: Problems of an Ontology of Cognition', *Sociologica*, i, Frankfurter Beiträge zur Soziologie, 1955.

'Paul Tillich and Carl Rogers: A Dialogue', *Pastoral Psychology*, xix (memorial issue), 1968.

'The Problem of Theological Method', *Journal of Religion*, xxvii, 1947.

The Protestant Era, University of Chicago Press, 1948: repr. Nisbet, London, 1952: abridged edn. 1957, 6th. imp. 1966.

'Realism and Faith', *PE*. Tr. of, Über Glaubigen Realismus', 1927.

'A Reinterpretation of the Doctrine of the Incarnation', *Church Quarterly Review*, cxlvii, 1949.

'Rejoinder', *Journal of Religion*, xlvi (memorial edn.) 1966.
'The Relation of Metaphysics and Theology', *Review of Metaphysics*, x, 1956–7.
'Religion and Secular Culture', *PE*.
'Religion as a Dimension in Man's Spiritual Life', 1954. In *TC*.
'Religionsphilosophie', 1925, *GW* I. English in *What is Religion?*
'The Religious Symbol', *Journal of Liberal Religion*, ii, 1940. Tr. of 'Das religiöse Symbol', 1928. Also in *Symbolism in Religion and Literature*, ed. R. May, 1961; and appendix to *Religious Experience and Truth*, ed. S. Hook, 1962.
'Religious Symbols and Our Knowledge of God', *The Christian Scholar*, xxxviii, 1955. Revised in *TC* as 'The Nature of Religious Language'.
'Reply to Gustave Weigel', *Theological Studies*, xi, 1950: repr. *Gregorianum*, xxxvii, 1956.
'Reply to Interpretation and Criticism', *TPT*.
'Schelling und die Anfänge des existentialistischen Protestes', *Zeitschrift für philosophische Forschung*, ix, 1955.
'Science and Theology: A Discussion with Einstein', 1940, *TC*.
The Shaking of the Foundations, Penguin Books, 1962 (1st pub. 1949).
'Sin and Grace', *Reinhold Niebuhr: A Prophetic Voice in Our Time*, Seabury Press, Greenwich, Connecticut, 1962.
Systematic Theology, Vol. 1, Nisbet, London, 1953 (1st pub. 1951).
—— Vol. 2, Nisbet, London, 1957.
—— Vol. 3, Nisbet, London, 1963.
Das System der Wissenschaften, 1923, *GW* I.
'Theology and Symbolism', *Religious Symbolism*, ed. F. E. Johnson, Harper & Bros., New York, 1955.
Theology of Culture, Oxford University Press, Galaxy, New York, 1964 (1st pub. 1959).
'The Two Types of Philosophy of Religion', 1946, in *TC*.
Ultimate Concern, S.C.M., London, 1965.
'What is Basic in Human Nature', *Pastoral Psychology*, xiv, 1963.
What is Religion? (tr. of early articles by J. L. Adams etc.), Harper & Row, New York, 1969.
'What is Wrong with the Dialectical Theology?', *Journal of Religion*, xv, 1935.
'Die Wiederentdeckung der prophetischen Tradition in der Reformation', *Neue Zeitschrift für systematische Theologie*, iii, 1961.
'The Word of God', *Language: An Enquiry into its Meaning and Function*, ed. R. N. Anshen, Harper & Bros., New York, 1957.

(*ii*) OTHER WORKS

AARON, R. I., *The Theory of Universals*, Oxford, Clarendon Press, 2nd edn., 1967.

ACTON, H. B., 'Foreword', in P. Bowes, *Is Metaphysics Possible?*, Gollancz, London, 1965.

ALEXANDER OF HALES, *Summa Theologica*, Dominican Fathers, Quarrachi, 1924.

ARISTOTLE, *Metaphysics*, tr. H. Tredennick, i and ii, Heinemann, London, 1933, 1935.

ARMBRUSTER, C. J., *The Vision of Paul Tillich*, Sheed & Ward, New York, 1967.

AQUINAS, Thomas, *Contra Gentiles*, tr. Dominican Fathers, Burns, Oates & Washbourne, London, 1924.

—— *De Ente et Essentia*, editio tertia, Marietti, 1948.

—— *On Being and Essence*, tr. Maurer, Pontifical Institute of Medieval Studies, Toronto, 1949.

—— *Summa Theologica*, i, Blackfriars, Eyre & Spottiswoode, 1948.

AUGUSTINE, *City of God*; *Confessions*; *Commentary on Psalms*; *On Freedom of Choice*; *Sermons*; *Soliloquies*; *On the Trinity*: see *Augustine, Works*, tr. M. Dods, T. & T. Clark, Edinburgh, 1871–6.

BERDYAEV, N., 'Unground and Freedom', in J. E. Earle (tr.), *Boehme: Six Theosophic Points*, Ann Arbor paperbacks, University of Michigan Press, 1958.

BERGSON, H., *Creative Evolution*, tr. A. Mitchell, Holt, New York, 1911.

BOAS, G., 'Being and Existence', *Journal of Philosophy*, liii, 1956.

BOEHME, J., *Aurora*; *Clavis Specialis*; *De Electione Gratiae*; *De Triplici Vita*; *Epistolae Theosophicae*; *Mysterium Magnum*; in *Behmen's Works*, i–iv, London, 1764–81.

—— *Signatura Rerum*, Everyman, Dent & Sons, London, undated.

—— *Six Theosophic Points*, see BERDYAEV, N.

BURNABY, J., 'Towards Understanding Paul Tillich', *Journal of Theological Studies*, v, 1954.

CAMERON, B. J., 'Some Nineteenth Century Sources of the Historical Problem in Paul Tillich's Christology: Hegel to Schweitzer', Oxford B. Litt. thesis.

CLARKE, B. L., 'God and the Symbolic', *Anglican Theological Review*, xliii, 1961.

CLAUBERGIUS, J., *Elementa Philosophiae sive Ontosophia*, 1647.

COPLESTON, F. C., *History of Philosophy*, vi, Burns & Oates, London, 1964.

CORNFORD, F. M., *The Republic of Plato*, Oxford University Press, 1955.

COUSINS, E. H. (ed.), *Hope and the Future of Man*, London, Teilhard Centre for the Future of Man, 1973.

COX, D. 'The Significance of Christianity', *Mind*, lix, 1950.

COX, H., *The Secular City*, Pelican Books, 1968 (1st pub. 1965).

CROSS, W. O., 'Some Notes on the Ontology of Paul Tillich', *Anglican Theological Review*, xxxix, 1957.

DAUBNEY, R. H., 'Some Structual Concepts in Tillich's Thought and the Pattern of the Liturgy', *TPT*.

DAVIDSON, T., *The Philosophical System of Antonio Rosmini-Serbati*, Kegan Paul & Trench, London, 1882.

DEMOS, R., 'Review of *ST* I', *Journal of Philosophy*, xlix, 1952: repr. *Journal of Religion*, xlvi, 1966.

—— 'Tillich's Philosophical Theology', *Philosophy and Phenomenological Research*, xix, 1958.

DESCARTES, R., *Philosophical Writings*, tr. E. Anscombe and P. T. Geach, Nelson, London, rev. edn. 1970 (1st pub. 1954).

DE DEUGD, C., 'Old Wine in New Bottles? Tillich and Spinoza', *Talk of God*, ed. G. N. A. Vesey, Royal Institute of Philosophy Lectures, 1967–8, Macmillan, London, 1969.

DIONYSIUS THE AREOPAGITE, *The Celestial Hierarchies*, London, 1920.

—— *The Mystical Theology*; and *On the Divine Names*, tr. C. E. Rolt, *Translations of Christian Literature: Dionysius the Areopagite*, S.P.C.K., 1920.

ECKHART, *Sermons*, in J. M. Clark, *Meister Eckhart*, Nelson, London, 1957.

—— *Commentary on the Book of Exodus*, in J. M. Clark and J. V. Skinner (tr.), *Meister Eckhart: Selected Treatises and Sermons*, Collins, Fontana, 1963.

EISLER, R., *Kant Lexikon*, Berlin, 1930.

EMMET, D., 'The Ground of Being', *Journal of Theological Studies*, xv, 1964.

FERRÉ, F., *Language, Logic and God*, Collins, Fontana Library Philosophy and Theology, London and Glasgow, 1970 (1st pub. 1962).

FERRÉ, N., 'Three Critical Issues in Tillich's Philosophical Theology', *Scottish Journal of Theology*, x, 1957.

FORD, L., 'The Three Strands of Tillich's Theory of Religious Symbols', *Journal of Religion*, xlvi, 1966.

—— 'Tillich and Thomas: The Analogy of Being', *Journal of Religon*, xlvi, 1966.

FORSTMAN, H. J., 'Paul Tillich and His Critics', *Encounter*, xxv, 1964.

FOSTER, K., 'Paul Tillich and St. Thomas', *PTCT*.

FOX, D. A., 'Eros and Logos', *Encounter*, xxix, 1968.

FRANKL, V., *Pyschotherapy and Existentialism*, Pelican Books, 1973 (1st pub. 1967).

GILSON, E., *Being and Some Philosophers*, Pontifical Institute of Medieval Studies, Toronto, 1952.

—— *The Christian Philosophy of Thomas Aquinas*, Gollancz, London, 1957.

GRENE, M., *Heidegger*, Bowes & Bowes, London, 1957.

HAMILTON, K., *The System and the Gospel*, S.C.M., Library of Philosophy and Theology, London, 1963.

HAMMOND, G. B., *Man in Estrangement*, Vanderbilt University Press, Nashville, 1965.

—— *The Power of Self-Transcendence*, St Louis, 1966.

HARTSHORNE, C., 'Tillich's Doctrine of God', *TPT*.

HEGEL, G., *Early Theological Writings*, tr. T. M. Knox, int. R. Kroner, University of Chicago Press, 1948.

—— *Lectures on the History of Philosophy*, iii, tr. E. S. Haldane F. H. Simpson, London, 1896.

—— *Lectures on the Philosophy of Religion*, iii, tr. E. Spiers and J. Sanderson, Kegan Paul, Trench, Trübner, London, 1895.

—— *The Science of Logic*, tr. A. Miller, Allen & Unwin, Muirhead Library of Philosophy, London, 1969.

HEIDEGGER, M., *Being and Time*, tr. J. Macquarrie and E. Robinson, Blackwell, Oxford, 1967 (1st pub. 1962).

—— *Ein Einführung in die Metaphysik*, Max Niemeyer, Tübingen, 1953.

—— *An Introduction to Metaphysics*, tr. R. Manheim, Anchor Books, Doubleday, Garden City, New York, 1961.

—— *Was ist Metaphysik?*, Frankfurt, 1949.

HENEL, I. C., 'Paul Tillich's Begriff der Essentifikation und seine Bedeutung für die Ethik', *Neue Zeitschrift für systematische Theologie und Religionsphilosophie*, x, 1968.

HICK, J., *Evil and the God of Love*, Collins, Fontana Library Theology and Philosophy, London and Glasgow, 1968 (1st pub. 1966).

—— 'Theology and Verification', in B. Mitchell (ed.) *Philosophy of Religion*, Oxford University Press, 1971.

—— and McGILL, A., *The Many Faced Argument*, Macmillan, Papermac, London, 1968.

HILL, D., 'Discussion [with WILLIAMS, D. D., DRIVER, T. F., DAVIES, W. D.]: St Paul and Tillich', *Union Seminary Quarterly Review*, xxi, 1965

—— 'Paul's "Second Adam" and Tillich's Christology', *Union Seminary Quarterly Review*, xxi, 1965.

HOOK, S., 'The Quest for Being', *Journal of Philosophy*, 1953.

—— *The Quest for Being*, St. Martin's Press, New York, 1961.

—— (ed.) *Religious Experience and Truth*, Oliver & Boyd, New York, 1962.

HUDSON, W. D., *Wittgenstein and Religious Belief*, Macmillan, London and Basingstoke, 1975.

INBODY, T., 'Tillich and Process Theology', *Theological Studies*, xxxvi, 1975.

KAINZ, H. P., *Active and Passive Potency in Thomistic Angelology*, Nijhoff, The Hague, 1972.

KANT, I., *Critique of Pure Reason*, tr. J. M. D. Meiklejohn, Everyman's Library, J. M. Dent & Sons, London and Toronto, 1934.

KEEFE, D. J., *Thomism and the Ontological Theology of Paul Tillich*, E. J. Brill, Leiden, Netherlands, 1970.

KEGLEY, C. W., and BRETALL, R. W. (eds.), *The Theology of Paul Tillich*, Macmillan, New York, 1961 and 1964 (1st pub. 1952),

KEIGHTLEY, A., *Wittgenstein, Grammar and God*, Epworth, London. 1976.

KELSEY, D., *The Fabric of Paul Tillich's Theology*, Yale University Press, New Haven and London, 1967.

KIERKEGAARD, S., *The Concept of Dread* (tr. W. Lowrie), Oxford University Press, 1944.

KIESLING, C., 'A Translation of Tillich's Idea of God', *Journal of Ecumenical Studies*, iv, 1967.

KILLEN, R. A., *The Ontological Theology of Paul Tillich*, Kampen, Kok, 1956.

KING, M., *Heidegger's Philosophy*, Blackwell, Oxford, 1964.

KNIGHT, T. S., 'Why Not Nothing?' *Review of Metaphysics*, x, 1956 1957.

KNOX, J., *The Humanity and Divinity of Christ*, Cambridge University Press, 1967.

KOYRÉ, A., *La Philosophie de Jacob Boehme*, Paris, 1929.

KRAEMER, H., *Religion and the Christian Faith*, Lutterworth, London, 1956.

KUHN, H., *Encounter with Nothingness*, Methuen, London, 1951.

LEFF, G., *Heresy in the Later Middle Ages*, i, Manchester University Press, 1967.

LEIBNIZ, G. W. *The Monadology and Other Writings*, ed. R. Latta, Oxford, Clarendon Press, 1898.

—— *Opuscules et fragments inédits de Leibniz*, ed. Couturat, Paris, 1903.

—— *Principes de la nature et de la grace fondés en raison*, Presses Universitaires de France, Paris, 1954.

LOOMER, B. M. 'Tillich's Theology of Correlation', *Journal of Religion*, xxxvi, 1956.

LOTZE, H., *Metaphysics*, i, tr. Bosanquet, Oxford, Clarendon Press, 1887.

LOVEJOY, A. O., *The Great Chain of Being*, Harvard University Press, Cambridge, Mass., 5th edn. 1953 (1st pub. 1936).

McDONALD, H. D., 'The Symbolic Theology of Paul Tillich', *Scottish Journal of Theology*, xvii, 1964.

McLEAN, G. F. 'Paul Tillich's Existential Philosophy of Protestantism', *PTCT*.

MACLEOD, A., *Tillich: An Essay on the Role of Ontology in his Philosophical Theology*, Allen & Unwin, London, 1973.

McPHERSON, T., 'The Existence of God', *Mind*, lix, 1950.

MACQUARRIE, J., *Existentialism*, Penguin Books, 1973.

—— *God Talk*, S.C.M., London, 1967.

—— *Principles of Christian Theology*, S.C.M., London, 2nd imp., 1970 (1st pub. 1966).

McTAGGART, J., *Studies in Hegelian Cosmology*, Cambridge University Press, 1918.

MARTENSEN, H. L. and HOBHOUSE, S., *Studies in the Life and Teaching of Jacob Boehme*, Rockliff, London, rev. edn. 1949.

MARTIN, B., *Paul Tillich's Doctrine of Man*, Nisbet, London, 1966.

MARTIN, G., *An Introduction to General Metaphysics*, Allen & Unwin, London, 1957.

MASCALL, E. L., *Existence and Analogy*, Libra Books, Darton, Longman & Todd, London, 1966 (1st pub. 1949).

MILLER, A. A., 'The Theologies of Luther and Boehme in the Light of their Genesis Commentaries', *Harvard Theological Review*, lxiii, 1970.

MITCHELL, B. (ed.) *Philosophy of Religion*, Oxford University Press, 1971.

MOLLEGEN, A. T., 'Christology and Biblical Criticism in Tillich', *TPT*.

MOLTMANN, J., *The Theology of Hope*, S.C.M., London, 1967.

MUNITZ, M., *The Mystery of Existence*, Appleton–Century–Crofts, New York, 1965.

NEVILLE, R. C., *God the Creator*, University of Chicago Press, 1968.

THE NEW CATHOLIC ENCYCLOPAEDIA, McGraw-Hill, New York, 1967.

NICHOLLS, W., *Systematic and Philosophical Theology*, Penguin Books, 1969.

NIEBUHR, Re., 'Biblical Thought and Ontological Speculation in Tillich's Theology', *TPT*.

O'MEARA, T. A., 'Paul Tillich and Ecumenism', *PTCT*.

—— and WEISSER, C. D. (eds.), *Paul Tillich in Catholic Thought*, Darton, Longman & Todd, London, 1965.

OSBORNE, K. B., *New Being*, Martinus Nijhoff, The Hague, 1969.

OTTO, R., *The Idea of the Holy*, tr. J. Harvey, Penguin Books, 1959 (1st pub. 1917).

PETERS, E. H., 'Tillich's Doctrine of Essence, Existence and the Christ', *Journal of Religion*, xliii, 1963..

PITTENGER, W. N., *Christology Reconsidered*, S.C.M., London, 1970.

—— 'Paul Tillich as a Theologian: An Appreciation', *Anglican Theological Review*, xliii (memorial edition), 1961.

—— *Process Thought and Christian Faith*, Macmillan, New York, 1968.

PLATO, *Meno*; *Phaedrus*; *Sophist*; *Symposium*, in Jowett, B., *The Dialogues of Plato*, i, 4th edn., Oxford University Press, 1953: iv, 2nd edn., v, 2nd edn., 1875. See also CORNFORD.

PLOTINUS, *The Enneads*, in McKenna, S. (tr.), *Plotinus, The Enneads*, Faber & Faber, London, rev. edn. 1956.

RADHAKRISHNAN, S., *The Principal Upanisads*, Allen & Unwin, Muirhead Library of Philosophy, London, 2nd imp. 1968.

RHEIN, C., *Paul Tillich, Philosoph und Theologe, Ein Einführung in sein Denken*, Stuttgart, 1957.

RICHARD OF ST. VICTOR, *De Trinitate*, Textes Philosophes du Moyen Age, vi, Ribaillier, Paris, 1958.

ROBERTS, D. E., 'Tillich's Doctrine of Man', *TPT*.

ROBINSON, J. A. T., *Honest to God*, S.C.M., London, 1963.

—— *The Human Face of God*, S.C.M., London 1973.

ROWE, W., *Religious Symbols and God*, Chicago, 1968.

SANTAYANA, G., *The Realms of Being*, iv, Constable, London, 1940.

SCHARLEMANN, R. P., *Reflection and Doubt in the Thought of Paul Tillich*, Yale University Press, New Haven and London, 1969.

—— 'The Scope of Systematics: An Analysis of Tillich's Two Systems', *Journal of Religion*, xlviii, 1968.

—— 'Tillich's Method of Correlation: Two Proposed Revisions', *Journal of Religion*, xlvi, 1966.

SCHELLING, F. W., *The Ages of the World*, F. de W. Bolman, Columbia, New York, 1942.

—— *Berlin Lectures* (1841–2), in J. Wilde and W. Kimmel (eds.), *The Search for Being*, Noonday Press, New York, 1962.

—— *Schellings Werke*, i–iv, Stuttgart, 1856–61: and i–vii, Munich, 1927-8.

SCHRÖER, H., *Der Denkform der Paradoxalität als theologisches Problem*, Vandenhoeck & Ruprecht, Göttingen, 1960.

SMART, R. N., 'Being and the Bible', *Review of Metaphysics*, ix, 1955–6.

SOMMER, G. F., 'The Significance of the Late Philosophy of Schelling for the Formation and Interpretation of the Thought of

Paul Tillich', Dissertation, Duke University, Durham, N. Carolina, 1960.

SPINOZA, *Ethics*, in *The Rationalists*, Dolphin, Doubleday, New York, 1960.

SPRAGUE, E., 'How To Avoid Being Professor Tillich', *Journal of Philosophy*, lvi, 1959.

STOUDT, J. J., *Jacob Boehme: His Life and Thought*, Seabury Press, New York, 1968. Retitled edn. of *From Sunrise to Eternity*, 1957.

SULZBACH, M. S., 'The Place of Christology in Contemporary Protestantism', *Religion in Life*, xxiii, 1953–4.

TAUBES, W. On the Nature of the Theological Method, *Journal of Religion* xxxiv (1954), 22.

TAVARD, G., 'Christianity and the Philosophies of Existence', *Theological Studies*, xviii, 1957.

—— *Paul Tillich and the Christian Message*, Burns & Oates, London, 1962.

THATCHER, A., 'Existence and Life in Tillich', *Scottish Journal of Theology*, xxvii, 1974.

—— 'Three Theologies of the Future', *Baptist Quarterly*, xxv, 1974.

THOMAS, J. Heywood, *Paul Tillich: An Appraisal*, S.C.M. Library of Philosophy and Theology, London, 1963.

TIEBOUT, H. M. (Jr.), 'Tillich and Freud on Sin', *Religion in Life*, xxviii, 1958–9.

VAN BUREN, P., *The Secular Meaning of the Gospel*, S.C.M., London, 1963.

WEIGEL, G., 'Contemporaneous Protestantism and Paul Tillich', *Theological Studies*, xi, 1950.

—— 'Myth, Symbol and Analogy', *PTCT*.

—— 'The Theological Significance of Paul Tillich', *PTCT*.

WHITEHEAD, A. N., *Process and Reality*, Collier Macmillan, Toronto, 1969 (1st pub. 1929).

WILLIAMS, D. D., 'Review of *ST* 2', *Review of Religion*, xxii, 1958: rep. *Journal of Religion*, xlvi, 1966.

WITTGENSTEIN, L., *Philosophical Investigations*, tr. G. E. M. Anscombe, Blackwell, Oxford, 1972.

WOLFF, C., *Philosophia Prima sive Ontologia*, Frankfurt, 1730.

INDEX OF NAMES AND SUBJECTS

panentheism, 164
pantheism, 44, 88
paradox(ical), 58, 89, 141–2, 144,
     149, 154, 157, 162
PARMENIDEA, 162
participation, 62, 64, 129, 138, 151,
     173
PASCAL, 26
PEARCE, G. J. M., vi
Penia, 45
PETERS, E. H., 148 n. 21
PHILO OF ALEXANDRIA, 110
philosophy, 3–4, 10, 12–13, 16–17,
     21–2, 25, 37, 40, 54, 66, 76, 81,
     90, 92, 94, 97, 100, 102, 117,
     153, 157, ch. 8
first philosophy, 4–5, 168
philosophy of religion, 27, 29, 40, 72,
     84, 92, 115, 171
PITTENGER, W. N., 133, 147 n. 14,
     149 n. 24, 162 n. 5
PLATO, Platonic, 25, 27, 29, 31,
     33, 41–51, 58, 68 n. 52, 70, 76,
     87, 95–6, 100, 102–3, 106, 108,
     110–16, 136, 149 n. 22, 155–7,
     169
Platonism, 44, 54, 88, 95, 110
PLOTINUS, Plotinian, 8, 25, 31, 33,
     50, 86, 95
polarity, polarities, 5, 56, 62–68, 99,
     113, 120, 128, 151
pole, polar, 9, 48, 52–3, 57, 62, 64,
     68–9, 95–6, 114, 120, 123,
     127–8, 138, 147, 160
Poros, 45
PORPHYRY, 111
positivism, 111, 168
potency, potencies, 46, 55, 65–7, 69,
     74, 81, 107, 127, 134, 155
potential, 55, 74, 126, 134, 145–8
potentiality, 54–5, 65–6, 68, 70, 72,
     95, 99, 103–8, 112, 114, 122,
     125–7, 130–1, 135, 153, 155–6,
     160
Potenz, 65
power, 27, 32–3, 41–4, 46, 52–3, 63,
     66, 68–9, 87, 104–6, 130, 137,
     144, 156, 160–1, 164

power of being, 12, 25, 28, 32, 34,
     36–7, 40–5, 48–50, 55–7, 64–9,
     76, 84, 87, 94, 99, 103, 106, 108,
     110, 124, 127, 160
principia per se nota, 30
prius, 28, 80–2
Protestant principle, 142–4, 152
protology, 7–8
Proton, 7–9
PSEUDO-DIONYSIUS THE AREOPAG-
     ITE, 32, 85–7
psychology, psychological, 22, 60,
     117, 127–31, 144, 173
pure act, *see actus purus*, 73–4
pure actuality, 67, 74, 160

quality, 41–2, 48, 50, 102, 108,
     117–8, 144, 173
question of being, 11–17
quiddity, 75

RADHAKRISHNAN, S., 130
rational, rationalist, rationalism,
     1–2, 5–6, 11–14, 18–19, 23–4,
     26, 37, 44, 141, 149, 163, 167
RASETZKI, N., 7
realism, 102
reality, 5, 9, 27–8, 39, 73, 76, 79–80,
     82, 90, 92–3, 97, 101, 103, 105–
     6, 110–1, 115, 127–8, 154, 156–
     7, 162, 164–5, 168–9, 171, 176
reality as a whole, 4, 168
reason, 2, 129, 168–9
religion, 26–7, 36–9, 78, 84, 94,
     143–4, 170
rest, 65–68, 114
reunion, 44–7, 89–90, 141
revelation, 52–3, 56–8, 83, 138,
     143–4, 162
RHEIN, C., 85 n. 39
RICHARD OF ST VICTOR, 135
RICHMOND, J., 175
RITSCHL, 162
ROBERTS, D. E., 133 n. 20
ROBINSON, E., 2 n. 8, 13 n. 30
ROBINSON, J. A. T., 104, 149
ROWE, W., 83 n. 34, 133 n. 20
ROSMINI, 2